CONVERSATIONS WITH LYNN JOHNSTON

**Conversations with Comic Artists** M. Thomas Inge, General Editor

# Conversations with Lynn Johnston

Edited by Jeff McLaughlin

University Press of Mississippi / Jackson

*For Lynn and all her peers who use their creative talents to bring us joy.*

The University Press of Mississippi is the scholarly publishing agency of
the Mississippi Institutions of Higher Learning: Alcorn State University,
Delta State University, Jackson State University, Mississippi State University,
Mississippi University for Women, Mississippi Valley State University,
University of Mississippi, and University of Southern Mississippi.

www.upress.state.ms.us

The University Press of Mississippi is a member
of the Association of University Presses.

**Publisher**: University Press of Mississippi, Jackson, USA
**Authorised GPSR Safety Representative**: Easy Access System Europe –
Mustamäe tee 50, 10621 Tallinn, Estonia, *gpsr.requests@easproject.com*

Library of Congress Cataloging-in-Publication Data

Names: McLaughlin, Jeff, 1962– editor
Title: Conversations with Lynn Johnston / Jeff McLaughlin.
Other titles: Conversations with comic artists
Description: Jackson : University Press of Mississippi, 2025. | Series: Conversations with
    comic artists series | Includes bibliographical references and index.
Identifiers: LCCN 2025028707 (print) | LCCN 2025028708 (ebook) |
    ISBN 9781496860217 hardback | ISBN 9781496860224 trade paperback |
    ISBN 9781496860231 epub | ISBN 9781496860248 epub |
    ISBN 9781496860255 pdf | ISBN 9781496860200 pdf
Subjects: LCSH: Johnston, Lynn Franks, 1947—Interviews |
    Johnston, Lynn Franks, 1947– For better or for worse | Women cartoonists—
    Canada—Interviews | Women comics artists—Canada—Interviews |
    Cartoonists—Canada—Interviews | Comic books, strips, etc.
Classification: LCC PN6733.J55 Z46 2025 (print) | LCC PN6733.J55 (ebook)
LC record available at https://lccn.loc.gov/2025028707
LC ebook record available at https://lccn.loc.gov/2025028708

British Library Cataloging-in-Publication Data available

# Books by Lynn Johnston

## Potlatch Publications
*David, We're Pregnant!* 1975

## Peter Martin Associates
*Hi Mom! Hi Dad!* 1977

## Meadowbrook Press
*Do They Ever Grow Up?* 1978

## Andrews & McMeel
*I've Got the One-More-Washload Blues.* 1981
*Is This "One of Those Days," Daddy?* 1982
*It Must Be Nice to Be Little.* 1983
*More Than a Month of Sundays.* 1983
*Just One More Hug.* 1984
*Our Sunday Best.* 1984
*The Last Straw.* 1985
*Keep the Home Fries Burning.* 1986
*It's All Downhill From Here.* 1987
*Pushing 40.* 1988
*A Look Inside . . . For Better or For Worse: The 10th Anniversary Collection.* 1989
*If This is a Lecture, How Long Will It Be?* 1990
*What, Me Pregnant?* 1991
*Things are Looking Up.* 1992
*There Goes My Baby!* 1993
*It's the Thought That Counts: The 15th Anniversary Collection.* 1994
*Starting from Scratch.* 1995
*Love Just Screws Everything Up.* 1996
*Remembering Farley.* 1996

## Andrews McMeel
*Growing Like a Weed.* 1997
*Middle Age Spread.* 1998
*Sunshine & Shadow.* 1999
*The Lives Behind the Lines: 20 Years of For Better or For Worse.* 1999
*The Big 5-0.* 2000
*Isn't He Beautiful: A For Better or For Worse Little Book.* 2000
*Isn't She Beautiful: A For Better or For Worse Little Book.* 2000
*Graduation: A Time for Change.* 2001
*All About April: Our Little Girl Grows Up!* 2001
*A Perfect Christmas: A For Better or For Worse Little Book.* 2001
*Wags and Kisses: A For Better or For Worse Little Book.* 2001
*Family Business.* 2002
*Graduation . . . Just the Beginning! A For Better or For Worse Little Book.* 2003 (By Lynn Johnston and Andie Parton)

*With This Ring*. 2003
*Reality Check*. 2003
*Leaving Home*. 2003 (By Andie Parton, with illustrations by Lynn Johnston)
*Suddenly Silver: Celebrating 25 Years of For Better or For Worse*. 2004
*Striking a Chord*. 2005
*Never Wink at a Worried Woman*. 2005
*So You're Gonna Be a Grandma! A For Better or For Worse Book*. 2005
*She's Turning into One of Them!* 2006
*I Love My Grandpa: A For Better or For Worse Book*. 2006
*Teaching . . . Is a Learning Experience!* 2007
*Seniors' Discount*. 2007
*Home Sweat Home*. 2008
*Just a Simple Wedding*. 2009
*Farley and the Lost Bone*. 2011 (By Lynn Johnston and Beth Cruikshank)
*Something Old, Something New*. 2011
*In the Beginning, There Was Chaos*. 2011
*Making Ends Meet*. 2013
*It's One Thing After Another*. 2014

## McGraw Hill
*Laugh 'n' Learn Spanish*. 2003

## Bowen Press (HarperCollins imprint)
*Farley Follows His Nose*. 2009

## Goose Lane Editions with the Art Gallery of Sudbury
*For Better or For Worse: The Comic Art of Lynn Johnston*. 2015

## IDW and the Library of American Comics
*For Better or For Worse: The Complete Library, Vol. 1: 1979–1982*. 2017
*For Better or For Worse: The Complete Library, Vol. 2: 1983–1986*. 2017
*For Better or For Worse: The Complete Library, Vol. 3: 1986–1989*. 2019
*For Better or For Worse: The Complete Library, Vol. 4: 1989–1993*. 2020
*For Better or For Worse: The Complete Library, Vol. 5: 1993–1996*. 2021
*For Better or For Worse: The Complete Library, Vol. 6 1996–1999*. 2022
*For Better or For Worse: The Complete Library, Vol. 7 2000–2003*. 2023
*For Better or For Worse: The Complete Library, Vol. 8 2003–2006*. 2024
*For Better or For Worse: The Complete Library, Vol. 9 2006–2008*. 2024

## Lynn Johnston Productions
*The Botshop: Book One*. 2023
*Marvellous Things: Book Two*. 2023
*A Dog with No Name: Book Three*. 2023
*The Big Trip: Book Four*. 2024
*A Little Kindness: Book Five*. 2024
*The Best Prize: Book Six*. 2024

# CONTENTS

# INTRODUCTION

## I

How long does it take to read a newspaper comic strip? One-two-three seconds, as Lynn Johnston posits in one interview? Ten seconds, thirty if it's confusing? This book is a collection of interviews presented in sequential order that clearly show how those few seconds captured millions of people's hearts. Early on, Johnston's *For Better or For Worse* was about new mom Elly Patterson and her struggles presented in gag-a-day form as she tries to manage a household that includes a husband who tends to wrongly dismiss her worries as silly. Later, as the children grew up, the strip became a very complex presentation of a family and almost an entire community. Nevertheless, the Pattersons managed through the best of times and the worst of times and the most mundane of times, always trusting in the love of each other. And when one of them didn't feel quite their best or felt like they didn't have all the answers, there was usually someone there to offer a kind word, a hug, or a humorous retort. Readers understandably returned day after day, year after year, *decade after decade*.

According to Johnston, it takes about three years to care about what happens to characters in a story-driven comic strip. Yet I suspect that when people turned to the funny pages on September 9, 1979, when her strip first appeared, they didn't need those three years. It took just those first few seconds.

*For Better or For Worse* was a long-running continuity strip with a complex community of characters with fully formed lives—albeit fictional ones. In managing to give us the Patterson family, not only was Johnston providing opportunities for us to laugh about the "for better" parts of their (and our!) lives, but she also offered up moments that required dedicated fans to pause and reflect (and even shed a tear) when she showed the "for worse."

## II

In my research for suitable pieces for this book, I discovered that because *For Better or For Worse* was a newspaper strip, most of the interviews with Johnston were themselves done by folks connected to newspapers. Thus, the conversations (if you can call them that) occupied relatively brief real estate on the printed page. Notably, there were interesting interviews and profiles in all sorts of media (television, radio, newspapers, magazines) done in Canada that many people outside the country have probably not seen. These early 1980s samples are fun, as they introduced her to the rest of her homeland just as she was getting established. In the 1990s there was a lot of print regarding two significant—for very different reasons—storylines: the reveal of Michael Patterson's friend Lawrence's sexual orientation in 1993 and the heroic death of the much-loved family dog Farley in 1995. Unfortunately, the newspaper articles about these two events tended to be very short and very repetitive. Indeed, they typically involved some sort of editorial response, as some complained, "How *dare* such stories be presented in the funnies, or be raised *at all*?" It should be noted, however, that such appearances aside (at least with Lawrence's story), the number of lovely letters of support Johnston received far, far outweighed the negative ones.

As we move towards the end of the book, you'll see the interviews typically getting longer; with the popularity of internet podcasts, interviewers now had the time to explore various topics and themes via hourlong (or more!) exchanges. One minor downside to this was that, for the sake of informing different audiences, some of the same questions get asked over and over again. Still, what stands out is Johnston's willingness to talk openly about so much of her professional and personal life—the better, the best, the so-so, and the worst—which reveals her strength, graciousness, and of course her expertise and sense of humor. It also highlights why she is acknowledged as one of the greats. I hope you all enjoy this collection!

Putting this collection together has taken me and my keyboard all over the place, virtually speaking. There are hundreds, thousands, of mentions of Johnston and her long-running strip *For Better or For Worse*, and while there were plenty of such references in (mostly) US newspapers, the ones from her (and my) home country were the ones I had the most excitement discovering. I knew that her fans outside of Canada would probably not be aware of them—until now.

In my search for materials I received the nicest emails from many of the people I wrote out of the blue looking for assistance. It might be a librarian in a small Canadian town where Johnston used to live or an archivist working for a huge database located in the USA. It might be a staff member at one of the Canadian universities where Johnston received one of her honorary degrees. Or it might even be someone who was unable to find (or grant copyright permission) for what I was looking for. Whether I was successful or not, the fact that so many individuals took the time to go look for me and then keep on looking (and write me later on with good or bad news) reassured me of not only how nice people can be, but also how many people wanted to make this book a success.

Although there were space restrictions and sometimes cost restrictions, finding some of the best interviews out there also meant not to giving up when there was a roadblock. Often it just meant trying another approach or direction. In fact, one of my favorite finds was the last one, and it took me more than six months of on-and-off-again work to track it down.

I found a promising interview with Johnston and visited the American newspaper's website to find out how to get reprint permission. I wrote the newspaper's contact . . . and I waited . . . and waited. . . .

Months went by.

Nothing.

I'm pretty patient, but I'm also very persistent. I revisited the company's website, and it said that if it was an urgent matter to state so in the subject line and they would get back to me within a few days. So naturally I did that.

A couple more months went by.

Finally, a nice employee wrote back only to tell me that they didn't hold copyright on the article—the freelancer did.

*Sigh.*

Well, at least I got an answer.

I asked if they knew how to reach that person, but they didn't have a clue, and besides, it was a long time ago.

So the hunt was on!

Originally, I was looking for one person out of 340 million. But I had three bits of information that narrowed this down: a name, the date of the article, and the location of the newspaper. I started with the assumption that the person might have stayed in the area and so sought out various persons with the same name to check their occupations. (Of course, two flaws in my reasoning were that not everyone is online and not everyone maintains the same vocation.) Unfortunately, of the same-named individuals, none had any connection to writing about pop culture, let alone comics. Then I saw one that alluded to having done some work (not writing) in film. To find any further information about him, I had to join LinkedIn and look there, but that could not provide me with an email or phone number. Still, I was given the name of a film production company. Close enough!

So off I went to look at the film company's website. No such person with the name I had was listed. But since not every employee (or past employee) would necessarily be mentioned on a website, I wrote to one of the contacts listed. A few hours later, they wrote back, telling me they recognized the name but didn't know if it was the individual I was looking for. However, they would forward my request just in case.

I wondered: How long should I wait? Should I just forget about it? I mean, the last time I tried to find someone, I discovered that they had passed away and there was no way of getting copyright approval.

Would the fellow get back to me?

Yes! Indeed, he did the very next day!

But would it be the right fellow?

Yes! Indeed, it would be!

And would he give me permission?

Yes! He would! So many thanks go to Alex Chun!

With that quest solved, there are many others I must also thank. I offer my deepest gratitude to all those interviewers and copyright holders whose work you will find herein.

I relied upon many folks to help me put this book together. Starting at my home institution, Thompson Rivers University, Brenda Smith was a wonderful resource. I'd ask her for help on one thing and, like so many other librarians, she would come back with that information and much more! Likewise, my research assistant Andrew Faulds was someone I could always rely upon. His handling of various tasks was greatly appreciated. It's also important for me to mention that when it came to transcribing the audio interviews, I listened to each one a few times through, and even though I often played them at slower speeds, I may have misheard some words. So thank you to another TRU student, Hunter Aiken, for doing one last "go through" for me.

Thank you also to the following individuals: Reginald Watson at *The Peterborough Examiner*; Teri-Lynn Janveau at North Bay Public Library; Kate McClancy; Randy Duncan; Mike Rhode; D. D. Degg; Jon Fulton, Erin May, Melissa Svendsen, and Karen Hetherington at Thompson Rivers University;

and Nadia Ditraglia, Jennifer Tran, Chantall Van Raay, and Brad Coburn at McMaster University. Then there is Dave Kellett, Heidi MacDonald, Shawn Gilmore, Steve Scher, and Tom Belton. There is Marcia Steyaert at Western University; Kristy Waller at Emily Carr University of Art + Design; the folks at the Ohio State University Collections; Jenn Kho at the *Chicago Sun Times*; Carly Johnston, Ed Driedger, and Maggie Horsfield at Nipissing University; Sara Janes, Farhan Yousaf, Yvonne Roussel, and Ashley Beda at Lakehead University; Courtney O'Hara; Moira Duncan at Library and Archives Canada; Kurtis Findlay at Library of American Comics; Kent Worcester; Ralph Drew, Dana Toby, and Nicole Mogar at the *Los Angeles Times*; Judy Hansen; Miles Baker; Julia Pohl-Miranda; Kate Beaton; Raina Telgemeier; Linda Steele at CBC; and Karen Thompson at Bell Media. I have to also give a very big thank you to Stephanie van Doleweerd at the official *For Better or For Worse* website (be sure to check it out!).

I am very happy to be working with the University Press of Mississippi again, so I want to acknowledge the talents of Sara Day, Corley Longmire, and Lisa McMurtray. I'm a big fan of the UPM Conversations series, and I strongly encourage you to buy the other volumes!

Last, and certainly most importantly, I must thank the subject of this book, the interviewee: Lynn Johnston. Lynn, thank you for your generous gift—drawing a comics strip 365 days a year for decades is truly an astonishing and exhausting feat. Indeed, you always gave us something to smile about—even if it was just for a few seconds a day. And personally, thank you for the gift of your time. Be it our email exchanges, our phone conversations, our Zooms, or our face-to-face chats, it was a great pleasure and privilege to get to know you a little bit more. With that, I hope readers also get to know you—and your work—even more.

**JM**

# CHRONOLOGY

1947     Lynn Beverley Ridgway is born on May 28 in Collingwood, Ontario, to Mervyn and Ursula Ridgway.

1949     The Ridgway family moves to North Vancouver, British Columbia. Mervyn starts working as a watchmaker and jeweler while Ursula, a talented artist and calligrapher in her own right, looks after the family and home.

1949     Brother Alan born (a.k.a. Uncle Phil in the strip).

1950s     Johnston's early artistic skills are noted by the family. By the 1960s she is aware of her aunt Unity Bainbridge's ability to be a full-time working artist, marketing her own creations.

1965     Graduates high school and is accepted at Vancouver School of Art (VSA). [Editor's note: *For Better or For Worse: The Comic Art of Lynn Johnston* gives 1965 as the date, but one of the drawings—page 56—is dated 1964.]

1966–67     During the summer between her second and third year at VSA, she finds work at Canawest Films, where she works on a cheaply produced Abbott and Costello cartoon. Still, she decides she wants to have a career in animation and leaves art school.

1967     Now twenty, Johnston marries Doug Franks. The couple, along with Johnston's close friend Cecily Sell and her husband, drive to Los Angeles looking for work at Jay Ward Studios. Both women are immediately offered jobs working on animation backgrounds, but their husbands refuse to make the move. Franks then loses his camera operator job at the Canadian Broadcasting Corporation (CBC), so they move to Hamilton, Ontario. Assuming they will move back to Vancouver when the job market improves, Johnston finds a part-time job at the Hamilton General hospital as a graphic artist. It lasts about six months.

1969     Recognized for her artistic talents, Johnston gets work with the medical teaching staff illustrating lectures at McMaster University

Medical Centre. Her graphic art teaching aids along with anatomy diagrams are a big hit for many professors and students.

1970/71    An Old English sheepdog puppy joins the couple and is named "Farley" after Canadian author Farley Mowat, whom Johnston had the pleasure of getting to know.

1972    Having left her job at McMaster because she wanted to return home—alone—to North Vancouver, she is talked into returning to Hamilton and her uneasy marriage. Now pregnant and doing freelance work for the hospital, Johnston is asked by obstetrician Dr. Murray Enkin to do some drawings for the ceilings above his examining tables.

1973    Son Aaron (a.k.a. *For Better or For Worse*'s Michael) is born April 11. Months later, Johnston and Franks divorce. Johnston spends two years working for a packaging company. As a struggling single parent, she sends Farley to his new home in the country.

1974    Dr. Enkin informs Johnston that he wants to help her publish her ceiling drawings. A total of 101 drawings are ultimately collected under the name Lynn Franks in *David, We're Pregnant!*, which eventually sells 300,000 copies. Sequels *Hi Mom! Hi Dad!* and *Do They Ever Grow Up?* come later, although Johnston struggles to receive royalties due to the publishers' unjustly withholding the funds. Watching planes take off and land at the local airport one day, Johnston meets Rob Johnston (a.k.a. John Patterson), who happens to be landing his small Cessna. He plans to finish dental school and move to Northern Manitoba where he wants to be a "fly-in dentist."

1975    Marries Rob Johnston.

1977    Gives birth to Katherine (a.k.a. Elizabeth) December 28. Johnston's three books on parenting find their way to Universal Press Syndicate. They reach out and ask her to consider creating a daily comic strip. She is presented with a twenty-year contract.

1978    The Johnstons move to the small northern community of Lynn Lake, Manitoba (some 1200 kilometers/730 miles from the Canada–US border), where they will remain for the next six years. Lynn is given six months to develop her strip. After her soon-to-be editor Lee Salem puts her in contact with *Cathy* cartoonist Cathy Guisewite, the proposed family strip *The Johnstons* is renamed *For Better or For Worse*.

1979    On September 9, *For Better or For Worse* comic strip makes its debut. While Johnston uses the middle names of her children and husband for their strip counterparts, she chooses Elly in honor of her childhood best friend Elly Jansen, who passed away in elementary school.

1980    The November 10 *For Better or For Worse* storyline deals with the Pattersons getting their dog Farley.

1983    In the Sunday, July 18, strip, Michael gets spanked. The last panel is later redrawn in the reruns so that Michael is instead punished by being put into the corner for a "time out." It is one example of when Lynn made alterations to the strip when republished (see also July 15, 2012). Sometimes these changes were due to a desire to update language or imagery, and other times they were in response to changing attitudes.

1985    The economy of Lynn Lake is hit hard by the closure of a local mine, so the Johnstons move to the town of Corbeil, Ontario (one-hour flying time from Toronto). Johnston participates in "November Draws" comics with forty others for a special Famine Relief strip during the US Thanksgiving. The *For Better or For Worse* animated Christmas television special *The Bestest Present* appears. The first of a handful of animated episodes to come, this would perhaps be considered the "bestest" of the lot, winning a Gemini Award for best writing in the Children's Entertainment Category. Interestingly for trivia fans, Aaron and Katherine voice their counterparts Mike and Elizabeth, while Rod provides the voice for the mail carrier.

1986    Wins the Outstanding Cartoonist of the Year Reuben Award by the National Cartoonists Society. She is the first female and first Canadian to receive this honor from her peers. Charles M. Schulz of *Peanuts* fame, whom she has met earlier, happily informs Johnston that he voted for her. They will become lifelong friends.

1990    The September 8 *For Better or For Worse* storyline deals with Elly's surprise pregnancy. Johnston receives an honorary degree, doctor of letters, from Lakehead University, Thunder Bay, Ontario.

1991    The body of Michael Vadeboncoeur, Johnston's friend and inspiration for Lawrence's coming-out storyline, is found in Toronto, Canada. He had been brutally murdered. Johnston receives the Inkpot Award for Excellence in Comics (San Diego Comic-Con).

1992    The February 1 *For Better or For Worse* storyline deals with child abuse. Johnston receives the Order of Canada (Canada's highest civilian award).

1993 The March 26 *For Better or For Worse* storyline deals with Lawrence coming out. *For Better or For Worse* now reaches fourteen hundred newspapers. Johnston is nominated for the Pulitzer Prize. Library and Archives Canada receives 580 original strips and drawings from Johnston. She receives an honorary degree, doctor of laws, from McMaster University, Hamilton, Ontario.

1994 The February 15 *For Better or For Worse* storyline deals with Elly hitting menopause.

1995 The April 5 *For Better or For Worse* storyline deals with Farley dying after saving one of the Patterson family.

1997 *For Better or For Worse* now appears in 1700 newspapers. On April 1, readers of newspaper comics see cartoonists switch workloads. Mike Peters takes over *For Better or For Worse* while Johnston tackles Peters's *Mother Goose and Grimm*.

1998 The January 19 *For Better or For Worse* storyline deals with the death of Grandma Marian. Johnston leaves Universal Press Syndicate for United Features.

1999 *For Better or For Worse* now appears in 2000 newspapers. Johnston receives an honorary degree, doctor of laws, University of Western Ontario, London, Ontario.

2000 The February 4, *For Better or For Worse* storyline deals with Elly getting a mammogram. On February 12, Johnston's dear friend and legendary cartoonist Schulz dies. A short-lived weekly animated series based upon the strip runs (Funbag Animation Studios). Johnston receives two honorary degrees: doctor of letters, Nipissing University, North Bay, Ontario; and doctor of letters, Emily Carr Institute of Art and Design, Vancouver.

2001 Presented with a special national award for her portrayal of human rights and diversity issues by the League for Human Rights of B'Nai Brith Canada. Unfortunately, she also discovers that she has dystonia, a movement disorder. The Farley Foundation is created to provide funding to help low-income seniors or people with disabilities pay for the veterinary care of their sick or injured pets. *For Better or For Worse* was awarded Comic of the Year, Editor, and Publisher.

2002 Receives Queen Elizabeth II Golden Jubilee Medal.

2003 Receives a star on Canada's Walk of Fame, as well as an honorary membership award from the Ontario Veterinary Medical Association for her work with the Farley Foundation.

| | |
|---|---|
| 2004 | The August 16 *For Better or For Worse* storyline deals with Elizabeth moving to the fictional Northern Canadian town of Mtigwaki. Johnston returns to Universal Press Syndicate. Johnston receives the Debwewin Citation from the Anishinabek Nation for excellence in Aboriginal-issues journalism. |
| 2005 | The July 26 *For Better or For Worse* storyline starts to explore Elizabeth's being stalked. |
| 2006 | The September 25 *For Better or For Worse* storyline deals with Elly's father Jim having his first stroke. Johnston is recognized as one of the "Giants of the North" as she is presented with the Doug Wright Hall of Fame Award. |
| 2007 | In May, Johnston receives the Order of Manitoba even though she hasn't lived in the province for some time. Lynn and Rod divorce. In September, the strip shifts focus away from Elly and John onto the children, and some older strips are used as flashbacks. |
| 2008 | The original run of *For Better or For Worse* ends on August 30; an epilogue Sunday strip appears on August 31 revealing the future of the major characters. However, the strip starts being republished September 1 as "new-runs," utilizing a mix of reruns and tweaked strips from the 1980s. Johnston is inducted into the Canadian Cartoonist Hall of Fame and the National Cartoon Museum Hall of Fame. |
| 2010 | In July, *For Better or For Worse* returns to pure reruns. |
| 2012 | Receives the Queen Elizabeth II Diamond Jubilee Medal. |
| 2014 | Library and Archives Canada acquires the Lynn Johnston Materials, receiving over 3000 original drawings. By 2023 the collection will grow to contain 7,686 pen-and-ink drawings, 296 watercolors, 3.54 meters of textual records, and 244 photographs. Other originals—including strips, proofs, and correspondence—will find their way to the Lynn Johnston Collection at the Billy Ireland Cartoon Library and Museum and the Ohio State University; these include materials on the death of Mrs. Baird, the child abuse sequence, the Lawrence story, Farley's death, and the death of Elly's mother. |
| 2019 | Receives the Sergio Award from the Comic Art Professional Society. |
| 2023 | April 14, Johnston continues to draw—and as the editor of this book contacts Lynn to finalize dates for their conversation in the upcoming weeks, she comments, "We are super busy at the studio right now. I'm trying to finish six children's books, do the |

backgrounds for four video games, and we are working on book seven of an *For Better or For Worse* anthology."

2024   In February, the first three books in her new children's book series Alottabotz appear. *The Botshop, Marvellous Things*, and *A Dog with No Name* follow the adventures of Timothy Bot, a nine-year-old robot boy who moves to the sprawling fictitious city of Cyberland.

2024   Volume 8 of *For Better or For Worse: The Complete Collection* comes out.

2024   Volume 9 of *The Complete Collection*—the last volume—is released.

CONVERSATIONS WITH LYNN JOHNSTON

# A Profile of Cartoonist Lynn Johnston

## ADRIENNE CLARKSON / 1980

From *The Fifth Estate* (September 22, 1980), CBC television. Excerpts aired on *Rewind with Michael Enright* (October 24, 2012), CBC/Radio Canada, from which this is taken. Reprinted by permission.

**Michael Enright:** I'm Michael Enright, and this is *Rewind*. . . . Today, a look at Canadian comic books and comic strips. . . .

George Henderson talked about the need for some Canadian voices in the comics and Lynn Johnston, the creator of the hugely successful comic strip *For Better or For Worse*, fits the bill. Back in September 1979, her strip, *For Better or For Worse*, appeared in a handful of newspapers across North America. This piece, from *The Fifth Estate*, caught her almost exactly a year after its debut, in September 1980, as she struggled to balance the demands of a daily strip with the pressures of being a mother. Interviewing her is Adrienne Clarkson.[1]

**Adrienne Clarkson:** Most of us make the same mistake when we're changing the diapers or mopping up the mushy popsicle from the new rug. We think that all we have is a mess. But there's a woman in Lynn Lake, Manitoba, who knows better. For her, household drudgery and the minutiae of family life provide her inspiration, her fame, and a very good income indeed. What happens around the house is all a rich vein of ideas—dare we call it her mother lode?—that Lynn Johnston shares with people around the world. Her cartoon strip, based on her own family life and called *For Better or For Worse*, appears in 187 newspapers in the United States and Canada with a total circulation of more than fifteen million, plus more papers in Italy, Australia, and New Zealand.

Now her syndicate is pushing for new spin-offs and new markets. And it all began with Lynn Johnston's ironic understanding that dog tracks in the fresh wax can be revealed truth.

The first Sunday, September 9, 1979. We meet Elly for the first time. FOR BETTER OR FOR WORSE © 1979 Lynn Johnston Productions. Dist. By ANDREWS MCMEEL SYNDICATION. Reprinted with permission. All rights reserved.

This is Northern Manitoba, fisherman's paradise, where there are so many lakes, some of them don't go by name but by letters of the alphabet. Planes are like buses here, and you find flying carpet-layers, flying pharmacists, and flying dentists like Rod Johnston. Wife Lynn says he's got muskeg on his boots and in his blood, so they settled in his hometown, Lynn Lake, a mining town, population three thousand.

Lynn Lake, for a Vancouver girl like Lynn Johnston, was a bit of a surprise. When she first arrived, she thought the town could take a bit of fancying up, but Lynn Lake remained unmoved. The main street is two rather rundown blocks with a Bay store that still trades in furs. It's three years now since Rod Johnston hung up his shingle, and he's busy with two practices and flying visits to Indian villages. So Lynn adopted the Northern uniform of jeans and plaid shirts and found that life in the North could be like suburban life anywhere, except for the number of black flies to be battled. But it's the ordinariness of her own experience which has inspired Lynn's best ideas.

**Lynn Johnston:** [*Pretending to be Elly*] "Whenever the kids are sick. I take their temperatures, read them stories, rock them to sleep. When John's sick, I rub his back and bring him stuff and keep the kids quiet. [*Whining*] I want my mom."

I always draw myself in her whether I mean to or not, but it started out as being me, and I feel very close to the character.

**AC:** This is *For Better or For Worse*, the bags-under-the-eyes look at family life, which is the new hit of the funny pages across North America. The sardonic hand behind it? That of Lynn Johnston. At this Toronto gallery, she's celebrating the opening of a show of her drawings from her cartoon strip. She's the best-selling female cartoonist in the US and Canada thanks to its wry humor. Lynn's touch with pen and ink has already yielded three collections of cartoons, and she's much in demand as an illustrator. Her theme is family life in its rockier moments and in its trials. You'll notice that Lynn even looks like Elly in the strip. And both have bespectacled dentists as husbands. Lynn readily admits that her inspiration is often very close to home.

[*In the background we hear fans talking to Lynn.*]

**LJ:** [*Speaking to a fan*] Well, some of the best lines are right out of the kids, right out of my husband, so I can't take credit for all of this.

**AC:** Fans like these aren't ashamed to admit they read the funny pages. Some of them even clip and keep the Johnston strip because they see themselves there.

**Fan 1:** She has such terrific insight where we can have a situation at home, and we might not think it's very funny. In fact, it's downright awful. And you read her cartoons—it's the same thing, and it makes you laugh about it. It's really good.

**Fan 2:** Shows you the comic side of what's really happening.

**AC:** Devotees of Johnston's humor date back all the way to Lynn's early days as a medical illustrator at McMaster medical school in Hamilton, where the surfacing of the cartoonist kept medical students amused. Then came pregnancy and pregnancy cartoons for Lynn's doctor. Published at his urging, *David, We're Pregnant!* sold over one hundred thousand copies and caught the attention of a cartoon syndicate in Kansas.

**LJ:** They sent me down to Kansas and gave me the greatest attention. I couldn't believe it. And I was terrified at first. In fact, my stomach growled so much I asked them to turn up the music in the office. After all the flattery subsided, I had found my right hand had signed this ten-year contract, and I went back to the hotel and was terribly ill.

**AC:** Lynn's emergence as the cartoonist of the warts and diapers side of family life would bring her $100,000 a year.

Lynn's readers may readily identify with the life in the strip, but they might well have a harder time with the rather rougher life Lynn Johnston actually lives. For Northern families like Lynn and her husband, the family plane has replaced the family station wagon. This is only two hundred miles south of the tree line, and when she arrived here, Lynn considered herself a pioneer. Now she says that living in the North is just like suburban life anywhere. There are still lots of neighborhood kids to be entertained, and they put Lynn's artistic skills to their own uses.

But now the daughter Katie, two and a half; husband Rod; and seven-year-old Aaron, Lynn's son by a previous marriage, and Lynn herself have all become cartoon characters. Anything that happens in the Johnston household can be grist for Mother's drawing board in the basement. Lynn's workroom, conveniently beside the laundry room, is where she has to be found every morning from nine until noon, scratching out those moments of domestic truth for the strip, which has become the *All in the Family* of the funny pages. Lynn nearly parted company with the syndicate at one point when she felt they wanted her to be too bitter. They want realism and a tart edge. And it's that realism which brings in the approving letters.

**LJ:** I just so much enjoy getting letters from other mothers who are so much like myself, and they say, "You've said it right!" And that happened to me yesterday. And one lady wrote and said, "Where are you? Are you under my fridge? Are you behind my piano? How do you know what happens in my house every day?"

**AC:** How does your life, your family life, relate to the strip? Are you living your life so that you'll have lines for the cartoon?

**LJ:** Not consciously. I guess I feel sometimes as though I tape-record it unconsciously because when I'm sitting there looking for material, things that have happened at home do come up and I remember them. Sometimes I come up with a good idea, and I race down and write it down right away. And that's wonderful.

**AC:** For example?

**LJ:** Oh, well, a couple of times, we've had arguments, and I'll say, "You bum! How can you say that to me? Let me write it down," and then I'll race downstairs, and for word for word, it will come out in the paper.

**AC:** But using your family and friends as material can cause injuries.

**Rod Johnston:** There was one particular one that really kind of wounded. I tried to be nice about it, but it really did hurt.

**AC:** You remember what it was?

**RJ:** Yeah, it was . . . Aaron was really rough with other kids, and he just finished beating some other little kid up. So he came home, and I spanked the daylights out of him for hitting. And I said, "There, that'll teach you not to hit anymore." And she, of course, published that one, and I felt a little foolish about that one. But that's really the only one that I've ever felt badly about;

the rest of them I kind of like to see. What I get frustrated by is [that] I come home with what I think are great lines and I tell her what they are at lunchtime and she won't use them. [*Everyone giggles*]

**AC:** Finding enough of those punch lines, one-liners, and gags to satisfy the demands of the daily strip is most of all what makes Lynn nervous. But since her subject is domesticity, there's always the possibility of getting ideas with the groceries. Lynn's always listening carefully. And she believes that the women in the North, who mostly don't have an escape from the housewife's daily grind because jobs are hard to get, are her best source of material on the frustrations of family life. There is no cosmopolitan glamour in Lynn's strip—only, as she says, eye bags and dandruff, and there are times when it's easier to see in Lynn the harassed cartoon housewife rather than the $100,000-a-year cartoonist.

What about your life in Lynn Lake now that you know you are a syndicated cartoon stripist? What do the other women think of you at coffee klatches and so on? How do they regard you?

**LJ:** Nobody talks about it at all. And the only time the subject comes up is when we're talking about a subject, and I find the subject good material, and I'll say, "Wait, that's a good line" or "Hey, let's talk about this more," and then they say, "Oh no, she's going to use it." And then people remember that I am open to their suggestion. Most of the time, no one talks about it. In fact, sometimes I think that nobody even knows here, which is good; I like that.

**AC:** Do you think they think of you more as the flying dentist's wife?

**LJ:** I hope so; I think so.

**AC:** You get any reaction to that?

**RJ:** Sometimes when I'm working on people, they'll say, "Ah-ha, I recognize that."

**LJ:** They're looking at his nose.

**AC:** What about the success that the strip has brought? I mean the monetary success. What has that meant to you, the money that's come in from it?

**LJ:** It's meant—well, first of all, I don't know how to keep a bank book anymore. . . . Well, you know, the first year I couldn't believe I had a salary because I'd worked sort of from hand to mouth freelancing out of a greenhouse at the back of my house. And this business of having a regular salary was wonderful. It's a tremendous freedom. We keep hoping that it won't change us because neither of us have ever been the type of people that wanted to live in a ritzy area. We've never wanted a big car. The only thing Rod ever wanted was a plane. And I love flying too. So we've bought the plane and I think that's [*sings*] "That's where, that's where the money goes." Yeah, there are times when I sit down in that plane and I say, "This plane is mine. I bought this plane and I did it!" You know, "Woo!" [*Laughs*] It's tremendous.

**AC:** For Lynn Johnston, life is more for better than for worse.

**LJ:** I know I'm very special and I'm very lucky. Because I have a job that I can do at home, and it's in my own time, and my kids are around me, and I make a good living. That's wonderful.

**Michael Enright:** That portrait of Lyndon Johnston first aired on *The Fifth Estate* in September 1980. Lynn Johnston is one of the most successful and celebrated cartoonists in history, Canadian or otherwise. Her strip is carried in more than two thousand newspapers in twenty-three countries and can be read in eight languages. She's also won a Gemini Award, been nominated for a Pulitzer Prize, is a member of the Order of Canada, and is the first woman to ever win a Reuben Award for Outstanding Cartoonist from the US-based National Cartoonists Society. In 2008, Johnston announced via the comic strip that she would take the story back in time to its beginning, with half of the material to be new, and the other half repeats.

Note

1.  After an illustrious career as a journalist, Adrienne Clarkson later became Canada's head of state as the 26th Governor General of Canada (1999–2005).

# A Cartoonist for Better or for Worse

## ANN FINLAYSON / 1980

Courtesy of *Maclean's Magazine* (November 24, 1980). Reprinted by permission.

Not long ago, in a flurry of media attention greeting the arrival on the funny pages of yet another accomplished Canadian cartoonist, Lynn Johnston was misquoted as lamenting, "*Mea culpa* is my middle name." Bewildered when she read it, she looked it up. "I couldn't have said it. I didn't even know what mea culpa meant," she says ruefully. "But I do now. And it's true, it's true." The rush of interest that puts words in her mouth and causes television crews to follow her all the way home to Lynn Lake, Manitoba (population: 2,225), hasn't exactly rattled her, but it has made her feel . . . well, a little guilty about the unexpected success of her family comic strip, *For Better or For Worse*, which delivers a daily message of domestic good cheer (with a feminist twist) to more than forty million readers around the world.

Fans of *For Better or For Worse* are perfectly right to identify the thirty-three-year-old Johnston with the wistfully guilt-ridden, slightly frazzled Elly—wife and mother of two—who struggles womanfully on the funny pages to exorcise, through goodwill, her sardonic view of marriage and motherhood.

"Lynn is firmly in the tradition of domestic cartoonists," says Jim Unger, Ottawa-based perpetrator of the diabolical carryings-on in Herman. "I see her strip as a Dagwood and Blondie for the 1980s." But Johnston's self-doubts, fits of pique, and tussles with changing roles blend tradition with introspection with the result that *For Better or For Worse* has attracted a mixed bag of fans—from teenagers who think it's "funny" and housewives who identify strongly with Elly to grown men who can see themselves in John, Elly's well-meaning but beleaguered husband.

"I do try to keep the situations real," says Johnston. "I've never been interested in doing pigs that talk, that sort of thing. I take real-life situations and give them a little twist. Elly has all the problems any mother with a couple of little kids underfoot has. She is liberated, but it's hard."

In her down moments, Elly brings to mind a saucer-eyed Woody Allen—forever coping, frequently misunderstood, puzzled that, in spite of husband John's willingness to share the load, the burdens of family life inevitably fall on her shoulders. When John tries to help by washing the kitchen floor, that great symbol of female oppression, Elly is torn between gratitude and the nagging suspicion that the floor should never have been dirty in the first place—and it's her fault that it is. When John surprises her by hiring a cleaning woman, Elly tears around like a mad thing, scrubbing and polishing in guiltstricken anticipation—an old theme that clearly strikes a responsive chord among the millions of women who see themselves portrayed with uncanny accuracy as they negotiate the shoals of domesticity in times of liberation. Old guilt, new perspective. "Most of my letters are from women," Johnston says, "and most of them are written as they would be to a close friend. There's something there that makes them think we all share the same problems. And, of course, we do."

"In a way, Lynn and I are dinosaurs," says *Toronto Star* columnist Gary Lautens, whose new book, *Take My Family . . . Please*, is embellished with thirty-three Johnston illustrations. "We both believe in the traditional values of family life and we both use family experiences for inspiration." But Lautens lives and works in downtown Toronto like many of the readers of *For Better or For Worse*, who chuckle over its big-city tone in every major market in North America as well as in Italy, Australia, New Zealand, and even Japan. They would be surprised to learn that the strip's domestic verities originate in Lynn Lake—a dot on the map 1,200 kilometers north of the US border.

Four years ago, Johnston and her dentist husband, Rod, returned to his hometown from Hamilton, Ontario, where she had been working as a medical artist at the McMaster University School of Medicine. "I began there doing straightforward illustrations," she recalls, "but occasionally I would do a cartoon if it seemed to make the point better." A series on the joys and irritations of pregnancy, done "for fun" for her obstetrician, were collected into her 1974 book, *David, We're Pregnant!*, and published in Canada. Two more collections followed—*Hi Mom! Hi Dad!* and *Do They Ever Grow Up?* Their success caught the attention of the Universal Press Syndicate in Mission, Kansas, which signed Johnston on for a daily strip with an $80,000-a-year, ten-year contract. "We had been looking for a contemporary family strip for a long time," says Lee Salem, who edits *For Better or For Worse* and also handles such funnies favorites as Garry Trudeau's cerebral *Doonesbury*, Cathy Guisewite's unhappily liberated *Cathy* and Jim Unger's *Herman*. "When we introduced it a year ago last May," says Salem, "Lynn's strip was an instant success, mostly I think because of its air of reality about [moments of] conflict within the marriage situation. She handles those with real precision. She's never saccharine and she keeps her material believable."

Not surprisingly, Universal has plans to bring out a collection of the strips next year. A television special is a possibility for the future, as is a line of spinoff products. "Right now I'm not even thinking about all that," sighs Johnston. "It was suggested that maybe I could introduce a dog into the strip. Well, I may do that—I had been considering it, in fact—but I would never do it just to sell a stuffed animal." Beginning November 11, the dog did appear. The pressures of producing a daily strip leave little time for extra projects anyway. Johnston works every morning in a spare room in the basement of her Lynn Lake home, submitting about six weeks' worth of material at a time. She mails copies to Lee Salem in Kansas, keeping originals at home for any revisions she agrees to in frequent telephone conversations. "Usually we don't change much," says Salem. "Occasionally I suggest tightening the dialogue, or once in a while I don't think an idea works."

Ideas, ideas. "I'm always looking for ideas," says Johnston. "Got any good ones?" Her own family is used to having private moments announced to the world, and most of her material originates at home with husband Rod ("He's a walking Pollyanna: he almost never objects to what I do to him in the strip"), son Aaron, seven, by her first marriage ("It wasn't great"), and daughter Katie, nearly three. "Aaron used to ask what he was doing in the papers, but now he seems to identify less with Michael. And Katie is too young to understand that she is the model for Elizabeth. Besides, I don't think my style is threatening anyway."

What is threatening are the public appearances that have come to dominate her career. "I'm not surprised," says Rod. "Lynn doesn't do too well in public. I think she really needs me around as a buffer." But the demands on Lynn Lake's only full-time dentist (who also serves four remote villages on a regular schedule) are heavy, and this time the buffer stayed home. When they travel together, which is often, they do so in the Cessna 185 they bought in July.

Johnston credits her earliest inspiration to the *Vancouver Sun*'s longtime editorial page cartoonist, Len Norris. But at the Vancouver School of Art (now the Emily Carr College of Art), her former drawing teacher Ian Macintosh remembers that "her talent as an illustrator was always apparent. She was always serious about her art, always likable, always responded to a challenge—a bright-eyed, versatile, funny person."

One of Johnston's lingering difficulties is with her mother, Ursula Ridgway, who now lives in Hope, British Columbia. "We're very proud of her now," says Lynn's mother, "but I do miss her letters. She used to write twenty or thirty pages about what she was doing. Now she phones a lot, but it's just not the same. I know she's very good, and we do enjoy the strips, but, really, ordinary was good enough for me." Sighs Johnston: "My parents think I've changed. They seem to believe that I must have because of the money and everything. Really, I'm pretty much as I've always been; they've just changed their view of me. I worry about it, I really do."

The toughest problem, though, is the question of new material. Unlike Dennis the Menace, who remains forever six, Elizabeth and Michael will grow up in the strip as Aaron and Katie do so in real life, thereby providing a steady flow of changing situations. "A strip like Lynn's can develop and change over time," says Jim Unger. "It may seem limiting, but look at *Doonesbury*. At the beginning Michael J. Doonesbury was the central figure, but now he rarely appears. Lynn could branch out if she wanted to, or she can keep it tight.

"Whatever she does, I think she's getting better and better as a cartoonist."

Welcome reassurance to a young woman who is still not quite able to believe her good fortune, who hasn't entirely worked out the relationship between success and pleasing her parents, and who worries about having enough ideas for the next nine years. But, as Salem points out, a ten-year contract looks longer than it really is. It takes several years to develop an audience, and in the end the creator has the upper hand: "A cartoonist can just stop drawing and there's not much anyone can do about it," she says. "But Lynn is handling it all very well. She'll be all right." Elly would be proud.

# Canadian Import with USA Appeal

### KATHY ALTER / 1988

From *The Hawk Eye*, Burlington, Iowa (July 1, 1988). Mississippi Valley Publishing. Reprinted by permission.

Elly, John, Michael, and Lizzie Patterson are probably celebrating today. Like families all over Canada, they take great pride in their country and enjoy this special day of celebration. Just as Lynn, Rod, Aaron, and Katie Johnston do. And though the first family is probably more celebrated, they owe their very existence to Lynn, the wife and mother of the second family.

The Pattersons, perhaps Canada's best known and best loved export, are the funny, sometimes frustrated, touching, loving—for the most part—and always honestly drawn characters that bring life to *For Better or For Worse* on nine hundred daily and Sunday comics pages around the world.

Lynn Johnston is proud of her creations. She "was for a while surprised" by the success of her comic strip. "Now, I'm terrified," she said in a recent telephone interview. It is a comfort, she said, "to know that others face the same problems" and for her, "it's almost like a therapy session to draw."

As a Canadian, Johnston sometimes used "Canadianisms," potentially confusing her international readers. FOR BETTER OR FOR WORSE © 2010 Lynn Johnston Productions. Dist. By ANDREWS MCMEEL SYNDICATION. Reprinted with permission. All rights reserved.

The reader identification with the strip, Johnston said, provides her with "a sense of connection" most artists can't feel because of the solitary nature of the job.

When readers praise the strip, she is of course pleased, she said, but it has also brought a sort of delicious terror to her. "There are so many readers, and people tend to expect a lot of you. In order to keep the standard up, you have to keep a sense of insecurity."

She attributes the appeal of the strip to "a certain sense of honesty. I try to show all the sides of a problem. I never show anybody all good or all bad. And for kids' sakes, I like to show that parents sometimes do things absolutely wrong." That honesty rings true for readers. In the comic poll conducted by *The Hawk Eye* in February, one reader said, "She must be looking in my back window." "Actually, what I'm doing is letting other people look in mine," Johnston said.

Family and friends often see their actions or words in the strip, Johnston said, and "they love it." But if the subject matter is controversial or potentially embarrassing, she checks with her source of inspiration. A recent segment showing Michael looking for armpit hair was "checked" with Aaron, Michael's real-life counterpart.

There is also much of Lynn in Elly, she said, much of Rod in John, and much of Katie in Lizzie, though other family members, friends, and acquaintances inspire bits and pieces of all the characters.

"My husband did recently buy a sports car," Johnston said, a chuckle rolling over the long miles from Northern Canada. "He also owns nine chain saws."

Physical characteristics, Johnston said, are most often gleaned from stock photography books, and she has "a family portrait" photo she uses for inspiration for the Pattersons.

Mrs. Baird, the elderly widow who was neighbor to the Pattersons until this year, "was [based upon] two women I knew and really loved. They were both widows, and because I loved them dearly, I always wanted them to meet the right men. Actually, both went into nursing homes, having a ball."

Mrs. Baird, regular readers of the strip know, also went into a nursing home and there did find "the right man." "That was my fantasy," Johnston said.

But Mrs. Baird also died. A topic you seldom find in comic strips. A topic that left readers wiping tears. Treading that unfamiliar water was a little frightening, Johnston said, "but it was a challenge to do something serious. I figured Mrs. Baird was in her eighties. What would happen if she just disappeared? And in terms of timing, it was time to do something serious.

"I was surprised by the number of people who were touched by it," Johnston said. "It was kind of neat."

A real-life situation also inspired the segment. "We had a friend who died of cystic fibrosis. . . . What a terrible disease," Johnston said, the pain of her friend's death still evident in her voice. "When Christine died, we were devasted by it. Katie said, 'Don't cry, Mom, now we know our own angel.'"

The strip, Johnston said, "is vignettes and short stories, insights. It's not a continuity strip, really, but I like to work in series. That's when I write best. When I first started, I wrote in spot gags, like *Herman*," but the series approach soon became her favored format.

"Sometimes," Johnston said, "the characters write the story themselves. Sometimes they fight you" if the storyline doesn't seem honest.

She also takes "the opportunity to preach occasionally," Johnston said. Strips this winter pictured Elly as the loneliest hockey fan in the world as she cheered Michael through his practices at the school arena.

The inspiration, Johnston said, was more consternation at the lack of parental involvement she saw at her son's real-life hockey practices and games. "I'd look around and wonder, 'Where are all the parents?' It meant so much for Aaron to have me there.

"I don't think anyone starts out to be a cartoonist," Johnston said, "It's just in your blood, like a disease or something. I really wanted to be a fine artist, but I'm just too silly for that. I love to laugh . . . and it gets me into tremendous trouble. It's hard for me to sit through a church service without thinking of one-liners." An assignment in college, Johnston said, was to take one subject and produce it in all possible art forms. "I chose the polar bear," Johnston said. "I did polar bears in every possible medium.

"When I did my sculpture, it looked so much like a Cessna, I put a propeller on the nose. Besides, I didn't want to part with anything serious that I did."

Art has always been an important part of her life, she said. Her mother and an aunt were artists, and her jeweler father "loved to do cartoon art. Dad introduced me to a cartoonist when I was only eight or nine. He took me to his house to see his studio." The visit made what might seem awesome seem possible, Johnston said. "I saw this cartoonist was just a man, just a person."

Now, "whenever there's a kid who wants to see the studio, I show him. It takes the mystery out."

Her studio is "in the basement with one small window. If I recognize the hubcaps, I know who's coming to the door. The dog's usually there with me, too." But it's not a Farley-type sheep dog. "When the baby was born," Johnston said, "I flipped a coin, and the sheep dog lost."

Her family, Johnston said, always encouraged her artistic efforts, as did many who surrounded her during those early years. "Wherever you go in life, there is always someone there who tunes in and encourages you." A math teacher she had knew she was "terrible in math," but always gave her an "'A' for the drawings I put alongside." *Peanuts*, *Archie*, *MAD* magazine, and *Little Lulu*—"because there was a girl who was winning, a girl who was smart"— provided early cartoon inspiration, as did other "classics," Johnston said.

Choosing a favorite strip or character now would be as difficult as then, she said. "*Calvin and Hobbes* is great, and I love *Mother Goose and Grimm* and *Hagar*," Johnston said. "There are just so many. Like candy, there are so many good ones, you'll never try them all."

Now, as a member—a board member, for that matter—of the National Cartoonists Society, she rubs elbows with her childhood and current cartoonist heroes. They are now her peers, and her peers gave her the ultimate honor in 1986, the [Reuben] Award as Cartoonist of the Year.

She feels inadequate as an expert on comic strip longevity, because, she said *For Better or For Worse* is "only ten years old. But I think it's that sense of insecurity. I try to be better than the day before. And honesty. If you lose it, it's time to stop. I hope I have the guts to stop."

Her readers hope she never has to face that decision. Meanwhile, they can revel in the fact Lynn and her creation mirror another of their thoughts: The daily newspaper comics page, she said, "is the only page that makes any sense."

# The Lynn Johnston Interview

## TOM HEINTJES / 1994

From *Hogan's Alley*, no. 1 (1994). Reprinted by permission.

It's easy to form a mistaken impression about Lynn Johnston. I should know. Thinking myself rather well-informed, I had known her to be a fantastically talented woman masterminding one of the most successful strips—critically and popularly—in recent comics history. I also knew she loosely modeled *For Better or For Worse* on her own family. And I was also aware that Universal Press Syndicate had sought her out, intent on convincing her to wield her unique talents in fashioning a new type of family strip—one done by a woman. (This was during a time when Cathy Guisewite's *Cathy* had shown the comics-reading public to be hungry for a female perspective.) To prepare for this interview, I read the autobiographical introduction to her strip's tenth-anniversary collection, where I learned about her childhood, which overall seemed healthy and normal. What I did not and could not know, however, was even more striking and served to heighten my already considerable admiration for the woman behind the drawing board. In achieving the pinnacle of success she currently enjoys as the creator of a strip appearing in more than sixteen hundred papers, Lynn Johnston had to rise above obstacles that would have shackled most people. If *For Better or For Worse* seems so honestly and genuinely realized, its characters so in touch with themselves and their world, it is because they are extensions of their creator's complex and perceptive personality. Lynn, forty-six, was born Lynn Ridgway in Collingwood, Ontario, Canada, and she grew up in British Columbia. She is married to Rod Johnston (whose middle name is John). She has two children, Aaron Michael, twenty, and Katie Elizabeth, sixteen. (Do those middle names sound familiar?) They live in Corbeil, Ontario. This interview—originally published in 1994 in *Hogan's Alley #1*—was conducted, transcribed, and edited by Tom Heintjes.

**Tom Heintjes:** As a child, you were something that a lot of cartoonists weren't—you were outgoing and extroverted, the class clown, the prankster.

**Lynn Johnston:** I was outgoing and extroverted in the wrong way. I was a fighter. I was angry. I wanted to fight, and I wanted to hurt people.

**Heintjes:** What was the source of that anger?

**Johnston:** I was very unhappy at home. You think about child abuse and you think of a father viciously attacking a daughter or a son, but in my family it was my mother. My mother, I would say, was a . . . very brutal disciplinarian. She was brought up with a "spare the rod and spoil the child" philosophy, and she was raised by a father who brutalized her. He didn't want daughters. He wanted sons. He had no time for daughters. He refused to educate his daughters. It was a waste of his money. And they all left home as soon as they possibly could. Some of them ran away from home, some left to join the armed forces. That's what my mother did. And my father was the first person she'd met who treated her kindly. She was terrified of men, and she married a very meek, kind, dear man. And she had the upper hand. She ruled the roost. My father was beaten as a child. His philosophy became "I refuse to lay a hand on my children."

**Heintjes:** That's the opposite approach of most abused children.

**Johnston:** Right. But my mother's philosophy was, the harder you beat them, the more they'll realize that what they've done is wrong. She would hit me until she was exhausted. She would use brushes, broomsticks, anything she could wield. I could look at the different bruises and tell what she had hit me with. If it was a black bruise with a red stripe down the middle, it was a piece of kindling. If it was a brown bruise with a certain shape to it, it was a hairbrush. If it was perfectly round, it was a wooden spoon. I used to go to school with bruises from the middle of my back to my heels.

**Heintjes:** And your father never interceded?

**Johnston:** Never. And my mother was so full of anger and hate. She was a brilliant woman. She could have done anything. She was a writer, she was an artist, she was a calligrapher, just a brilliant, talented lady with potential beyond belief. Right after the war, she married a man and had a family. But she wanted a career. She wanted to be a doctor. God help you if you got sick, because her home remedies would kill you. Poultices, enemas, and God knows what else. But at that time it was not appropriate for a woman to go to work. Her work was in the home. Everybody saw these magazine ads with the lady in the dress who stayed at home all day. But even though all this was going on at home, if someone had tried to take me away and put me in a children's home, I couldn't have handled it. Even though my mother was very brutal, it was my home.

**Heintjes:** Did your mother feel a need to always be in control of any given situation?

**Johnston:** Oh, yes. You talk about women in the military . . . she would have gone over the hill first. She would have held the machine gun until the last bullet was fired. She was a fighter.

**Heintjes:** What were your parents like when there wasn't strife?

**Johnston:** My mother was a very literate person who had educated herself. She had an exceptional vocabulary. And my father was a comic. He could play any musical instrument. He loved to perform. He was a wonderfully comedic character. He had the ability to dance and sing and charm and analyze poetry. He was an exciting person to have in your home. When he got a few drinks in him, he was on. And he wasn't an alcoholic. But he was a performer, and all he needed was a beer in his hand and he was gone. So the two of them together were very witty, very funny. And we never dealt with anything straight out in our home. If something happened, it was over and done. But there was an undercurrent of anger and hate and unresolved problems, all the time. For example, my mother would look at you, and you would ask, "What's wrong?" and she would say, "Well, you should know." And it might be about something you said two weeks ago. But she would never tell you why she was angry with you. She might be angry with my father or my brother or someone else, and then something like a spilled bowl of cereal or a bad word would make her strike out, and she would beat and beat and beat and beat and beat you. You could see this look on her face that was pure rage.

When I got too big for her to beat, she would scream things at me like, "You fat cow! You ugly duck!" She just didn't know any better, because that was the sort of thing she grew up with. Back then, there were no parenting groups. There were no books. All she knew was "I have to get this ugly thing into line. I have to force this thing to toe the line."

I haven't told many people this because my parents were still alive and I didn't want to reveal it, but I want you to print this, because it happens in so many families! She really cared, though. It's hard to describe. On the one hand, she beat the living crap out of me. On the other hand, though, she was bright and witty and well read. Neither of my parents ever stopped encouraging my brother and me from pursuing our creativity. They let us take all kinds of art classes. My dad made forty-seven dollars a week at the jeweler's shop in Vancouver. If there was any money left over, we would go to see a movie or something like that. My mother used to shop for clothes at the Salvation Army. She would buy trench coats there and remake them to fit us. She made us the most wonderful clothes. We never realized how poor we were! She was a survivor. We grew our own food, and we were never hungry. My mother saved every scrap of food either for the compost heap or for the birds. People never knew we were poor, but out of that poverty came the most incredible inventions—board games, recipes. . . . We never stopped inventing.

**Heintjes:** Both of your parents had come through the Great Depression.

**Johnston:** That's right, and they had a Depression mindset. After I got this job at the syndicate, I started sending them money so they could go on trips and do the things they could never afford to do. All the while, I never knew that my mother was socking money away. And when my mother passed away, I found she had a bank account with $60,000 in it!

**Heintjes:** How long ago did she pass away?

**Johnston:** It's been four years now.

**Heintjes:** It sounds as if you've reconciled your feelings toward your parents.

**Johnston:** It's taken a long time. You know, when she died, I didn't cry. I stood by the bed she had just died in, and I remember being very clinical, thinking, *She is still warm*, folding her arms across her body, tilting her head. It was very strange. Then I came home from the hospital, and I was sitting on the side of her bed, looking into her closet. I looked at her clothes, and you know what I thought of?

**Heintjes:** What was that?

**Johnston:** I thought of the Wicked Witch of the West, who turned into a puff of smoke after the house crushed her, and all that was left of her were her shoes. That's what I thought. And it took me a long time before I could see past that and see her as something else—a strong, positive influence on me in many ways.

**Heintjes:** I'm having a little bit of trouble reconciling what I'm hearing now with what you wrote of your childhood in the tenth anniversary *For Better or For Worse* collection.

**Johnston:** That book was written before my parents passed away. I was very, very protective of my parents. We were never able to resolve all these issues. We never talked about it. I remember after my mother's death, I thought my father would talk to me about it. It was a perfect time to talk about it. One beautiful sunny Saturday he and I were taking a walk along the river, and we were talking about our lives together and growing up. And I said to him, "Dad, I want to talk to you about Mom beating us." And he said, "I will not talk about it." So part of him was acknowledging that it happened, and part of him was saying that it never happened at all. So when something goes unresolved, you have to resolve it some way. One way to resolve it is with the death of the people, because there is a certain romanticism that comes with death. I know it sounds crazy, but I have had far more connection with my parents after their deaths.

I'm not a great driver. I often get extremely frustrated with great big trucks in front of me and people driving too slowly. And just the other day, I almost killed my daughter and myself because I didn't wait for a sensible place to pass. I was thinking that somehow there's a hand on me that's keeping me safe. One time I was on an airplane in a terrible storm. The woman sitting next to me had white knuckles, staring anxiously out the window. And I wanted to say to her, "We're not going to crash—you're with me!" I lead a charmed life, I really do.

**Heintjes:** Are you religious?

**Johnston:** I don't like organized religion where people tell me I have to follow a certain dogma. I don't like other people interpreting Scriptures for me. I like to interpret them for myself. Not that I feel that I'm the only one who can, but I just feel. . . . Let's put it another way. Only a couple of times have I ever been to church and felt enlightened by it. When I was a kid, I was in the choir, and I remember the politics of the choir. The favorite kids got to sing solos, the kids who were not favorites didn't. When I was sixteen, I was in the choir, and I was taking off my surplice after a performance, and this old gray-haired guy from the bass section grabbed my breast from behind. I spun around and said, "What are you doing?!" and he said, "Oh, I'm sorry, I was helping you off with your surplice." And the way he said it, I thought, *How can I believe that he wasn't trying to help me?* But when I got out of church that day, I thought, *How could that happen in church, of all places?* So church for me was always politics and lies.

**Heintjes:** Did your household have a pretense of being religious?

**Johnston:** It was "do as I say, not as I do." Mom and Dad would stay in bed on Sunday morning, but the kids would have to go to church.

**Heintjes:** Really?

**Johnston:** Oh yeah. They went to church on holidays.

**Heintjes:** Did you mind going to church under these circumstances?

**Johnston:** Well, I loved to sing, just loved it. I loved to sing harmonies. So the choir for me was wonderful. The dogma of the church was secondary. After I proved I could keep a tune, I loved getting to sing solos.

**Heintjes:** Did you devise any sort of escape mechanism for the life you had?

**Johnston:** I was very reclusive. I spent hours and hours in my room drawing. That was my release, and that was my way of surviving. You see, anything I imagined, I could draw. And I found that if I was in a terrible depression and I closed my eyes, the blackness would appear to go on forever. But if I put it down on paper, it was no bigger than 8.5 × 11 [inches], and I could deal with that. If you have a horror inside of you, it goes down to your marrow. But on paper, it's not so bad.

**Heintjes:** So drawing became a form of therapy.

**Johnston:** It was a way to survive. If I was in love with someone, I would get their picture out of the school yearbook and do portraits. If I was curious about sex, I would draw pictures of it. There were no books for me to look at. Then I would go find my father's matches to burn the paper. [*Laughter*] If I wanted to draw funny pictures, I would draw them, and I remember loving watching my brother laugh at them. My brother was a great audience, and if he liked the picture, he would laugh and laugh and laugh, and he would want to keep the picture. Making people laugh with an image I had created . . . what power that was!

**Heintjes:** How did your upbringing affect the way you rear your own children? Do you find yourself reacting against the way she brought you up?

**Johnston:** [*Pause*] I treat my children both like my mother and myself. But I really need to answer that question later, because I had to go through so much before I learned how to raise my children.

I had a terrible marriage the first time around because I had no self-confidence, even though I had tremendous self-confidence. That was the strange thing. That's why I'm a perfect Gemini. One part of me says that no matter what happens, I have a talent that no one else has. I could sing, I could write, I have so many gifts that I could fall back on. I knew I wouldn't have to work at Woolco. I could go into show business. I knew, deep down inside, that I was never going to starve.

The other side of me said, "You're fat, you're ugly, you don't deserve the best." I never believed I was in love with a guy unless I was crying into my pillow. Any kind man who brought me flowers and remembered my birthday, I thought, *You wimp!* Any guy who treated me like shit, I wanted! "Please God, don't let him go! He said he'd call me!" So I went for these guys who treated me like shit, and I married one of them! The guys who treated me badly were the funny guys, and I always went for the guys with the sense of humor. But I married a guy who treated me very badly, but I was happy. I was miserable, so I was happy.

**Heintjes:** This was Doug, the man who gave you Aaron?

**Johnston:** Yes, and when I had Aaron, he left me, and I didn't know how to raise a child. And I wasn't close to my parents, and because I was too proud to go to my parents for help, I mistreated that little baby. I didn't want a baby. I wanted the stability that a family was supposed to represent. And a baby can't say, "Thanks, Mom, for feeding me and keeping me warm and dry even though I screamed my lungs out all night last night." And they want and they want and they want and they want. The only satisfaction you have is that they're fed and they're warm and they're safe and they're thriving and they smile at you every once in a while. They're not going to thank you until they're forty-five [*laughter*].

I remember once when he was very unhappy and he was screaming and screaming, and I threw him out into a snow bank in his pajamas. This was in Ontario, and it was not warm here. And he put his hands against the window of the front door, pleading to be let in. And I was inside, screaming at him, "If you don't want to sleep all night, you can friggin' sleep outside!" And this was a teeny baby. And I don't know what it was—it was almost like at that moment, my guardian angel put his hand on my shoulder and said, "Open the door."

The next morning, I called a very good friend of mine who was working at the hospital. I had also been doing some work for this hospital on a free-lance basis. And I said to my friend, "I need some help. I don't known how to parent." Now, you say to yourself, "I'm a mature adult—I should know how to parent." But raising a child is not like training a dog. [*Laughter*] I was not a sensible mother. I just didn't know what I was supposed to do. I didn't know about time out. I didn't know to say, "Okay, we're both out of control, let's have time out for five minutes and calm down."

I was in a very unhappy situation. I was lonely, I was single, and I had all the elements set against me. I had no support. And it didn't help that I had a very irritable, difficult child. He's going to go into the theater [*laughter*]. He's a performer. He's witty. He could go into stand-up comedy. He's taken all his anger and turned it into something creative.

**Heintjes:** Sounds like he got those traits honestly.

**Johnston:** He did. Aaron and I will be joined at the hip until the day we die. We have loved and hated each other since the day he was born. He's very much a part of my heart. He's going to broadcasting college now, and he'll do fine. But he came into a world that did not welcome him. I was exactly like my mother in that sense. I just didn't know how to raise him. I had grown up with all the anger, the frustration, and I didn't know how to raise a child.

**Heintjes:** Did you ever physically discipline Aaron?

**Johnston:** I only hit him once. Hard. I felt myself becoming my mother—and I couldn't bear that! I did shout a lot, and I cried a lot. I didn't want to hit Aaron, because he was so small. I can remember my mother dragging my brother around by his arm, like a little monkey. That image was very clear in my memory, and I could never do something like that to my own child. That's one thing that's always served me well as an artist—I could draw that scene right now, because I can recall it so well. I don't forget things like that.

**Heintjes:** Has your husband helped you shape your approach to child rearing?

**Johnston:** Oh yes. I was lucky enough to marry the dearest man in the whole world who, without a psychologist's papers, is able to observe a situation and . . . I won't say analyze it, but see the dynamics and help me figure out why I'm doing something in a certain way. It's taken me a long time to become the person I am, for all the ugliness to fall away. The rotten flesh is gone, and the seed is there. I can touch that now.

**Heintjes:** Contrast Aaron's upbringing with your daughter's, Kate.

**Johnston:** When Kate was born, she was born into a world of joy and happiness and confidence. The difference between the children is night and day. She's happy, she's thriving, she's full of self-confidence. I tell her she's beautiful every day before I send her off to school. When I had her, I was happy, and when you're happy, you can look in the mirror and say, "You know, I'm not so bad." But when Aaron was born, it was different. My husband would say things to me like my mother did. "You're fat and ugly." And he treated me like garbage. His girlfriends would call him at home, and when I would pick up the phone, they would giggle at me. And I would look in the mirror then and say to myself, "If only I were pretty. If only I were thin." So I decided to get thin, and boy, did I get thin—I went down to 110 pounds. I was anorexic. I would go to bed and my stomach would be cramped.

**Heintjes:** What cured you of the anorexia?

**Johnston:** I think it was because a friend of mine did the same thing. We would call each other late at night and say, "I'm starving, are you starving? Okay, don't eat anything and I won't, either."

**Heintjes:** You were each other's codependent.

**Johnston:** That's right. She was from Germany. Her name was Brunhilda. She ran away from home to come to Canada, and we became best friends. We went on this incredible diet where we both became skeletons. I remember looking at her at one point and saying, "You look terrible!" Here we were, trying to become the models we saw in magazines. We wanted the pointed hips and the angular elbows—we looked like Biafrans.

When I first met Bernie, she was wonderful, sexy, beautiful . . . every man's dream. She wasn't fat, but she was rounded, just a delicious-looking woman. Beautiful blue eyes, just perfect. And here she was after this diet, her back covered with bumps from her spine.

**Heintjes:** I don't imagine that you were much better off.

**Johnston:** No, I wasn't. But I looked at my friend Bernie and said, "This is it, we're killing ourselves." I quit dieting, and she didn't. Her period stopped, and she just got worse.

**Heintjes:** What ultimately happened to her?

**Johnston:** She married a doctor, and that was a crazy relationship. They moved back to Germany, where they split up, and I lost touch with her. I know her father owned a pub in Germany, and I have a crazy idea that she's working at that pub. I'd love to go there and see her again; she was a wonderful person.

**Heintjes:** You are a very successful, much-admired woman. And yet you suffered so much in your childhood and early adulthood. Since so much of a person's self-esteem is formed during this period, I wonder how you feel about yourself now.

**Johnston:** I've always felt that life is a novel, and part of it is written for you, and part of it is written by you. It's up to you to write the ending, ultimately. I've had some tremendous adventures, good and bad. It's part of the novel, and a novel isn't interesting if it doesn't have some good and bad. And you don't know what good is if bad hasn't been a part of your life.

Years ago, one person wrote to me and accused me of being an amateur psychologist. I wrote back to her and said, "Yes, I am an amateur psychologist." We all are. That's how we get through life. That's how we figure out our relationships with people. And I wrote to her, "As an amateur psychologist, I wonder what is upsetting you so much that you would be angered by a comic strip? What else in your life is upsetting you?" I'm sure she was miffed by that.

Sure, I've had some bad times, but everybody does. But people don't get to talk about them like I do, unless they do to a therapist. People don't get to put them in the paper like I do. At forty-six, I'm still making mistakes, but I really think people are enriched by the bad stuff, and it should not motivate you to do bad stuff in return. I'm a product of my home, and I have wonderful friends, a wonderful husband and a wonderful family. All of that is good. I could easily have been torn apart by another bad marriage. I was just so lucky to have a wonderful life after a tough marriage. I often think you bring unhappiness on yourself, because if you don't like yourself very much, you allow yourself to be influenced by people who reinforce that.

**Heintjes:** That's what prompted my question, because in years past you seemed not to really like yourself a whole lot.

**Johnston:** Oh, I didn't. And I still don't. In a way, a certain amount of self-criticism is a good thing, because it keeps you humble. Realizing that no matter what success you've achieved, you can still make enemies makes you humble, too. The Lawrence [arc] has been a very humbling experience!

**Heintjes:** I want to switch gears here and talk about your early interest in comics. I find it interesting that some of your earliest comic influences were comic books and not comic strips. In fact, you and I share some of the same early favorites—*Little Lulu, Uncle Scrooge, MAD* magazine.

**Johnston:** Well, those were all fantasy comics. I was never interested in superheroes, though. In the superhero comics the men were always all-powerful, and I was surrounded by weak men. My father was meek, and every male teacher at school that I could browbeat into tears, I did. The men were my adversaries, in a sense.

**Heintjes:** Did you enjoy Wonder Woman comics?

**Johnston:** No. Wonder Woman was perfect, and I was fat and ugly. I knew I could never look like that, so I didn't want to look at her. I loved the Little Lulu stories, where she would fantasize that her bedroom rug would turn into a pool of water, and she could dive down into the center of the world. Or Scrooge McDuck with his money bin. I loved all that stuff. It was wonderful fantasy that seemed achievable by a child. And it wasn't ugly. There were no villains with guns. The bad guys were the ones who were going to steal your lunch money or who were going to stop it from raining forever.

**Heintjes:** Were comics permissible in your household when you were a child?

**Johnston:** Yes, they were, all the time. Because they were creative. The only thing that caused a problem was *MAD,* and that was only with my mother, because my father had a more raucous sense of humor.

**Heintjes:** At that time, *MAD* must have seemed like an underground comic.

**Johnston:** It was absolutely an underground comic. To my mother, it was like having a porno magazine. It was gross. She also didn't approve of the Three Stooges because they were so coarse. My mother was a lady.

My grandfather had been a philatelist for King George V. He was probably one of the leading experts on forgeries. My grandmother was an opera singer who worked for a portrait painter who worked for the royal family. So of course they hobnobbed with the upper crust. And my mother married a guy whose father was a shipyard worker in Collingwood, Ontario. My father's vocabulary was so big only because he was a voracious reader and taught himself to speak properly. So my mother was from the aristocracy and my father was from the bush, so she was shocked when we were captivated by something as crass as the Three Stooges. One time I whacked my brother over the head with a piece of celery to see if it would shatter as effectively in reality as it did when the Three Stooges did it, and it did! It has to be fresh, though. [*Laughter*]

**Heintjes:** Did you ever poke him in the eyes?

**Johnston:** No, but my brother and I tried to kill each other many times. My father would encourage us to stage-fight behind my mother's back. He knew how to do the pratfalls without hurting himself, and he didn't mind the Three Stooges.

**Heintjes:** What sort of creative influence did comics have on you? Did you ever try tracing any of your favorites?

**Johnston:** No, never. I never wanted to trace people's work. I would try to draw cartoons from time to time based on other peoples' stuff, but I just wasn't happy copying anybody. If I took elements of anybody's work, it was Len Norris of the *Vancouver Sun*. He was my father's absolute idol; he just adored the man and had all of his books. He was an editorial cartoonist, and his drawing was just exquisite. It had a British sort of sarcasm to it. He had been an architect, so his renderings were just absolutely beautiful. He always gave you extra stuff to look at. If there was a painting on the wall of the ocean and the painting was tilted, the water was still perfectly horizontal. If there was a bird cage, all you would see of the bird was its feet, because it was obviously dead. I always appreciated that, because not only did you have all of these extra jokes, but you had ten minutes of looking at all of these drawing thrills.

**Heintjes:** You've mentioned in the past that your grandfather would sort of pontificate on each of the Sunday comics, and you differed with him over *Peanuts*.

**Johnston:** Well, when I was a kid, my grandfather was not a nice guy. If you talked to other people who knew him, he was a great guy with a sense of humor, and he was somebody they enjoyed knowing. But to me, he was a sadistic, black, haughty, unattainable ogre. I always felt his disappointment in me. I hated him and wanted him to love me at the same time. As a child, you work so hard for the approval of a grandparent or a parent. You want them to love you, and you'll do anything, even if it means being silly or acting out. You want them to notice you and you want them to care, even if it's not positive care. You want something out of them.

My grandfather used to lavish all sorts of attention and affection on my brother, while he virtually ignored me. He would give my brother fifty cents, and he would give me a nickel. Right in front of each other.

My grandparents lived on this wonderful piece of property that ran up to the train tracks behind their house. It overlooked a very rocky landscape. Behind the house they had peach trees, and we would grab the peaches and wait for the train to go by, and if the peaches were rotten enough, they would smack off those passenger trains' windows like you wouldn't believe! [*Laughter*] We'd get bull's-eyes and yell, "Yahoo!" And that seed in the middle of the peach would hit the window with that satisfying *click*. One day in the peach trees I found a robin's nest with a perfect little robin's egg in it. I came running down the hill with it, and my grandfather was sitting in front of the house with my brother, and they were making string baskets with their fingers. I guess I was about eight and my brother was about six. Anyway, I said, "Look what I found! Look what I found!" I was so excited! And my grandfather said, "The way to keep this is to make a tiny hole in the end of it and blow the material out so you can preserve the shell." So he got a needle from the house, and I was so excited that I would have this robin's egg. As he was about to puncture it with his needle, he turned to my brother and said, "And I will give this to you." And I said, "But I found it! It's mine!" And my grandfather turned to my brother and said, "As I said, I will give this to you." Then he lifted up the bird's egg close enough to his face so he could see what he was doing, and he popped the needle in, and the egg must have been rotten, because it blew up in his face and covered it in the yuckiest muck. I was thrilled! I remember thinking, *There is a God*.

**Heintjes:** Wow—that is perfect!

**Johnston:** But you see, I wanted his approval. I would do anything for his approval, because as a grandparent I saw him every other weekend. No child wants to be out in the cold. My grandfather loved the comics, and he would analyze the Sunday comics. This was something between him and me, because my brother never cared for the comics. He would analyze *Pogo*, and he would analyze *Momma and Miss Peach*. He would talk about why they were drawn that way and what the artist really meant. I was into this, because it was attention from him. I remember thinking that nothing could be worse than *Henry*. It was boring to read; it was drawn so boring. His tongue would appear out of his chin when he was eating an ice cream cone. I remember thinking, *I could do better than that*. That's the sort of thing that really spurs you on to try it.

The one strip my grandfather really didn't like was *Peanuts*. Now, I remember when *Peanuts* first appeared in our paper. It was in the mid-1950s. I was sitting next to my grandfather on the couch, really enjoying the fact that I was close to him, it was warm, and he wasn't pushing me away. He was going through the comics, and I always tried to agree with him, just to make him happy. He finally came to *Peanuts*, and it was a strip where Charlie Brown talks about how depressed he is, and Lucy comes out with a smart remark, and my grandfather said, "No child talks like that. No child has these thoughts. This is ridiculous." And I thought, *You're wrong. We may not use the same words, but we have the same thoughts and the same feelings*. Everything about that strip seemed right. And what appealed to me about it more than anything is that all the women were strong! Lucy was a crank, but she was strong! Peppermint Patty could go out there and play ice hockey and win! One thing I know about Charles Schulz is that he really likes strong women. Many women in his life have been strong. He's encouraged his daughters to be strong, as well. I think he was taking little risks in the strip. You know, there's a formula to comic art, a formula to the gag. It's not predictable necessarily, but there is nevertheless a formula. I think Charles Schulz was willing to forgo that formula with punch lines like "Whatever . . ." and the psychiatrist's five-cent booth.

**Heintjes:** The characters would cast their eyes upward in response to a remark—that was all new.

**Johnston:** Right! I was looking in a copy of *Bartlett's Familiar Quotations*, and they only give him two quotes out of the whole thing. Of course, they only give Jesus one. And I said to myself that I was going to take five minutes and come up with more than two quotations. So I opened up—I think it was the thirty-fifth anniversary book, and in five minutes I wrote down six or so others that could really have been in *Bartlett's*. They were really fine, brilliant, quotable quotes. And I told that to him. I couldn't believe they gave him only two quotes. Cathy Guisewite is someone else who writes very quotable quotes. Why aren't they in *Bartlett's* friggin' *Quotations*? They've got all these things by Aristotle that no one ever heard of before.

**Heintjes:** I think it all comes down to something that you and I and everyone who loves comics have to battle on a daily basis, and that is the general public's dismissal and trivialization of anything associated with comics. I was showing some of my cartoon work to a coworker who is a fine artist. She didn't really know I could draw before I showed her my stuff, and she looked at it and said, "Wow, Tom, if you have this kind of talent you might be able to do some real art one day!" And she wasn't trying to offend me. It was just a natural thing for her to say, because it was comics and therefore not "real" art.

**Johnston:** She actually said that to you . . . wow. Here's an anecdote for you. The first time I went up to Charles Schulz's house, the first time I had spent any real time with him, the first thing he wanted to show me was a drawing he had done of a street in France he had seen while he was there during the war. I looked at this beautiful, sensitive illustration of the houses and the cars, and he looked at me and said, "I really can draw." All of us feel that way.

The editorial cartoonists razz us, and we razz them. They say to us, "You don't have these tight deadlines every day, and you don't always have to be topical, you can do stories about whatever you want. You can draw a strip and then go play golf." And we say to them, "Yeah, but you have an infinite amount of resource material, and you have real space to draw in! We have these little postage-stamp areas, one-third of which has to be the dialogue."

**Heintjes:** That leads me to my next question. You obviously have a real passion for drawing. It shows in everything you do. Do you ever feel constrained by the size of the strip?

**Johnston:** Not really. I've found that I can use that space effectively. I do think, though, that if they reduced it any more I would simply throw my hands up in the air and find another business. We'd lose our readers. Most people can't see that small.

**Heintjes:** I want to talk about *For Better or For Worse*, just in case you thought we were never going to get around to it. Tell me about your early career in cartooning and how this eventually manifested itself into the strip.

**Johnston:** When I was a kid, I always cartooned. When you're a kid, you eat when you're hungry and you laugh when you're happy and you do stuff on the spur of the moment that's a thrill. I cartooned. It was something I did without thinking about it. So when I went to art school, it was the linear, visual arts that intrigued me and the commercial art was the thing that came closest. I was not going to be a painter, and I was not going to be one of these experimental artists who cast body parts in rubber. I wanted to do something that was fast and funny and would make a statement and sold stuff.

**Heintjes:** Most art schools think that comics work is pretty despicable as a career goal.

**Johnston:** Exactly. The people who went into the commercial field were called "the hacks." Meanwhile, these other people were spending fifty dollars on paint—actually, they were requisitioning from the government, which was enough to make you puke—throwing it on thirty-foot canvases, hanging them in local galleries and getting medals for it! The rest of us are painfully doing tuna casseroles in black and white ink. But the ones who did the casseroles are making a living. The people who threw paint onto canvases are either on welfare, drugged, or went into the retail business. I don't know.

But it was a fine arts college. They put no money into the commercial art area. You know that adage "Them that can't do, teach"? It was so painfully, pathetically, unhappily true. The guy who was teaching commercial art was looking at it from the 1920s. We were still rendering in black and white when color television was happening. We were begging for color, and he was making us render in black and white with frisket paper and smudged charcoal and things that people didn't do anymore. We wanted to do stuff in airbrush and colors. Then, when I got a summer job in an animation studio, I can't tell you how I suddenly woke up! There are people in this world who are as nutty as me! There are other people who act and sing and perform and bang their heads against the wall and laugh and draw and dream and bring things to life!

So I quit art school and took on a full-time position at the animation studio. I worked there for two or three years, and I met and married a cameraman, and moved to Ontario looking for work. In those days, there was no work in BC [British Columbia], and all the work was in Ontario. Now that we have an NDP [New Democratic Party] government, BC is where all the work is, and there's none in Ontario! So we moved to Ontario, and I tried to get work as an animator out here. But there was no work in animation unless I wanted to freelance for *Rocket Robin Hood*, which was garbage! I thought maybe I'd go back into the jewelry business, because my dad was a jeweler, and I'd grown up working for him. So one day I took my folio in the store with me for the hell of it, and the guy who ran the store said, "Look, I'll hire you if you can't find any-thing else—you've got too much talent to work here." I took that as the most wonderful compliment; it filled me up. I could've kissed the guy right there. About a day later, there was an ad in the paper for a medical artist at McMaster University, and they were simply looking for someone who could do charts and graphs for medical students. Black-and-white diazo slides, illustrations for lectures, things like that. So I spent all night making charts and graphs up out of my head, and I copied out of my anatomy books, and I padded my port-folio with all this phony-baloney stuff. And I went into this place to apply for this job, and this animal just looks at my legs. It was miniskirt time, and it was a time when I didn't weigh much, and I guess he liked what he saw. He hired me for my legs—they were really lucky that I could draw. At the time, I was really glad of the sexist attitude. "I got the job 'cause I've got legs!" [*Laughter*] So they hired me and another guy who could draw quite well, and they put us into medical school along with about twenty brand-new medical students who were being trained in an exceptional way. They were completing a four-year course in two years. So a lot of the stuff was already done for them. All the dissections were completely done—it wasn't like they had to do the dissec-tions. So I took a detailed anatomical course so I could illustrate and label the dissections. I did the most unbelievable stuff for five years. I did reconstructive plastic surgery, genetics, growth and development of the fetus, I worked with people as they were having angiograms, I animated a whole kidney biopsy. . . . It was a real serious medical professional's job I had. And in my spare time I would do posters for the university. It was wonderful, because at home, I had this terrible marriage; things were falling apart there.

One of the doctors in epidemiology and biostatistics had a dad who was cartoonist. He said, "I've seen your posters around the school," and he asked me to do some cartoon art to illustrate his lectures. I did them, and it was so much fun! Dave Sackett was a delight to work with. The other doctors were infuriated, though. They thought it was making fun of their profession, but the students who looked at these cartoons memorized the information one hundred percent quicker than the students who didn't! And they did an analysis of the cartoon work versus the plain diazo slides, and suddenly I did nothing but cartoon art for the university! I was no longer doing the detailed anatomical and surgical work. I did that freelance at home, and I started a little freelance commercial art studio where I branched out and developed a huge clientele.

When I had my son, I was thinking I would be able to stay at home and do my freelance work. Then my husband left. Aaron was six months old. I was left with the baby, the house and my freelance work. I was making $7,000 a year in 1973. At the time, you could survive on $7,000 a year. If I spent any more than twenty dollars a week on groceries, I was over budget, but I was managing on $7,000 a year as long as welfare was paying for Aaron's daycare. I was so proud of myself that I could survive as a cartoonist, and I could support myself and my baby and pay my mortgage and my groceries. And the last people I would ever ask for help were my parents. I would never ask them for help. I always wanted them to think that I could make a living by myself. So that's where I was right before I met Rod Johnston. You see, I love to fly, and I love small aircraft. The smaller, the better. One stormy day in March, Aaron was sitting in the car seat, and this little plane flew overhead. He said, "Airplane, Mum!" So I turned the car and drove up the hill to the airport so we could watch the plane land. The fellow who flew the plane came over to me and started a conversation. And he invited me to fly with him the next day. We flew to the next airport for hamburgers. A year later, we were married. Now, you can't tell me that somebody didn't say, "The guy in that airplane is your guy." [*Laughter*]

Rod wanted to move to the Northwest Territories. He wanted to be a flying dentist. He was in his second year of dental school; he was brought up in the Arctic. His father was a miner and a prospector, and his mother had been one of the first teachers to go up into the Arctic. I thought, *I don't want to lose this guy*. And he was going to have a rough time accepting Aaron, because Aaron was a very difficult child who wanted his mother all to himself. He did not want Rod around, so he'd scream all night and throw these temper tantrums where he'd foam at the mouth and bang his head against the wall. And one day, Rod said to me, "Look, I'll take on Aaron, and you take on the bush, and we'll make it." And we did. I've been married to him for seventeen years now, and I'm still crazy about him. We had an interesting life up there, and that's where the strip began. While I was freelancing, I had done three little books, one of which was done while I was pregnant with Aaron. I had done them for the ceiling above my obstetrician's examining table, and he convinced me to turn them into a book.

**Heintjes:** Who published these?

**Johnston:** Oh, there are some horror stories. The first one, *David, We're Pregnant!*, was published in Hamilton, Ontario, by a publisher who never paid me. For the second book, *Hi Mom! Hi Dad!*, I signed up with a second publisher in Toronto, who ended up being such an alcoholic that he went bankrupt and lost his business, and the second book disappeared.

**Heintjes:** The second book just ceased being published?

**Johnston:** That's right.

**Heintjes:** Did you ever get your originals back?

**Johnston:** Oh no. Then, the third book, *Do They Ever Grow Up?*, was done through a Minneapolis guy.

**Heintjes:** What happened to the first book?

**Johnston:** I ended up hiring a lawyer to buy the rights to my first book back for the amount the guy in Hamilton owed me, which at that point, three years later, was $25,000. To date, *David, We're Pregnant!* has sold more than 300,000 copies. And he'll go to his grave telling everybody what a shit I am because if it wasn't for him, I wouldn't have the job I have now. "Once they get big, they dump on the little guy," that kind of stuff. The second guy in Toronto died. The third guy in Minneapolis got the rights to all three books and did a wonderful job publishing them, but we've since had a . . . difference of opinion. So he keeps publishing the books, but I don't do artwork for him anymore.

But he was the one who sent my books to the syndicate, saying, "If you don't publish her, I will."

**Heintjes:** That was to Jim Andrews at Universal.

**Johnston:** That's right. It was Lee Salem who called up and asked for twenty samples, and I thought, *How crazy! How could they want so much so fast? They've got to give me time!* So within two weeks I sent them twenty comic strips. At the time, we were living out of packing boxes, I had a brand-new baby girl, and we were really living in chaos. And I didn't hear from them forever, and then a twenty-year contract arrived! Later, I found out that the reason they wanted the twenty strips right away was to see if I could produce fast and produce under pressure. That's something new people aren't prepared for. It might have taken them six months to put together the twenty samples they're sending in, but the syndicate doesn't know how long it took them to do those twenty strips, so they test you.

**Heintjes:** That's part of the value of the development period, too.

**Johnston:** Exactly. I know a young man who's just had a very frustrating time. He signed a development contract with a syndicate, and then the syndicate finally turned him down. Well, I've seen the work he's submitted over that six-month period, and the problem is, no matter how hard they worked with him, he never improved. Yet he was under the delusion that he was getting better, that he could simply turn in more of the same stuff. And how do you say to somebody, "You're not funny enough?"

**Heintjes:** It's hard to hear.

**Johnston:** It's hard to hear, and it's hard to say. He recently sent me a block of stuff, and he draws very well, but he's not funny enough. He said, "Please give me some advice, and I will frame it." It's almost like people will succeed by osmosis. "I really want to meet so-and-so, because if I meet so-and-so, maybe then my work will be published." It doesn't come from connections, it comes from inside. I was brutally honest with him and said, "You're not funny enough." In today's awful, competitive world where the comics are shrinking and the newspapers aren't buying any more and the syndicates aren't willing to risk anymore, you have to be good now. They're not willing to take someone with potential and pursue and develop it. And that's how I got in. I got in at a time when they said, "Well, it's a little rough, but let's see what the kid can do." Now, I look at that early stuff and I wonder why they ever hired me. But I don't think they have the time, money, or energy to do that as much anymore. Comic strips are shrinking, and whenever a new strip is introduced, an old strip has to be bumped. And many of the old strips that can be bumped have been bumped, so they're up against the good stuff. And to compete with the good stuff, you have to be really good. So I was lucky. I entered the field at a time when I needed to develop, and I was allowed to.

**Heintjes:** Even from the earliest days of *For Better or For Worse*, when the strip was still evolving, to its current incarnation, you've managed to bring a lot of what I would call subtlety into a medium that is generally not known for its subtlety. One of my favorite strips you've done was the Sunday where Elly was standing on the patio brushing her hair, reminiscing about how she used to watch her mother do the same thing, and all the while Elizabeth is watching Elly. It was so understated and poignant, and I think the reason it stayed with me is because comics have traditionally not dealt well with subtle themes and topics.

**Johnston:** I think maybe it's because I'm a girl. [*Laughter*] There are so many men in the business who are good at the comedy part, but the subtle, gentle, nuance part, you don't see that much. I think Brian Bassett, who does *Adam*, is very capable of that. I think Sparky [Charles Schulz's nickname] does that. I do it. Cathy Guisewite is far more brazen, but you'll see that gut-wrenching insight in *Cathy*. They have their finger on that sensitive pulse. They make you say, "Yes, I know how that feels." It's not necessarily funny, but it's real.

**Heintjes:** One other sequence that I think was a particularly well-done slice-of-life piece was the story of the rubber band around Farley's leg. That one really rang true.

**Johnston:** Oh, that one was based on something that really happened! We don't have a Farley type of dog—Farley is based on a dog I used to own that I gave away. But our dog kept favoring its leg, he kept licking on it, and when you looked at it, you could see that he was licking at a wound. But it looked like a bad cut, maybe a wire cut. He never leaves the property, but he does have free roam of the bush, and who knows? Maybe he cut himself on some wire down there. We don't really know what might be in the bush. So I was treating it and looking after it, but it wasn't healing. I finally took him to the vet's, and he couldn't find out what it was, either. Very fortunately, one of the two vets at the clinic decided to take a really good look. He opened the wound up and found an elastic band. It turned out that my son had at one point put a rubber band around the dog's leg and forgot about it, and the darn thing worked its way through the hair until it was against the skin, and it eventually worked its way into the flesh, right down to the bone.

It affected all of us. It affected the kids deeply, because they had lost sight of this rubber band, and none of us knew what was happening. And I did that strip to alert people about this potential problem. It's like Ann Landers telling people to watch their babies around toilets, because they can drown. "Well, gosh, I didn't know that!" And here this was such a simple thing. For readers, nothing affects them like something happening to pets. You can show people being blown off the face of the earth every day on daytime TV, but show a dog with a thorn in its paw, and you've got readers sending in volumes of mail.

**Heintjes:** Are we left to conclude, then, that perhaps subtlety is not commercial and that's one reason for the relative lack of women cartoonists?

**Johnston:** I think there are lots of women cartoonists. I think they're working at ad agencies, and other people are getting credit for their brilliance. They are animators, they do cards, they are everywhere, wonderful, talented women cartoonists. But very few have come into this comics field, for whatever reason. I never thought that I could do this. I never applied for this job. I never sent anything in and said, "Hey, check this out, give me a job." When I signed a contract at Universal Press Syndicate, the people around that big rosewood table were interested in celebrating. They wanted to take me out to lunch, but I went back to the hotel and—swear to God—got physically ill.

**Heintjes:** You realized what you'd gotten yourself into.

**Johnston:** How could I produce material every day, 365 days a year? How could I do that? I could see producing a book now and then, but a daily comic strip? I was going to have readers every day who would expect a certain level of quality work, and I think that maybe that's why I segued into the little vignettes that have moralistic and motherly values, like little parables. I might not be able to have a joke every day, but I could have a thought every day.

When you're very young, you often find yourself completely devoted to something, whether it's Elvis Presley or a father figure or whatever. You become a cult member of some sort. And when I was very young, I wanted to be married to a minister. I didn't want to be a minister, but I wanted to be the wife of one, because I wanted to write his sermons. I was about eight years old, and I would lie in bed and pray, "Please, God, make me a minister's wife," because I wanted to write something that would mean something to people!

I was brought up believing that everyone was bathed in sin. You would arrive at church, the day would be beautiful, the birds would be singing, everything would smell like fresh morning dew, and you'd feel great! And when you walked out after the service, you'd feel like you had nailed some poor sucker to a cross! "Wait a minute! I was happy until I came here!" [*Laughter*] And I don't think spiritual guidance necessarily means shredding your self-confidence and destroying your day. You should come out of church wanting to carry on and care about people, pursuing your dreams and being positive. And when I was that little girl, I wanted to write pieces for that audience that would lift them up and make them feel great! And do you know what?

**Heintjes:** Yeah—in a very real way, you ended up doing just that.

**Johnston:** And I never even married a minister! [*Laughter*]

**Heintjes:** When you started *For Better or For Worse*, did you have in mind the passage of time that would allow your characters to age and change over the course of years?

**Johnston:** I had no plan when I started. My only focus was "please let me write something that would be worthwhile to read every day. And let me meet my deadline." When I first started the strip, the characters were my family. I used all the same names. And when I signed the contract, I went crazy. I asked for time to learn how to write dialogue, to learn how the characters looked from all angles. Elly Patterson had to look like Elly Patterson from the front and the back. She has to look like Elly Patterson whether she's being introspective and gentle and sweet or she's got multiple eye bags with dandruff popping off her head. She has to look the same. I needed time to learn the characters and breathe life into them. I couldn't just go with them right off the bat.

**Heintjes:** How much time did you have to do all this?

**Johnston:** I had about six to eight months.

**Heintjes:** What happened during that period?

**Johnston:** During that time, I learned how to daydream and become part of that second family, because the family in that strip is an imaginary family. That daydream family is as real to me as my flesh-and-blood family. I know how they feel, I know how they think, because I am one of those people. To have them have their needs, their anxieties, their foibles and their faults, I had to become one of them. I know where the school bus parks. I know what the school looks like. I know what Connie does for a living, and I know that Anne's husband messes around on her. I know that Gordon's father is an alcoholic and that Lawrence is gay and has known about it since he was eleven. I know these people intimately, and because of that they've taken on lives of their own, independent from my family.

**Heintjes:** And the syndicate had no problems with any of the structure you had set up.

**Johnston:** They had just realized what a wonderful find Cathy Guisewite was. Here was a woman who was saying things no one else was saying. They were naked, barebones, grit-your-teeth truths! And they loved that! And they also loved the fact that Cathy was Cathy [Editor's note: Cathy is the title character of Guisewite's newspaper strip]. And they loved the fact that the Pattersons were me and Rod and Aaron and Kate. And yet, the closer the date of publication got, the more I felt it was unfair to my children to have their names running in the papers. I thought they needed a buffer between themselves and this chronicle that would happen every day. When they were little, it was just Mom's work, but as they got older, it was like an exposé. They would have to convince their friends at school that "No, I don't have a girlfriend named Martha" and "No, I didn't have to have an appliance put in my mouth to stop me from sucking my thumb—these are figments of my mother's sick imagination, and they have nothing to do with me, thank you very much." I could see it when they would bring their friends over. They would enter the house like they were coming into some incredible place! Then they would look around and think, *Well, it's got a leaky faucet, a mother who yells at you, crumbs on the floor*, and the magic was gone. So it was important for the kids to bring their friends home. It was important for their friends to see Rod and me first thing in the morning, looking like we'd been hit by a Mack truck.

I would go to my kids' school to talk about comic strips, how they were colored and produced and so forth, but it was really for the purpose of saying, "See? Aaron and Kate Johnston are Aaron and Kate Johnston, and they have nothing to do with Michael and Elizabeth Patterson." For one thing, Michael is a much more confident, comfortable teenager than my son ever was. Aaron was just flying off in all directions. Like Aaron, however, Michael is sensitive. He's going to be a writer. He's very emotional. They're different people. And yet, given a very specific situation, Michael would react the way Aaron would. For example, in April last year, Lawrence told Michael that he was gay, and Michael handled it the way I know Aaron would. He was shocked at first, and then he said, "You've been my friend since the age of three. The only thing that's changed here today is me. You haven't changed; therefore, I have to deal with this." And that's the way Aaron would deal with this.

**Heintjes:** You haven't always portrayed Michael and Elizabeth in the most flattering light. You've dealt with the awkwardness of a date, the pain of rejection, peer pressure, and the general tempestuousness of adolescence. Do their schoolmates ever have anything to say to them about this sort of portrayal?

**Johnston:** At first they did. Years ago, the kids were asked about whether their dad was a dentist, whether they had a shaggy dog, and so on. Now, the fact that we've lived in a small community for ten years has been very helpful to my children because they have friends who have known them for ten years, and those friends know the truth. They know that Kate Johnston is not Elizabeth Patterson. What's interesting is that Kate's friends will read my work much more avidly than Kate will. Neither of my kids read my work at all. Kate's more likely to read *Luann*. Aaron always loved *Garfield*. When Aaron was about eight years old, he was asked by an interviewer if he liked the fact that I did *For Better or For Worse*, and he said he'd be more impressed if I did *Garfield*. [*Laughter*] I thought that was hysterical. People ask me if I'm hurt because my children don't read *For Better or For Worse*, because both of them will tell you, "Oh, hell, I never read it. I don't know what she's writing about." What that says to me is that they trust me. They don't have to check up on me every day. They don't have to ask, "What did you embarrass me about today, Mom?" I am so protective of them. Any time I broached a subject that I thought they might feel uncomfortable about, I would talk it over with them first.

Here's an example: My son had a problem with acne. Oh, he was just miserable with it. But I never broached it in the strip because I didn't want to hurt him. And one day he said to me, "Mom, you never do anything on zits! You've got to do that!" He thought I should do one about a zit on the end of Michael's nose, and I did. Also, Aaron has glasses and Katie does not, and Aaron begged me, "Please, please, don't have Michael have glasses." But the whole thing with glasses is so important—losing them, the expense, and so forth. And Katie sees very well without glasses, but Elizabeth wears them. So there's a difference there. And Katie has jaw-length brown hair, and Elizabeth has blond hair that's in a ponytail. And April looks exactly like Katie did when she was a baby. I loved having that baby so much. My first baby was a nightmare. It was a nightmare for both of us. Aaron's childhood . . . we both look back on those days as war-zone days. And I can't have children anymore, and I'm going through that awful pre-menopausal stage of saying, "I want another baby!" So to satisfy my own mumsy, nurturing needs, I did the next best thing and had one in the strip. And it's been wonderfully therapeutic.

**Heintjes:** As we conduct this interview, the controversy over Lawrence revealing his homosexuality is raging. What has been the reaction to it from various people: readers, newspaper editors, your colleagues?

**Johnston:** It has been mixed everywhere. To begin with, when we announced that the storyline was going to run, people who had no access to the material became violently opposed, saying it was pornography. Very few newspaper editors took that position, though—most newspaper editors are schooled to see both sides of an issue before you make a stand. Yet some were outraged. They were not expecting this. They did not read the literature that came with it. They don't feel that comics are anything more than icing on the cake, they don't have to read them—they just wax them and stick them down. The editors who didn't read the notice alerting them that they might want to run some alternate material were caught off-guard. I really do feel for them, because it was an unusual subject for the comics page. Not that it's unusual for *For Better or For Worse*, but they just don't like the comics to deal with issues, and especially not this one.

**Heintjes:** What was your intent in creating the sequence?

**Johnston:** I wanted to challenge myself to write a good story about something that's largely misunderstood and to show that it's the kid next door, anybody in any neighborhood. It's a story about friendship and acceptance; there was not one mention of sex. Not one mention of anything that could not be talked about comfortably. Considering the climate of the 1990s, when you can turn on any average sitcom and you get vulgarity and explicit sexual discussion, open talk of body parts, naked people in bed, you wonder where the humor is in today's comedy writing. And considering that a most unfortunate view of sexuality is seen every day on every channel, with the exception of PBS and Disney, I guess, where are the family values we're talking about?

**Heintjes:** I was thinking that in a so-called family newspaper, the most depraved events can be described in lurid detail—the Jeffrey Dahmer case, mass murders, all sorts of horrific events—and yet this sequence in *For Better or For Worse* is deemed unacceptable.

**Johnston:** Fortunately, many people did not find it unacceptable. Many editors said, "This is interesting. This is a challenge. Let's see if people are reading, and let's see how they respond." Generally, that was the attitude in the big markets. The *Chicago Tribune* has been wholly supportive. *The Boston Globe*, the *Toronto Star*, *The Winnipeg Free Press*, the *Vancouver Sun*, the *Los Angeles Times*—on and on and on, there has been tremendous support from the bigger centers. In the smaller centers, and especially the centers where there are a lot of very strong fundamentalist beliefs that this is evil and that homosexuality is a matter of choice and all this stuff, the hatred runs so hot and heavy. There is so much fear. And in those centers, the editors are part of the community. In a community of twenty thousand people, the editor goes downtown for coffee, and everyone knows him and can attack him. And from the privacy and obscurity of my home, I can produce a series of drawings and I will receive a certain amount of mail attacking me, but I am comforted by the fact that I don't have to face these people personally day after day. So I understand the position of editors who said, "I'll cancel it" or "I'll run it on the editorial page" or however they decided to handle it. I think everybody handled it as well as they could under the circumstances. One interesting thing is, right at the very beginning, the angry, bitter, vicious attitude of "I will not admit this into my home! I will not acknowledge that this exists! I am blindly forcing this entire issue out of my life!" was overwhelming. And I thought, *What have I done?* I really believed that people in this century would be willing to take the time to look at what I was doing before they fired both barrels. But this happened before the strips even began to run.

**Heintjes:** This attitude was predominantly among the readership, not the editors?

**Johnston:** The readership. It started off with *The Detroit Free Press*. The bulletin had come through with the artwork many weeks in advance of publication. One young reporter there, who was gay, was really excited about the prospects of the strip's publication. He wanted to do an article immediately, so he interviewed me and put the article on the wire service, which goes everywhere. It was very supportive, and it went out to editors who hadn't even had a chance to review the comics. A lot of editors ran the wire story, and it turned on the nonthinking but reacting readers, people who are blindly devoted to a belief that has no other side to it. "There is no other question involved, this is just the way it is, and you have no right to introduce this into my home." So that's what rose like a Medusa out of the clouds, and from my perspective, I could see why people do not take a stand on issues in a community like that, because the fear of reprisal from these incredibly strong groups who are so powerful. . . . Religious fervor is like adrenaline, and it can over-power almost anything in its way. Because of this, I can see why information is suppressed, why people are oppressed, why so much goes unachieved. It's because of blind intolerance. Lee Salem told me this would happen. Especially when he saw the second half of the series, he said, "You really have no idea how vicious and angry and hateful people are in the United States about this subject." Canada is far more tolerant. And I argued with him. I said, "This is the nineties—people are so much more aware! People are talking about it! Look at television and newspapers!" There are articles here covering, word for word, trials of child molesters, and they describe it in detail. And I thought that in a climate where people are talking about sexuality in so many unsa-vory ways, let's do something positive for a change and show that this is the kid next door. This is the kid who walks your dog. This is the young person who operates on you at the clinic! Who knows? It's everywhere, and you can't discriminate against something that is there by birth.

**Heintjes:** I guess your faith in human nature was a little shaken when you found out the truth about people in the nineties, eh?

**Johnston:** In fact, that's the truth. I was surprised by this blind hatred that I guess is born of fear. There is a fraction of society that wants to believe in "a leader" and not believe in themselves. They don't want to trust their own judgment; they would rather blindly follow the leadership of someone else. That's the easy way out, I think. It's much harder to say, "Okay, let's think. Let's not simply obey." It took a while for the thinking people to come together. They waited until it was published before they responded, and when they read it, the positive response happened. They responded partly to retal-iate against all the negative stuff, but partly also to say, "This is appropriate, because of all the teenagers who kill themselves, one-third of them do it over their sexuality." They knew that these people who are discriminated against are not part of an evil power but are simply people who must be acknowl-edged, accepted, and respected. They are simply a part of our lives. They are a part of society. There is an undeniable population. So the thinking people started making their opinions known, and many people who had never talked openly about this subject before were defending the story. Some papers were even being picketed in favor of running the strip. Before the strip had really started to run, some papers were being picketed against the strip, but after it began to run, a lot people really wanted to read it. I know it took the syndicate quite awhile to respond to people who want to see the story because their own papers had prevented them from seeing it.

**Heintjes:** How did Universal satisfy them?

**Johnston:** They printed up a little booklet, and anyone who wants to see the story can send them a self-addressed stamped envelope, and they'll send them the literature.

**Heintjes:** When you decided to create this sequence, did you consult with Lee Salem so he would have an idea of what you were getting into?

**Johnston:** Yes. I wrote out the dialogue first, and I faxed him the dialogue. Then I drew up the first section of it, to where Lawrence confides in Michael, and that section ends with Michael punching Lawrence in the arm playfully. That was sent off about eight weeks ahead of deadline, and that was well ahead. Generally, we're about six weeks to the good, and I can get by with about four weeks or even three weeks. So there were plenty of weeks there in case I needed to backtrack and produce something else. Lee was very matter of fact about accepting it, and I told him I was going to go ahead with the rest of the story. He wanted to see what I was doing, so I faxed him the pencil roughs to the next section. He was concerned at that point. He said, "Maybe this goes on too long—do you know how angry people are going to be?" But he left it up to me, and said that if I wanted to do it, they would give their support and stand behind me. But he said, "Keep in mind that you are going to take some flak." I asked him if I would lose papers. He said, "Absolutely." I asked him how many, and he said he didn't know. I asked him, "[Will] I lose ten?" He said I probably wouldn't. I asked him if I would lose six papers, and he said probably not. I said, "Three?" and he said I maybe would lose three. I told him that even if I lose three papers I think the story is worth telling, and he said it was my decision, and they would stand behind me. And the rest is history.

**Heintjes:** How taken aback was Lee by the overwhelming reaction?

**Johnston:** He wasn't taken aback at all. He was steeled for it. He's used to dealing with Garry Trudeau's detractors. I thought the people at the syndicate might be angered by the extra work, but they were kind of charged up by it.

**Heintjes:** Any publicity is good publicity?

**Johnston:** Well, in fact, that's what John McMeel said to me. He was kind of enjoying it. Now, I haven't spoken to him over the past week! [*Laughter*]

**Heintjes:** This is pretty much the first major bump you've encountered in your career, isn't it?

**Johnston:** I've had a pretty easy life as a cartoonist, and that's part of the problem for me. I get letters now and then that complain about the way I do things, and I generally think, *Get a life!* If you don't like the way I punctuate my sentences, tell me what else is interesting in your life. And most other people say, "I love your work, you're on my refrigerator, my dog is just like yours," and so on. So I was bathed in this wonderful, warm glow of acceptance for so long, and yet *For Better or For Worse* had always dealt with relevant subjects. I had always challenged myself to write a story that included both sides. For example, when Gordon's father beat him, Gordon's father does not appear as an ogre, but he appears as a man who can't control his temper and he cries over that. I try to see things from both sides. I tried to see Elizabeth and her smoking from both sides. I try to be nonjudgmental in the stories I tell so that where there is a resolution, it's up to the reader. I try not to use the strip as a platform from which to preach, and I don't think this sequence is a preachy one, either. It is simply a story that happens. It happens every single day in the world. Every day, someone is discharged from the comfort of their home because that person does not conform to the lifestyle that that family planned. And the story doesn't say that anyone was wrong or that the situation was right. What the story tells is that this is a very difficult lifestyle for anyone to be part of. It's not a life glamorized by partying and orgying. It's a life, and a life deserves to be respected and applauded for whatever it can contribute. So I don't think I was preaching as much as I was telling a very honest and true story. In so doing, perhaps it has run on a little too long, and that has been painful for me, because it lengthens the time I'm under fire. But it tells the whole story, and I can't imagine broaching the subject without telling the whole story, from my impression of it as I felt it needed to be told. And to prove, I suppose, that it's not a matter of choice, because who would choose to go through that?

**Heintjes:** How is your mail running, now that a large part of sequence has run?

**Johnston:** At this point, it's overwhelmingly supportive. The negative letters have been very angry or very religious. One very fine letter came in from a very religious lady who told me that I was misguided and that, with love and understanding, she wanted me to know that. She hoped I'd find peace in Jesus. I thought that was a wonderful letter. I really appreciate this lady, because she was still loving and kind and accepting of me, no matter what my beliefs were, and that to me was wonderfully valid. But then you get letters from people who say, "Do you realize that all serial killers are homosexual?" One hysterically funny letter came from a man who was in his sixties, and he began by explaining what an upright, Christian man he is, and that he doesn't believe in a debauched lifestyle, and if I only knew what these people did to each other, I would be so disgusted and repelled that I would never consider socializing with them. And he added that what they did was so horrific that he didn't want to even think about it, and then he followed it with four pages of detailed descriptions!

Some moments from Lawrence's coming-out storyline. FOR BETTER OR FOR WORSE ©
1993 Lynn Johnston Productions. Dist. By ANDREWS MCMEEL SYNDICATION. Reprinted
with permission. All rights reserved.

I've gotten very few letters from people who are gay. I think the people who will be particularly affected by this story are waiting until it's over before they say whether or not it was good. For the most part, I'm hearing from families, psychiatrists, doctors, teachers, very open-minded people who are saying, "Good—we have left this in a closet for far too long, and it's time we allowed people a life." And I've gotten letters of support from people of all ages. There are teachers who are going over this a day at a time with their students, with the approval of the students' parents. They're writing and phoning to tell me that it's an educational tool. One letter was from a mother who said that because of the strip, her son had the courage to tell her that he was a homosexual, and because of the strip, she had the courage to handle it well. I also got a letter from a woman in Edmonton who said that if the strip had run last year, perhaps her son would still be alive, because then he would know that he was not the only one in the world with this problem. It's that kind of response that makes me think it's been worth the roller-coaster ride it's put me on. It would be so much easier not to make a statement, not to tell a story, to continue to be that yellowing page on the refrigerator.

**Heintjes:** If you had it to do all over again, would you have proceeded with the story?

**Johnston:** Yes, despite the fact that it has been quite horrible. I have not slept, I have not eaten, I've lost ten pounds, I've lost nineteen papers, I've lost many readers. It was not something I did for joy or something I did for publicity. I did not say, "Damn the detractors" and go ahead, intending to upset the editors. I did it because it was a story I really, fully believed in, and when you write a story that is perhaps a controversial one, you have to expect to take the heat. And I have. And I also have to realize how soft I am. I am not unmoved by the spears and arrows that are coming through the mail. I'm not immune to those. It absolutely is an attack on me, and it's from people who are thinking, feeling people. As a cartoonist who is very optimistic and who wants to be approved of, I am not unaffected by it. It has been an ordeal. Again, I've lost ten pounds.

**Heintjes:** A new quick weight-loss method! [*Laughter*]

**Johnston:** I figure that if I ever get fat again, I'll do the abortion issue. [*Laughter*] It's pretty well gone. I can feel all my ribs.

**Heintjes:** What has the reaction of your colleagues been?

**Johnston:** I talked to Mike Peters yesterday, and he said it's not very often that a cartoonist can make such an overwhelming statement and influence so many people to talk, whether it's for or against what you say. It's an issue that needs to be talked about. He said, "You've made people talk, and that's a very enviable position for a cartoonist."

**Heintjes:** Probably the only cartoonist who does that on any sort of regular basis is Garry Trudeau.

**Johnston:** I spoke to Garry Trudeau. I called him up and said, "Well, Garry, now I know just a little bit about what your life is like." He laughed and said, "They've given up on me. They still held out hope that you could be another gag-a-day cartoonist, but they long ago gave up hope on me." He also said that most people don't realize how thoroughly he researches everything he writes about. When he puts something in the paper that is very pointed and of a name-dropping nature, it is not done without hours and hours of thorough research. He said he knows that he has detractors, but he said that he's always confident that he's told the truth as he sees it. He was very comforting, and he said, "If you want to make a statement, you have to make it with all honesty and truth and be comforted knowing that it was made with your own strong sense of values and truth."

**Heintjes:** You're handling this sequence so deftly and so honestly, with a perceptiveness that seems so authentic. I'm left wondering if you simply wrote it from out of your imagination.

**Johnston:** I didn't. I wrote it from experience. My brother-in-law is gay. It certainly has not been by design, but so very many of my friends have been gay, all the way through school, art school, even in my husband's dental class—our very best friend, who graduated with Rod, was gay and is now HIV-positive. He's been thrown out of his home. We've been part of the private lives of so many people who have had to deal with this. I know this story. I know it's a true one, and I know the dialogue by heart.

**Heintjes:** That explains why it seemed so palpably real.

**Johnston:** It is real. That's why I can stand tall and know that I am not making up a story simply to shock people. I produced a story that is so true that it's painful. You know what it's like? It's like lancing a boil and taking out the thing that won't allow it to heal. Not that I intended to do that, but I had the confidence that I could tell this story from the side of the people who had experience. In that way, I was being very true to myself, my strip, and to them. The strip's always been very honest.

**Heintjes:** Have you heard from any other colleagues?

**Johnston:** Well, the first person I sent it to, before I sent it to anyone else, was Sparky. We tease each other all the time, because we're forever giving each other advice, and we never follow each other's advice. But if he had said to me, "Do not do this," I wonder if I would have. But he said, "This is good, and it deserves publication." He's been doing interviews to that effect. I have never mentioned his name, because I never wanted to involve anyone else in my situation, but I suppose reporters called Sparky because they wanted to get the point of view of someone they respect. He called me yesterday and said, "I've been doing interviews because of you!" [*Laughter*] Of course, he's been very supportive. I spoke to Greg Evans, who does *Luann*, and he's another cartoonist who has touched on some issues. Like myself, Greg is a very gentle soul who doesn't enjoy controversy and doesn't like the angry letters. He was feeling for me. I told him yesterday what a roller coaster it's been, and I was feeling pretty down. He sympathized with me, and we talked about how comic strips are changing and how far we have to push that envelope. He said he believes we have to nudge that envelope once in a while, but that he wasn't prepared to nudge it as far as I did. I also talked to Bill Amend, who does *FoxTrot*. He said that although he really wants to cover real issues, he wasn't prepared to push the envelope. Now, I've always felt that way as well. I have always strongly pursued the laughs, but my thoughts never pursued the laughs. The laughs always became a more objective look, or the other side of the coin. I didn't think that I would do something as radical as this. I knew that I would eventually touch this subject, but I never saw myself in the situation I'm in now. But perhaps that will happen to Greg, and perhaps that will happen to Bill. Perhaps one day they will feel very strongly about something and write what is in their hearts, and they too will discover that there are readers out there who are intolerant, who just want their laugh a day.

**Heintjes:** Do you think that what is happening to you will serve as a disincentive for comics creators to deal with their characters in a mature, realistic way?

**Johnston:** I think that something like this always sets some kind of a limit, always sets some kind of an example. I will be interested to see what other people will do. But at the same time, people who do comic strips are very optimistic, very easygoing people who generally want to be loved and approved of. So I can't see anything being done without love and care, and if cartoonists are going to do more relevant work, it will always be done within the context of family entertainment. I don't think it will become the deplorable, very basic humor you see on television, which has to say gross, four-letter things to elicit a laugh. People have been programmed to laugh at smut. I am so thrilled with *Comedy on the Road* and *Caroline's Comedy Hour* on A&E because these people are forced to be clean in their humor, and they are generally funny. I am very prudish. I am very conservative. I believe that sex is a private thing and that all of this gulping, gasping muck you see on television is too much.

**Heintjes:** When you describe yourself as "conservative," how do you mean that?

**Johnston:** I don't go to Dangerfield's in New York and laugh at the smut and filth they think is funny. Now, I love a dirty joke if it's really funny, but I can't laugh at filth anymore. I'm a very objective, open-minded, "mom" type of person. I'm modest in my dress, I'm modest in the way I speak, and I'm modest in so many ways.

**Heintjes:** Let me ask a couple of quantifiable questions: How many papers are dropping only the sequence, and how many are dropping the strip for ever and ever?

**Johnston:** I believe forty or fifty took alternate material, but they haven't dropped the strip. Nineteen have dropped the strip for ever and ever, amen.

**Heintjes:** What was supplied to the papers who elected to run alternate material?

**Johnston:** They chose a five-week run from 1991, something that fit right into that slot. And I don't know what the breakdown of dollars is—I don't know if Universal charged them for it; I never asked. I may well be charged for a great deal of this. It's a expense that we share.

**Heintjes:** As if creating *For Better or For Worse* doesn't keep you busy enough, now you're having to cope with this.

**Johnston:** It's starting to die down now. The phone never stopped ringing for the first couple of weeks. I would hang up the phone and it would instantly ring again, to the point where I had to take the phone off the hook just to take a shower, eat a lunch, do anything.

**Heintjes:** Did you resort to screening your calls?

**Johnston:** I did leave my answering machine on for a while, but the calls were almost all from editors and reporters, and I wanted to talk to them. I thought that if I'm going to produce this material that causes them a lot of phone calls, then I have to respond to them and be there for them. They need my support as well.

**Heintjes:** How did you get any real work done?

**Johnston:** I didn't. What was wonderful was that somehow I had been able to get a couple of weeks ahead, so I could afford to lose the time. And I did lose the two weeks. For two solid weeks, I answered the phone all day on the same subject.

**Heintjes:** I imagine your household was in something of an uproar.

**Johnston:** It was! We were all in a state of shock, but now we're looking forward to it all being over. Enough is enough, especially for my husband, who has his own concerns. He runs a very busy clinic with a huge staff, and he's got his own worries and anxieties, and he would very much like me to rub his back and ask him, "How was your day?" I say to him, "I turned down *Good*

*Morning America* and *Maury Povich* today." And he says, "Uh, I had a banana with lunch today." [*Laughter*] It's been difficult for him to be undermined as part of my life. This has taken over my life for the past two weeks.

**Heintjes:** Have media outlets that large really been wanting you to appear?

**Johnston:** Oh sure—today, *Good Morning America*, *Maury Povich*, *The National*, which is huge in Canada. But I turned them all down. I work in a print medium, and I am responsible to our client newspapers and to others who want to talk about this in the print medium. I felt that once I went on television, it would look as if I were crusading, that I am there for purposes other than writing a good story.

**Heintjes:** Next thing you know, you'd be known as "Lynn Johnston, AIDS activist."

**Johnston:** Yeah, something like that. I didn't want that to happen. I felt that the people who are in the forefront of this movement will take up the battle. If this has done anything to open a door, they'll go through the door themselves. I want to do comics.

**Heintjes:** You've discussed the pleasure that rendering things like razor stubble, bulges, baggy eyes, and things like that bring to you. Why is that? What does it all signify to you?

**Johnston:** [*Laughter*] Because it diminishes the stuff that's really there. I am not an overweight person. I am the typical ten pounds overweight that every forty-six-year-old woman is. I have ten pounds to lose. But there are days when those ten pounds hang off me like great rubber dewlaps. And there are some days when it is insignificant. On the days when I feel like Roseanne Barr, I draw it, and it feels great! It's like when there's a bald-headed comedian, the first thing he's going to do is draw attention to the fact that he's bald. "No one is going to hurt me, because I'm going to call attention to it myself first." Once the hurt is dealt with and gone, then we can get down to the fun of the comedy. People will think, *Why can't I be as capable as this guy is at dealing with his shortcomings?* If Phyllis Diller didn't feel like an ugly person, she never would have made those wonderful comments. If she hadn't felt ugly, she never would have said anything. Phyllis wouldn't want you to find out from another source that she'd had a facelift. She's going to tell you about it, and you're going to crack up over it. Then it will be dealt with, and then we can get down to the other stuff. I don't like being ten pounds overweight. I would like to look as perfect as the women in the magazines. So when I draw that ugly character, it feels wonderful, because . . . remember when I said that if you shut your eyes, the hurt and anger and blackness go on forever, but if you put it down on paper you can deal with it? So I draw this saggy, baggy character, and it looks so funny! I could never look that bad! I can laugh at that. People say to me, "Lynn, you're so attractive! Why do you draw Elly so ugly?" Well, shoot, there's a reason right there! [*Laughter*]

**Heintjes:** Do you ever get the feeling that your family thinks you're looking at them, waiting for material to happen?

**Johnston:** Never. That would be like looking at an oven, waiting for a cake to happen. You have to make it up.

**Heintjes:** That question came to my mind recently when I was reading about the early days of Motown and the success of the songwriting team Holland-Dozier-Holland. One of them said that people felt self-conscious talking to him because they felt he was always waiting for someone to say something that would trigger a song lyric in his mind.

**Johnston:** I think they were lying. I think that what they were really hoping is that they would say something that would trigger a song idea in his head and they could forever say they were responsible for that. That's what happens to me. Every day I get a letter from someone who says, "This morning, little Rupert said this gem over his Shreddies, and I think you could use it." Well, I don't, but they're hoping that you will. People do affect you in that they are your material and you record what's going on all the time. If you're having a tense, deep, tear-filled discussion with a best friend, you're not going to chronicle that in the paper, but you're going to observe the way they furrow their brows. Not because you're an analyst, but because you're "on record" all the time. I remember crying really deeply, walking over to the mirror, and thinking, *Wow—that's what I look like.* The way they fold their arms, put their elbows on the table, all of that goes into your memory. And what you are is an actor, and you're getting the body language of your characters down. Wonderful little things like a baby leaning out of a shopping cart saying, "Want dat, want dat" goes into "record."

**Heintjes:** The characters' body language adds so much to the feel of a strip. You know, I make no secret of my profound admiration for Will Eisner. In the years I've worked with him writing a column for *The Spirit*, he's taught me so much about how the medium works, and one thing he always stresses is that not only does the dialogue convey character, so does the character's body language.

**Johnston:** Will Eisner is the artist's artist. He is one of the best. You look at his work and you wonder, "How could anybody do so much with lines and shadows?" He not only gives a beautifully structured image, he gives you an emotion. And he is a consummate actor.

**Heintjes:** I think one of his earliest contributions to comics was his portrayal of very strong women who could make their way in the world without men. And this was in the 1940s, when this wasn't done much, especially in comics.

**Johnston:** I also think he was an innovator because he created women who had a certain anatomical credence. They were idealized, sure, but they were achievable. They weren't Wonder Woman bodies. At one NCS [National Cartoonists Society] convention, I was sitting at the same table with him, and I was looking at his hands. His hands are wonderful.

**Heintjes:** They look like the hands of a man half his age.

**Johnston:** One time, I was walking down the street with Charles Schulz and he took me by the hand. I remember as I swung my left hand forward, I thought, *The hand that draws Peanuts is holding mine*. It was such a thrill. So we hold hands all the time now [*laughter*].

**Heintjes:** I've been thinking recently about how, in some ways, taboos in comics are being shattered. But its a "two steps forward, one step back" process. No newspaper cartoonist today could render the kinds of women Eisner and Milton Caniff did back in the 1940s. Do you perceive a shattering of taboos in comics today?

**Johnston:** Women were idols then. Today, we are shattering every idol we ever had. They have now sent Kitty Kelley to England to destroy Prince Philip, the husband of Queen Elizabeth. We're really happy shattering our idols. We're happy destroying the Kennedy family. We all know they have multiple warts, but why can't we just leave JFK as a god? Let us have our heroes. And women are shattered every day on television screens.

In the time of Milton Caniff, even though women were drawn with a sensuous stroke, there was still an ideal of reverence toward women. That they were all virgins until proven otherwise. You would open a door for them. You wouldn't swear in front of them. There was a sense of courtesy and chivalry, which I can still appreciate.

**Heintjes:** What is harder for you—writing or drawing?

**Johnston:** Writing.

**Heintjes:** Why?

**Johnston:** It's the thing that furrows my brow, upsets my stomach, and takes the longest.

**Heintjes:** What method do you use to write?

**Johnston:** I write dialogue the way you would for a sitcom. I put the family in a situation, and I exist as a phantom in the room, and I hear them speak and I watch them move, and I follow them around, and I wait for the things to happen. Some things I coerce into happening, and some things happen spontaneously. I often never know where this completely independent family is going to take me. The stories often write themselves. It's a wakeful dream state. Mike Peters says the same thing. Even Joan Rivers admitted the same thing. When you're writing, it's like you're under a general anesthetic, where you'll wake up and say, "I don't believe it—the sun went down!" It's like a state of suspended animation. You are transported into a dream state so your body exists as a shell during the time you're writing. When the character April was born, a group of eight of my women friends decided to give me a surprise baby shower, and the day they planned it was a writing day. I was sitting in my studio, and my studio overlooks our driveway. Four cars pulled into my driveway, and people walked into my living room, and I still didn't know they were there. One of the women walked into my studio and said, "Lynn, there's something I want to show you." I said, "Hi Beth, how are you?" not noticing that someone had walked into my house. When she led me into the living room, I had to blink several times before I could adjust to the fact that my living room was full of balloons and friends and gifts! That's how anesthetized you are. When I draw, I can talk to a friend, I can listen to the radio, I can talk on the phone, because it's like dancing to a tune I've loved to dance to before.

**Heintjes:** So you're never just walking through the mall when a gag comes to you.

**Johnston:** Sure! And when that happens, it's wonderful. More than likely, it's the state of mind you're in. There are times when I intend to write and nothing happens. Then there are other times when I have the flu and I feel crummy and depressed, and I write two weeks' worth of stuff. About two weeks ago, I came up with eleven Sunday comics in one day! And you wonder, if there is some spiritual connection here, where were you guys last week?

I like complete quiet when I write, though. I have to have no interruptions. I can't work if there's background noise. Well, that's not always true. We live in a forest, and there were a number of trees that were dead, and they were in danger of falling over onto the house. So we had a couple of guys come over and take them down. They chainsawed all those trees as I wrote, and I didn't see them and I didn't hear them. I went outside later at about two o'clock and said, "Holy smoke, look at all the trees you cut down!" They said, "You were right there by the window the whole time!" And I never even was aware of any of it—the noise, the chatter, the trees falling, nothing. But that's unusual. Normally I have complete quiet. If I played a radio, I'd hear snippets of conversation or song lyrics that would distract me.

**Heintjes:** How is it different when you draw?

**Johnston:** When I draw, I have a studio that is very small, with a drafting table I've had for twenty-five years. On top of that I have one of those cutting mats. I like to work on a cutting mat because I often will cut things out and reshape them. I often make greeting cards for friends—I'm forever making little things like that—and I like to have a cutting mat for those things, too. I listen to the radio when I draw. I like to listen to the CBC because it's got all kinds of comedy and radio plays and commentary and phone-in shows. It gives me a sense of connection to the outside world. I know some artists have a TV on. John Reiner, who inks *The Lockhorns*, has a TV on while he works, but I can't imagine having a visual stimulus in the room—unless it's my dog!

I know Sparky likes absolute silence when he draws, because he draws and thinks up new material at the same time. One time I was out in California and I was late on my deadlines and I had all kinds of things to do. I said to him, "Look, I'm just going to stay in the hotel and work." He said, "Why don't you use my studio? I'll give you half my studio space." And I told him I didn't want to, because I was afraid I wouldn't be able to concentrate. And he insisted— but he said, "I don't want you to play a radio, I don't want you to talk to me, I don't want you to come over to my side, I want you to just mind your own business and stick to your side of the studio." And I said, "Okay, that's fine. You won't bug me and I won't bug you." He was over talking to me every five minutes! [*Laughter*]

**Heintjes:** Is there anything you hate to draw, anything you'll go out of your way to avoid drawing?

**Johnston:** I used to hate drawing feet. Now I've practiced them so much that I think I do them fairly well.

**Heintjes:** Is it shoes you dislike drawing or bare feet?

**Johnston:** Shoes more than bare feet. Shoes are very difficult for me. I find that hands aren't difficult for me at all, but for some artists they're difficult. The other thing I hate to draw is bicycles. One of the problems I have with my character in a wheelchair is that I hate to draw the doggone wheelchair! That was a whole insight to me. There are a whole bunch of disabled people who are saying, "We're here! Draw us! Joke about us, have fun with us! We have funny things to talk about, too—don't ignore us!" And I want to say, "I want to draw you, but I can't draw your chair!" [*Laughter*] It's not so difficult drawing someone who's sitting down; it's difficult drawing all those levers and wheels and lines.

**Heintjes:** Have you ever done a piece of work and felt so good about it that you've said, "This is it—I can't get better than this"?

**Johnston:** I have done work that I feel that good about, but what I say to myself is, "I look forward to the day when I do the level of work again." You know how it is when it's another regular, ordinary day, and then out of the blue someone phones you who you haven't heard from in years, or somebody invites you to something, and you say, "Wow! Isn't this great! Thank you for calling me—you've made my day!" You don't hang up the phone saying, "Well, that'll never happen again." You just look forward to it happening again someday.

Every day it's a joy. Every day it's a surprise package. There are some days when my work is so covered with Wite-Out that I don't want anyone to see it. And there are days when I can write and I feel pretty smug. There are also days when I feel like I'm going to quit and go work at Woolco. Or "It's gone—I've used it all up!" The trick is to stay far ahead enough of the deadlines so when you hit a dry spell, you can survive them with confidence.

**Heintjes:** How do you deal with writer's block?

**Johnston:** I try to switch to another channel in my "computer programming." If I'm having a real hard time doing dailies, I'll do a Sunday. If I'm doing a storyline and I can't figure out how to segue from school to the kitchen, I'll put it aside and let my mind drift or do work on a Sunday. If it's one of those days when nothing is happening, I have all kinds of other things I need to do—answer my fan mail, do illustrations for people I know who are getting married. . . .

**Heintjes:** Even work for *Hogan's Alley*. . . .

**Johnston:** Well, yes. [*Laughter*] That's the kind of stuff I will do when the gas has run out.

**Heintjes:** Which do you enjoy creating more—a daily or a Sunday?

**Johnston:** I enjoy both. I often think the Sundays are funnier, because they stand alone. In a week of dailies, I might have two humorous one and the rest are thoughtful ones. The Sundays are, if not humorous, at least wry. And I never, ever connect them into the storylines I do in the dailies. So I suppose that for something you would want to own for your wall, the Sundays are a much more whole statement.

**Heintjes:** Do you ever want to do something apart from the slice-of-life humor of *For Better or For Worse*?

**Johnston:** I am doing other types of material. I do a comic panel called *Chuffers* about an old guy who has a train. My husband is a model railroad fanatic, and he goes to conventions and meetings and builds trains to ride on. He's spent time on movie studio lots while they blow up trains. The guy is train-bonkers. He does a quarterly article for *LGB Magazine*, so I figure, "Well, if he played golf, I'd play golf," so I do a regular cartoon for this magazine. I do greeting cards for the clinic, and it's fun to do. It's like changing from one exercise to another.

**Heintjes:** Do you find that it gets something out of your system that otherwise wouldn't be gotten out?

**Johnston:** Yes—I get to draw things other than *For Better or For Worse*! I find that what I need almost more than anything else is connection with other cartoonists. It's like a self-help group. Very few people know what we go through. Look at a famous actress. Everyone says, "Oh, I wish I were you— you're beautiful, you're glamorous." But from her point of view, it's "I work so hard, I don't have a family life, I'm hounded and I have no privacy." The only people who can understand how they live are other actors. And cartoonists can say to each other, "God, I couldn't think of a thing last week." One editorial cartoonist told me that he's so engrossed when he's working that he doesn't know he's ignoring his wife until she bursts into tears and runs out of the room. He was so focused on what he was doing that he didn't hear her say, "I'm depressed and I need to talk to you." So we all get together and we commiserate. And Rod gets together with the other cartoonists' spouses and says, "Living with these people is a zoo!" because they not only live with us, they live with the fantasy world we create.

If I think my husband is angry at me and doesn't want to talk about it, I'll argue and make his half of the argument up while he's at work. I do it every day for my work anyway! And by the time he comes home from work, I'm furious! "You said this, and then you said that! And when I said this, you said that!" So cartoonists can be very difficult to live with. I remember the first time I went to a Reuben Award ceremony. I thought it would be like a Hollywood gala, with air kisses and "Hello, dahling!" I'm sure Hollywood isn't really like that, but that's the popular impression. The public is driven to believe that there's a lot of superficiality in Hollywood and that nobody trusts anybody and there's no true friendship there. If someone says "Welcome," it's because they really just want your job. I never expected the joyous feeling at the Reubens, the feeling that we all knew each other. How can you read *Cathy* and not feel like you knew Cathy Guisewite? How can you read *Peanuts* and not have a sense of what Charles Schulz is like? Or even *Garfield*? Jim [Davis] is as sarcastic as Garfield can be from time to time. When I went to this thing, I was overwhelmed by the sense of family and acceptance. And affection for my work as well. The competition is between the salesmen. If my salesman is trying to get an editor to drop *Blondie* for *For Better or For Worse* and says terrible things about *Blondie* to try to persuade him, I don't hear it. If his agent goes to an editor and says about *For Better or For Worse*, "Are you carrying that moralistic crap? Why don't you give them *Blondie*, which is a proven strip that people have laughed at for decades?" We don't hear that. So we can be wonderfully good friends. You get charged up by each other.

When I first saw *Calvin and Hobbes*, the first thing I thought was, *This guy can draw!* And I desperately wanted to meet him and shake his hand and see his studio. I think that when he began that strip, another era started. I talked to Bill [Watterson] not long ago, and he said, "What worries me about the fantasy aspect of *Calvin and Hobbes* is that people think I've cornered the market on fantasy. And if someone thinks up a character who sometimes goes into a fantasy world, they're accused of copying me." And he said he never invented the idea of a fantasy life—that was invented thousands of years ago, with the invention of people.

**Heintjes:** What is your daily schedule like?

**Johnston:** I work nine to five every single day. I have a deadline, and I make sure I am so many weeks ahead of that deadline. If it means that I work late one day so I can take off early another day, I do that. I almost never take a morning off. This is the first morning I've taken off in more than two years. It's a full-time job. I have an assistant who comes in three days a week, and she does the Zipatone [Editor's note: a type of shading or pattern sheet using in comics drawing], she colors all my Sundays, files, and helps with the mail, and she does our business. She doesn't do any drawing. Between the two of us, we have a full-time job here.

**Heintjes:** Does she choose all the Zipatone patterns?

**Johnston:** Yes.

**Heintjes:** It's all up to her.

**Johnston:** That's right.

**Heintjes:** Do you break your day up in some way, like morning is penciling, afternoon is inking? How do you structure your day?

**Johnston:** I will have a writing day. For example, the last two days have been writing days. I have a sunroom that has some plants, a reclining chair, and a coffee table, and I'll sit in there and write. When I have written the number of weeks that I am comfortable with, then I pencil. A good day for me is to write a week's worth of dailies. I'm happy with that. If I can write two weeks' worth of dailies in a day, that's a great day, and I'm tap-dancing at the end of it. The next day, I often find my batteries are too low to concentrate on drawing what I wrote, so I'll do other things, like answer mail. The next day, I'll be ready to do the drawing. And I can pencil two weeks in a day, and that's pretty exhausting. Then I can ink two weeks in a day. It takes Nathalie a full day to do all the Zipatone. Then, of course, I have all my Sundays to do, so it is a full-time job. People say, "Well, you just do a drawing a day and then goof off." They don't realize that it's a technical feat just to stay ahead of the deadline, and every day you don't produce is one day you get closer to falling behind your deadline.

So let's say it takes me two to three days to write two weeks' worth of dailies. It takes me a day to pencil two weeks, a day to ink two weeks, and Nathalie a day to zip it and get it on a courier. That's a week! So it takes me a week to do two weeks of work, but then I have Sundays, book covers, calendars, coffee mugs.

**Heintjes:** Not to mention correspondence.

**Johnston:** Oh, the correspondence. If I don't do it during the week, it takes me a full Saturday to get through it, because I like to answer every letter. I believe that if someone took the time to write to me, I feel it's important for me to write back. A number of times I've heard that people have my letter hanging framed on their living room wall. And these are people who are telling me how I'm doing. I'm not doing stand-up. I don't have an audience who will boo and hiss or applaud at my performance. So the only gauge I have of my performance is the response I get from readers. So I want to give them the courtesy of responding back to them, and that is a huge responsibility.

**Heintjes:** Your artwork has a looseness, a spontaneity that's very fun to look at. Do you pencil loosely and do most of the drawing in the inking stage?

**Johnston:** No, my pencils are quite tight. The way I look at it is the pencil is the ghost and the ink is how I bring that ghost to life. That's the solid, living being you can touch and feel. And when I put my pen to the cheek of that ghost, I touch that cheek.

**Heintjes:** What do you draw with?

**Johnston:** I use an H-B lead in a mechanical pencil. I like the feel of it. You see, my hands perspire terribly. I find that I can't stand the feeling of certain things in my hand, and wood is one of them. I wear animator's gloves when I work because my hands perspire so badly. It's a real problem. So on my right hand I always wear an animator's glove when I work. It's so funny, because I cut the first three fingers out. I buy them from the local photo shop, and I throw them in the wash. So I've got a drawer full of these stupid gloves with the fingers chopped out. Sometimes I'll wash them with the dark clothes so they'll all come out purple or green. I often don't like people to watch me draw because these gloves look so silly, but I really do need something on my right hand to keep the perspiration from affecting the line of my work. For paper, I use Strathmore bond. I work just a little over actual size. I don't work very big at all. In fact, one of Sparky's old strips is exactly twice the size of mine. He gave me all his old paper. I was over at his studio one day and he showed me this big stack of paper. "Look at this," he said. "I've gone to a different format and I'm going to have to waste all this paper." I measured it, and it was exactly double the size of mine, so I asked him if I could have it. So he had his assistant cut it in half, and he mailed me about five hundred dollars' worth of this beautiful, heavy paper. And it had the *Peanuts* logo printed on the back of it, so I did *For Better or For Worse* on the back of *Peanuts* paper for about two years. It was wonderful! I loved it.

**Heintjes:** What about inking?

**Johnston:** I use a flexible C-6 Speedball nib. It has a little well on it, which I love, because it gives you a little more time before it runs out. I use the ink that's commonly used for acetate sheets because I find it's more opaque and it doesn't smudge as easily. I often work on vellum when I'm doing finished art for coffee cups or art that's done for other purposes. I do a pencil rough on a piece of bond pad, and I put a piece of tracing vellum over top. I really like that ink for the vellum surface. The Wite-Out I use is animation paint. I think it's called Cartoon Color. I love the texture of it, I love the way it dries. I find it's better than any other Wite-Out product. You can draw over it with pencil or pen, and it's just like you're working on paper again. It's a beautiful tool.

**Heintjes:** Do you use a Rapidograph [pen] for straight lines?

**Johnston:** Yes, I do. I wish I could draw like Pat Brady or Bill Watterson. Things like furniture, the way they use those wonderful freehand lines, but I cannot do it. I also cannot draw circles or ovals very well, and I use templates for those. I curse myself every time I try to draw a freehand circle or straight line. I just screw up every time! I wish I could draw things as fluidly as I draw beings.

**Heintjes:** Whose work do you currently enjoy?

**Johnston:** One of the problems is that I don't see everything. I don't get all the editorial cartoonists, and I don't get all the dailies. Of the ones I see on a regular basis and really read and enjoy, I would put *Rose Is Rose* at the top of the list. I admire Cathy Guisewite's writing ability. I read the work very closely for her innovative punch line ability. I read *Cathy* as much as a technical guideline as for anything else. She gets into some things—weight, clothing—that some people may find repetitive, but I find she has a skill for writing that not many other people have. I still think that *Calvin and Hobbes* is one of the best-drawn strips there is. I'm interested to see how Bill Watterson is going to develop in the future as a writer. It will be interesting to see where *Calvin and Hobbes* goes from here. That's what I'm looking for. I'm also enjoying

*Jumpstart* by Robb Armstrong. I think that's exciting. I know Robb and his wife just had a baby, so I'm reading it to see when a baby is going to creep into the strip. And knowing the cartoonists is part of loving their work. Charles Schulz is probably my dearest friend in the industry, and it's such a thrill to say so. When I'm down I call him, and he calls me. We send books back and forth, and when he's mad about something he'll call me. And I just adore that connection. I know all about the red-haired girl, and I know his wife very well. I know that his poor little dog is blind and deaf now. I see things happening in the strip that I know personally about him. There's a connection there that's sort of a spiritual bond. Losing his work from the paper and losing him personally . . . it would be such a blow. It would be very tough for me to recover from that. There are very few things that reduce me to tears at the drop of a hat, but thinking about that does.

**Heintjes:** How do you feel when you look at your early work?

**Johnston:** Oh, I'm embarrassed by it, of course. [*Laughter*] But that's good, because if you're not always improving, you might as well quit. I am forever getting sent stuff by young guys and women asking for a critique. And to the ones who get outraged by an honest critique, I want to say, "Hang up your pen, Jack, because you're never going to go anywhere, because you're not insecure enough to improve." The ones who say, "That really hurt, but I'm going to try," those are the ones who give you hope, because you have to look at everything you do and say, "I can do better than that."

**Heintjes:** Do you have any words of advice for aspiring cartoonists?

**Johnston:** You have to be brutally honest with yourself if you want to be in the world of strip cartoons or editorial cartoons, because you have to be so many people wrapped up into one. You have to be a writer, a humorist, an artist, and an actor. You have to be a superb actor, because you have to breathe life into all these characters. If one of your characters is laughing, you want that mouth wide open and the tongue out, eyes crinkled up, and you want to convey that expression so that it goes into the eyeball of the reader and straight to the brain. You have to be able to act that well. If your mom says you're doing fine and the guy down the block laughs at your stuff, that isn't enough. It has to compete with the stuff out there now, and the ability of so many people only goes so far. And they try. And they try. And they try. And they send you stuff again and again. And you want to say, "But you're not listening. You're not getting any better. You're not standing back from it from an objective point of view and saying to yourself, 'It's not funny enough.'" How do you say to somebody, "You draw well, you're witty, you're a swell guy, but you're not funny enough!"? It's awful hearing that from somebody in the business, but you've got to say it to yourself. And how do you get funny enough? You get funny by watching and studying people like Bill Cosby, who say funny things, make funny faces and use funny body language. You don't look at successful cartoonists' work and say, "Gee, why are they there and I'm not?" You look at their work and say, "They're there and I'm not because the line does this and the words do that."

You also have to involve the audience in the gag. You can't hand them a gag. You have to let them get the gag. Here's a very bad example—two nuns are sitting on a bus and one of them is doing a crossword puzzle. One of them says, "Sister, what's a four-letter word ending in 'it' that you find in the bottom of a bird cage?" The other replies, "Grit." "Oh," says the first nun. "Do you have an eraser?" The audience has to "think" to get the joke. Why does she need an eraser? The answer to what she wrote, obviously, is "shit," but it's never spelled out. The audience laughs because the audience is involved. So many people don't do that—they want you to get the gag so badly that they hand it to you. Even a five-year-old wouldn't think it was funny, because he'd see the gag coming before he got to the punch line.

You have to be able to write poetry, because the way you write a strip is with an economy of words, a flow and a choice of words, that the reader reads straight through. There's no stopping and starting.

And you're drawing for the reader. You're not drawing for you. So many cartoonists are so selfish and are enjoying their work so much that they don't realize it's a performance for an audience. If you don't connect the forehead to the nose, for example, and those eyes are forever floating, and the hair is kind of a chicken's crop up on top . . . you, the artist, can see the character because in your "computer printout" all of that works for you, but the audience might look at it and just see a series of worms. Your gag is lost, because the audience is still looking at the character and saying, "Is that a nose, or is that part of his hair? What am I looking at here?" You're performing for an audience, and you've got to draw for that audience. The characters have to be somebody the audience cares about. When you're doing a comic strip, people tend to assume the readers will instantly relate to their characters, but that's not true. It takes three years before Joe Blow the reader will say, "That character will always respond in this way." Over time people realized that Dagwood would always miss the bus.

A new creator might do a strip about a farmer and his talking animal and have all kinds of gags about it. Meanwhile, the readers are saying, "Why does this animal talk? Is this guy married? Why is this happening?" And they can't relate, because the cartoonist never gives the readers enough information, and for three years, every single day, you have to say, "Hi, my name is Jack and I have a talking moose." Every single day. And three years later, people are going to say, "Hey, did you read the strip about Jack and his talking moose?" People assume that because they know their characters intimately, their readers will. But the readers are skeptical. They want what they're used to. They don't want *Rex Morgan, M.D.* to go away. "I don't want to lose *M\*A\*S\*H!* Don't give me a replacement for *M\*A\*S\*H*—I'm going to hate it!" To buck that attitude, you've got to be so appealing, so understandable, that the reader's going to say, "Well, that one's intriguing. I'll read it again tomorrow." And if they read it tomorrow, they have to find it equally intriguing. Often, new creators are so comfortable with their own stuff that they don't realize they have to spoon-feed the audience. It's one statement a day. In a sitcom, for example, you can have a full understanding of the characters in a half-hour, but in a comic strip, you've got to hook the reader a little bit, day by day. It's like fishing—you've got to use the right hook and the right bait, and you wait, wait, wait, wait.

**Heintjes:** And it's that patience that eventually leads to the readers' identification with the characters.

**Johnston:** That's exactly right. And once your readers identify with your characters, you know they're going to look forward to seeing them every day, and that's the rewarding part—knowing that your characters are a part of your readers' lives, even if it's only for a few moments each day.

# Parenting Ups and Downs with Cartoonist Lynn Johnston

SEAMUS O'REGAN / 2003

From *CANADA AM* (June 9, 2003). Copyright 2003 CTV Television, Inc. Interview provided courtesy of © BELL MEDIA INC. All rights reserved. Reprinted by permission.

**Seamus O'Regan:** Well, the comic strip *For Better or For Worse* has been breathing life and humor into more than two thousand—that's right, two thousand—newspapers worldwide. Twenty countries, eight different languages. And now one of Canada's beloved cartoonists, Lynn Johnston, is back with not one, not two, but three new books.

We have got *Leaving Home*, *Graduation*, and *With This Ring*. And it's a pleasure to welcome Lynn Johnston into our studios this morning. Good morning.

**Lynn Johnston:** Good morning, Seamus.

**SO:** It's great to meet you.

**LJ:** You too.

**SO:** You are so prolific and such a marvelous cartoonist.

**LJ:** I have help.

**SO:** What's that?

**LJ:** I have help.

**SO:** You have help. Tell us about the three books. Maybe we'll start with *Graduation*, this petite little book here.

**LJ:** It's just a minibook. But it's one of those things you give your graduate or you give the family of the graduating family. Just something to say "thanks" and "go for it" and "you did it."

It covers little-kid graduations. I mean, kids graduate from kindergarten with the whole thing, the hat and the gown. And then they graduate from grade eight. They graduate from grade twelve. They graduate from university. And grade thirteen—no, not grade thirteen now.

**SO:** Not grade thirteen anymore. Only the grade twelve.

**LJ:** So they have got the double cohort.

**SO:** You've got the double cohort. You also have got this great juxtaposition. . . . On one side you have poetry and some sayings, you know, nice little passages to think of, you know, during this special time, not only for the graduate but for the family. And on the other side it's usually a cartoon from you that, you know, is just kinda funny. The reality of it.

**LJ:** The poetry was written by the same girl who wrote *Leaving Home*. And she is a wonderful friend. For thirty years we have known each other. And she would tell me all these things about her kids. And she works with young people who are learning how to live on their own and young moms who are keeping their babies. And I said, "Andie, why don't you write a book?" So she did. And I illustrated it.

**SO:** *Survival of the Hippest*. Tell us about this book.

**LJ:** Well, it is a book on how to leave home. How to break a lease, how to find a roommate, how to keep a check book, how not to buy a car and have to live in it.

**SO:** Pay your phone bills.

**LJ:** Pay your phone bill. It's really full of great advice. But it's through her voice. And she knows an awful lot.

**SO:** There is a lot of great, practical information there, you know, for a parent to buy for their kid. It would probably save on long-distance calls you make to home saying, "What do I do now? What do I do now?"

But one of my favorite cartoon illustrations in there is one that you did of a girl. Yeah, this one here. I don't know if we can get it on camera. It's probably a bit too white. . . . Anyway, you can barely see it. But basically it shows a girl here in this kind of not-the-best-decorated apartment, let's put it that way. Kind of haphazard. And the mother is standing there despondent while the daughter says, "Wow, it's perfect!" Just so delighted to have her own place.

**LJ:** Well, the more dilapidated it is, the better. Like, my daughter's place right now is in such a shape that somebody tried to cook something and they were blown across the room because the stove shorted out. So everything shorted out. And they think the place is going to catch fire any minute. But they love it there.

But it rains a lot in Vancouver, so it will put the fire out. So she is really happy.

**SO:** You have always looked to your own family for your inspiration, for Michael and for Elizabeth and for all the Pattersons. Have you not?

**LJ:** I have been given their approval. But it doesn't copy their lives. It doesn't follow their lives. No, I make it up. Really. You have to.

**SO:** Yeah, and you have friends of your children.

**LJ:** Yeah.

**SO:** But was that ever a concern for you? Or for your family?

**LJ:** Yes, it was.

**SO:** The privacy issue.

**LJ:** Yeah, it was a lot—

**SO:** I mean, your son being compared to Michael, your daughter being compared to Elizabeth.

**LJ:** Always, yeah. Yeah, the kids were always getting teased about it at school and all that kind of thing. And I think that's why they are both in Vancouver now, is to try to—

**SO:** Get away?

**LJ:** —become their own people without having us sort of in the background.

**SO:** They left home.

**LJ:** They've gone. They've gone. But they're still calling home for the occasional bit of advice and a check once in a while.

**SO:** [*Laughs*] *With This Ring* is fantastic. And on the front, of course, it shows Michael getting married. Boy, how time flies.

**LJ:** Getting married. Isn't that something?

**SO:** Elizabeth is living with a guy. My goodness.

**LJ:** Well, here is where I really allow myself to just go right into the fantasy world. I would have loved one of my kids to get married.

**SO:** Not that there is any pressure. If they are watching in Vancouver.

**LJ:** No pressure. No pressure whatsoever.

**SO:** No pressure.

**LJ:** He has lost two great girls already! [*Laughter*] Am I going to get bitten for the one.

**SO:** Oh yeah.

**LJ:** Anyways, what's neat about this book is that the girl who designed the wedding dress really designed a wedding dress for Diana. Her name is Ramona Keveza, and she designed this great dress. And it really exists.

**SO:** It's a great compilation. And I just can't believe that so much time has gone by. But you certainly branched out into doing all sorts of other things. So that's great.

**LJ:** Well, we've got some dolls that we're doing with the Robert Tonner Doll Company. And Edgar the dog is coming out. We got all kinds of stuff on our website, which you can find in small print—

**SO:** At LynnJohnston—

**LJ:** No, "fborfw.com." You can see it on the comic strip if you read it. And thank you so much for having me here.

**SO:** Well, it's great to meet you, finally. Thank you so much for coming on. And I'm sure we'll see you again.

**LJ:** You actually read the books. I'm thrilled! [*Laughter*]

# Life's Issues Are Just "Stuff" for Lynn Johnston

**KAREN GRAM / 2004**

From the *Vancouver Sun* (September 25, 2004). Material republished with the express permission of *Vancouver Sun*, a division of Postmedia Network Inc.

"Everyone thinks I'm dying," protests cartoonist Lynn Johnston, her voice lifting off from the professional interview tone for the first time since our phone conversation began.

We'd been trading social niceties and talking about how pleased she is to be part of the Word on the Street festival at Vancouver's Library Square tomorrow, when she revealed that her short-term memory isn't what it used to be.

I spotted a journalistic red flag and jumped in.

"Oh really, you can't remember short term any more?"

Memory problems, a revelation that she has a painful autoimmune neurological disorder that makes her head jerk, plus news of impending retirement. The cartoonist's story suddenly didn't seem so comic anymore.

"No!" she cries, her voice betraying a frustration with the way media can misread things. For the record, the North Vancouver-raised, Northern Ontario-based, fifty-seven-year-old creator of the comic strip *For Better or For Worse* is not dying, and she can still remember what she had for breakfast. She explains she meant that should she ever lose her memory, she hopes it's the short term that goes, because she treasures the memories of her early childhood and the Lower Lonsdale streets she played in as a kid.

Much ink has been spilled over Johnston's childhood—especially the strict, uncompromising mother who regularly used a wooden spoon to discipline her. But Johnston wasn't the only child in the 1950s who felt the heat of a wooden spoon. The tough-childhood-begets-creative-artist narrative makes a good myth, but Johnston doesn't really go along.

Sure, her mom was tough and belts and spoons aren't recommended to raise a child, but she admits she was a difficult kid and says her mother only knew what her own British parents had taught her.

Johnston wasn't always this magnanimous about her upbringing, though. She had lots of anger earlier in her life, anger that her mother had never shown her love, just impatience, perfectionism, and, much later, respect. But she let it go when her mother died fourteen years ago.

"I don't have to describe my mother like that anymore," she says, adding that she is bored with it. "I can now look at my mother's face and appreciate her for who she was and what she did and know that she did the best she could."

Less has been made, however, of Johnston's father. Although he died the year after her mother, he is now immortalized in the comic strip as Gramps, the guitar-playing rock and roller who found love again late in his life. Her real-life dad was the funny guy in the family, she says. Her mom enjoyed a good joke too, especially puns and word plays, but her dad was a hoot. Resurrecting him in the strip has been a pleasure for her.

"I've loved drawing my father over and over again," she says. "I've absolutely loved it. I think had he been healthy and lived to a ripe old age, this is likely the way he would have enjoyed living his later years."

A watchmaker who played every musical instrument with strings and then some, encouraging his two kids to play as well—Lynn on classical guitar and her brother on trumpet—Johnston's dad was the parent who goofed around with her and her brother, making them laugh.

It was good tonic, and she says it shaped the way she has handled life ever since. "A lot of our serious discussions were laughing matters around the dinner table. A lot of our truths had to come out as a joke," she says.

Not surprisingly, that attitude works well in a comic strip that covers death, illness, bullying, growing pains, love, and everything else that goes on in life—for better or for worse.

And writing a real-time strip about the Pattersons, loosely based on her own family, has allowed Johnston to play God just a little. (In the strip, Johnston becomes Elly, the family matriarch; real-life husband Rod, a dentist, takes the name John but remains a dentist; son Aaron becomes son Michael; daughter Kate turns into Elizabeth.)

Besides resurrecting her father, Johnston was also able to have a third child, albeit a virtual one, through the comic strip. April, born into the strip in April 1991, helped Johnston, then forty-five years old, to accept that she and Rod would not be having a third. April, now thirteen and entering high school, is also Johnston's way of reliving her own childhood. In another storyline, she transforms something sad from life and makes it better—a true Aaron story in which he arrived at the scene of an accident as a TV camera man to discover that the fatality was a woman he had dated. In the strip, the woman lives and becomes Michael's wife.

But you can only play God so far, she says. Which is why we haven't seen any storylines about single parenthood, even though Johnston went through that herself when after eight years of marriage, she left her philandering first husband soon after Aaron was born. For several years, Johnston lived the classic single mom existence, struggling to make ends meet before hooking up with Rod, an old acquaintance. Single parenthood would make a good storyline, but, she adds sagely, "It's material, but it just has to happen. If you force something to happen it looks like it's a story that you put it in there because you haven't before."

Johnston says she doesn't set out to write about particularly difficult life issues, though she's done it frequently, most notably when she brought Lawrence, Michael's childhood buddy, out of the closet or when she killed off Farley, the family dog.

"It's just stuff," she says. "Stuff that happens to everybody."

Maybe so, but much of the "stuff" Johnston is notorious for including in the strip had never before appeared on the comics page. She neatly works controversial issues into the narratives of her characters. Introducing a gay character gave fundamentalist readers conniptions and landed Johnston reams of angry mail. However, with this storyline she effectively normalized the gay experience for a legion of readers, proving that indeed "it is just stuff."

With Gramps's life-affirming attitude, in which he finds love and rock and roll and groupies all in his eighties, she took on ageist attitudes. She normalized disabilities when Elizabeth had a teacher in a wheelchair, and she confronted schoolground antics when April had to deal with a bully.

In 2001, the B'nai Brith Canada and the League for Human Rights presented Johnston with a national award for her portrayal of human rights and diversity issues.

She also is a member of the Order of Canada. But one of the best forms of recognition she ever got was from Charles Schulz, author of *Peanuts*, who called her out of the blue one day to tell her how much he liked her strip.

While she denies being on a mission (many of her stories come from her own experience, including fighting off the bullies as a kid), Johnston admits she wants to demonstrate—lightly—that human beings of all races, beliefs and language groups are essentially the same.

Johnston's fictional world is populated with diverse individuals, just like the real world.
FOR BETTER OR FOR WORSE © 1991 Lynn Johnston Productions. Dist. By ANDREWS MCMEEL
SYNDICATION. Reprinted with permission. All rights reserved.

Recently she sent Elizabeth up to a small northern Native village to teach, a storyline she drew from her own far north experiences, when she, an urban dweller, and Rod lived for six years in the tiny community of Lynn Lake, Manitoba.

"People have a preconceived idea of what it's like to go to a village or go to a Pow Wow or something like that. I was the same as everyone else feeling it was almost foreign ground. But it's families and reunions and celebrations and birthdays and communion just like any other household.

"Once you start to say, 'Well, there is no difference between my household and a household where people speak Chinese or Lebanese or Sudanese,' there is no difference, there is no difference. I mean, there is no difference."

Although Johnston grew up near the Squamish nation, but she had very little contact with any of the kids who lived on the reserve.

"I felt and feel now that as a non-Native person I've been robbed of a culture I should have known about. I should have known about the residential schools. I should have known about the genocide. I should have known why Natives turn their eyes away, mistrusting of non-Native people."

With a comic strip that keeps topping the charts all over the world even after twenty-five years and has won all kinds of awards, it's understandable that Johnston might be tempted to make a few comments about society, but her big goal in the next few years is to find a way to wrap the whole thing up.

"I'm getting tired of the deadlines, and I know that a good story requires that it have a time when there is closure everywhere.

"It's turned into a soap opera, which I never intended," she says. "The characters have become so real that you couldn't just have an event happen without saying, 'And then what?' Then what? What happened next?'"

Johnston has to find a way to close each character's story. It won't be easy, especially when she can only make one statement a day.

She's tired of the restrictive format too, she says. She envies writers and journalists and fantasizes about writing novels. But she's not making any promises. Writing is the hardest part of her job, she says. As an Emily Carr graduate, the drawing comes naturally. She treats it like a reward after sweating through the writing.

In three years, she says, the strip will die. But like Gramps, the Pattersons will come back to life in a new form, on the web. Johnston didn't want to reveal too much, but she said it will involve animation and reusing old material in new ways.

Meanwhile, she is coming to terms with a neurological disorder that can be quite debilitating.

It's called dystonia. "It sounds like some small European country," she quips, adding it means "muscles out of control." It can take many forms, but in her case, it causes her head to twist with the force equivalent to hands wringing out a towel. It happens whenever she lies down or rests her head and is especially noticeable when she is tired. Her neck muscles are incredibly big and powerful as a result.

It makes it hard to draw, and among her staff of six women, Johnston now employs a creative director, Laura Piche to help her. Johnston still draws all the characters and scenes, while Piche inks in the background and does all the lettering.

"I could do it myself," she says. "But it would take me twice, three times, four times as long."

Back on the soap box for moment, she says she wants to spread the message that anyone experiencing similar symptoms should not settle for just any old doctor. They should find themselves a neurologist who specializes in movement disorders, such as Parkinson's or Tourette's Syndrome.

"Others will just tell you it's stress. Or you. You are just nuts," she says. "After a while you believe that. For many people it causes marriages to break down because one of side effects is you can't sleep and feel depressed."

Botox is one of the treatments known to give some relief to the condition, and Johnston tried it, but if she had kept it up, the Botox would have frozen her muscles and she would have had to wear a collar around her neck to support it. Besides, while money is not really an issue for her, having made multiple millions over the years, the treatments are expensive and don't always work.

"So I decided 'Well, that's the new me now.' We call ourselves 'the movers and shakers.' It's just part of life (for better or for worse)."

# It's for the "Better": As Lynn Johnston's Comic Strip Marks Its Twenty-Eighth Anniversary, It's in for Some Changes. But Then, So Is She.

**ALEX CHUN / 2007**

From the *Los Angeles Times* (September 10, 2007). Reprinted by permission.

In a letter sent to editors last month regarding the fate of her long-running semiautobiographical comic strip, *For Better or For Worse*, Lynn Johnston, borrowing a quote from Mark Twain, wrote, "Rumors of my demise have been greatly exaggerated!"

Ironically, it was Johnston herself who started the rumor almost a decade ago when she stated in interviews that she would be retiring this month, the twenty-eighth anniversary of her strip. Instead, *For Better or For Worse*, which runs in more than two thousand papers, including the *Los Angeles Times*, and chronicles the lives of the Patterson family will continue in a hybrid format that weaves together new plots with previously published material.

"I love a challenge, and this is the biggest challenge I've had since Farley the dog died," Johnston says, referring to the emotional 1995 death of the Patterson's beloved family pet. "All these characters are delightful people who live and breathe in my head, so I wanted to say a little more about each of them."

Loyal readers will notice many changes, starting with new art that will be used to introduce reprint material, told with photo albums and flashbacks. And one of the strip's hallmarks, the aging of the characters, will come to an end. Elly and John will be relegated to a backup role with the focus shifting to their son Michael, his wife, Deanna, and their two children, who, not coincidentally, are about the same age as Michael and his sister, Elizabeth, were when the strip began.

Comparing Johnston's earlier, simpler drawing with her later, more complex work. FOR BETTER OR FOR WORSE © 1987 Lynn Johnston Productions. Dist. By ANDREWS MCMEEL SYNDICATION. Reprinted with permission. All rights reserved. FOR BETTER OR FOR WORSE © 2005 Lynn Johnston Productions. Dist. By ANDREWS MCMEEL SYNDICATION. Reprinted with permission. All rights reserved.

"John and Elly have told their story, so this is about the next generation and comparing today to yesterday," Johnston explains from her Corbeil, Canada, studio, about two hundred miles north of Toronto.

To smooth the transition, the ratio of material will favor new work at the outset before tilting toward classic strips as Johnston gets more comfortable integrating strips rendered in two completely different styles. "Some of the gags are good, but I could have drawn them so much better," she notes.

Although she's excited by the challenges the new format presents, Johnston says that up until a few years ago she fully intended to retire, citing a desire to travel (she's already scheduled a trip to South America to work with medical missions), her age (she turned sixty in May), and her health.

For a number of years, she battled a neurological condition called dystonia, which has gone into remission since she went off hormone therapy. She experiences double vision caused by eyestrain and has an essential tremor—a condition that also afflicted her friend and mentor Charles Schulz—which causes trembling in her hands and makes it difficult for her to draw a slow, even line.

As a result, Johnston relies on assistants to help with coloring and inking. For her part, she doggedly continues to write and pencil the strips and inks all the characters, "because I really want that expression or body gesture to reflect what the story is about."

When she initially thought about retiring, Johnston planned simply to end the strip. Later, she toyed with handing the strip off to another artist—one artist was actually offered the job but turned it down, Johnston says—or letting the strip run as a strict reprint a la *Peanuts*.

In the end, however, Johnston decided she just couldn't let go.

"I'm not dead yet, so I thought if the classic strips do run again, there are some things I would fix and change and add to [them]," she says.

By utilizing classic strips, Johnston has been able to bank the free time she craves (she's already two months ahead on her dailies and Sundays); at the same time, continuing the strip has helped Johnston cope with her separation from her husband of thirty-two years, Rod Johnston.

"Working on the strip and in the studio with a staff I love are things that are familiar to me," she says. "Being a single woman is not something that is familiar to me."

Although this will not be the first time a cartoonist has reused previously published material—toward the end of his run on the strip *The Heart of Juliet Jones*, Stan Drake sometimes cut figures out from his older originals and pasted them into new art—it's the first time that it's being used as a storytelling device. But if anybody can pull it off, it's Johnston, says Lee Salem, Universal Press Syndicate president and editor. Johnston is the 1986 Reuben Award (cartooning's highest honor) winner and a 1994 Pulitzer Prize finalist for her story on Michael's friend Lawrence coming out of the closet.

Although the new format was "a little ill-formed when we first talked about it, she's really developed it during the last year," says Salem, who was Johnston's editor when she first became syndicated. Despite Salem's assurances, fans such as longtime reader Sandra Leonetti, thirty-seven, are taking a wait-and-see approach. "I can't say whether I'll like it or not, but I want to give it a chance," says Leonetti, who runs a Live Journal from her North Hollywood home dedicated to deconstructing the strip. "I'm hoping it's more than just Michael looking at photo albums and saying to his daughter, 'Yes, Meredith, your Aunt Liz and I had a snowball fight.'"

According to Johnston, readers like Leonetti need not worry. The strip will include some reminiscing, but it will also expand on incidents via voiceovers and new plot lines. "For example, Michael met Deanna when they were in grade two, and then she disappeared," she says. "Well, where did she go? This will be an opportunity for a story on what happened to her."

Before she moves on to the new plots, however, Johnston still has a few loose ends to tie up, including Elizabeth rekindling a romance with her high school friend Anthony. Johnston originally planned to wrap up the current storylines by the time the hybrid strips began in September, but by July, when she was writing the September strips, she realized that she hadn't said everything she wanted to say and that the current storylines would continue at least through the end of the year.

"The characters just wouldn't let me stop—it's like a train going downhill that you have to stop slowly, slowly, slowly before you reach the station or you'll go right through," Johnston says. "Well, I kind of went right through."

# *Maclean's* Interview: Lynn Johnston

ANNE KINGSTON / 2008

Courtesy of *Maclean's Magazine* (August 27, 2008). Reprinted by permission.

Cartoonist Lynn Johnston returns to the drawing board this month with *For Better or For Worse*, North America's most popular comic strip, syndicated in over two thousand newspapers. She had planned to retire the twenty-eight-year-old strip that chronicles the domestic lives of the Patterson family. But the unexpected breakdown of her thirty-year marriage last year prompted her to return to work. In an unorthodox experiment, the North Bay, Ontario, resident will recast the story from day one via a mix of old and new drawings.

**Anne Kingston:** Retelling the Patterson family story with new storylines is either supreme artistic catharsis or supreme regression.

**Lynn Johnston:** [*Laughs*] Actually, it's one of those neat experiments that you know is working as soon as you get started on it. At first I thought, *Maybe it should go back and forth in time*. But the year that I tried that was a year that I had some personal chaos and found it awfully hard to concentrate. It didn't flow. Also, I would have to keep developing the characters, and I would have even less time than I have now to do it. So I ended the story. It comes to a full stop the last week of August. The whole month of August has been the wedding of Anthony and Elizabeth. Some people are thrilled with the wedding, some people aren't. I don't care. They're happy, they want to get married, and it's going to be good. And, really, the whole story is about marriage and how you deal with the for better or for worse, and that was what I wanted to point out.

**AK:** Is that an allusion to your own marriage suddenly ending for "the worse" a year ago?

**LJ:** Oh yeah, that was a shocker! I had no idea, you know? I knew that there were things not working, but I kept thinking, *When I'm retired, we'll*

75

*work it out*. But there was no conversation, no discussion, and suddenly I find that there's another woman in the picture. So I sat there when I found out, absolutely stunned, thinking, *Who's writing this story?!?*

**AK:** You've said you expected to be retired, traveling through the Mediterranean with your husband at this point in life.

**LJ:** And had made those plans, and to have that, you know. . . . You know, I was in shock for several days. My eyeballs were open and my mouth was open saying, "What?!? I don't believe this, I don't believe this!"

**AK:** Did you ever consider incorporating the breakup into your work?

**LJ:** No. It's far too personal, and it's far too stressful, and if I can enjoy a fantasy world along with everybody else, then I should just keep doing that. You know, if I start to put what really happened in the strip it's unfair to my family.

**AK:** But you've touched on significant issues in your life before—a character who comes out of the closet, abusive relationships. . . .

**LJ:** But not divorce.

**AK:** No, not divorce, which makes me wonder if one of the reasons the cartoon has been such a sanctuary of comfort is because the Pattersons have their ups and downs but remain solid at the core.

**LJ:** That's what I thought I had! I was divorced once before, so all of that memory is still there. I was thinking of using that, in that Anne—Elly's neighbor—her marriage is not working too well, but I never worked it into the strip.

**AK:** But recently you recycled an old strip in which Elly has a recurrent dream that [her husband] John leaves her for another woman.

**LJ:** Yes, it was so prophetic. I thought, *You know what? I'm going to just throw that in there.* I think it's funny; it's so déjà vu.

**AK:** So that was a dream that you had during your own marriage?

**LJ:** Well, [my former husband] worked with beautiful women ever since I met him. He's a dentist. He has hygienists and front-desk girls, and there are usually eight girls around him all the time, and he used to travel to the Native villages taking his staff with him, and people in the town would look at me as if to say, "Well, girl, join the club," because in a small northern mining town there's a lot of horsing around, and the joke was you can steal a man's wife, but you don't touch his woodpile, you know? It was rampant up here.

**AK:** Adultery is a form of entertainment where you live?

**LJ:** It was recreation. It was like a high school, all these different personalities thrown into this one inescapable place where you had to be there together all the time, whether you wanted to or not, and someone you hated might turn out to be the guy in the bar that you're hitting the sack with next year, you know? I didn't have time for that, nor did I want it, but it was there in the town. But I thought there was safety in numbers if he was with a bunch of girls. And they were all really nice people. But I thought to myself, *If I'm going to be a jealous wife, I'll drive myself crazy.*

**AK:** Later-in-life divorce is rampant. I wrote a story last year for *Maclean's* about it titled "The Twenty-Seven-Year Itch."

**LJ:** I've also heard it called "the Viagra divorce."

**AK:** This is your second divorce. The terrain must be so different at this stage; you were a young mother of one son the first time; now you have two grown children.

**LJ:** Well, thank goodness they're adult children. It was terribly hard on them anyway. My heart goes out to the younger moms who have children at home who are thrown between the two and have to spend time between two families. It's so difficult. But [my husband and I] had very individual lives. He had lots of hobbies, and I spent a lot of time on my own, and so being on my own is not something that I'm uncomfortable with. I think I've coped really, really well. When I was divorced the first time, I met another young woman who was also divorced. Actually, what happened with her was her husband took her to the hospital as she was having her second baby and she never saw him again.

**AK:** Wow. Really?

**LJ:** Yeah, and the two of us were looking at each other saying, "You know what? We're really fine people, we're worth keeping," and we supported each other through being brand-new moms with new babies and on our own. We were hoping to help other people through this once we'd survived. We had our survival mechanism, which we thought was superb. And the first thing was never go to bed ugly, because if you look in the mirror at three in the morning and you've been crying all night, [then] you're saying, "Well, no wonder he left me. Look at you!"

**AK:** That's such a female response, to blame yourselves.

**LJ:** Yeah. We had no money, so we went to the Salvation Army and we bought the best negligees. I mean, who wears a negligee? You wear it one night, it goes to the Salvation Army, so that's the best place to go to buy a fancy, swanky negligee. So we would go to bed and we would do our hair, our makeup. We'd call each other at eleven o'clock at night: "Hey, babe, you look good?" "Oh, I look great. Did you do your nails?" "Yeah, I did my nails." "Great." Then we'd go to bed looking great, feeling good, and we'd call each other in the morning.

**AK:** You were ramping down *For Better or For Worse* when the marriage dissolved. Do you see any connection?

**LJ:** I think catching someone [being unfaithful] is . . . it's the end.

**AK:** Certainly adultery is a recurrent marital theme.

**LJ:** Do you know what it is? It's cowardice. If you're not happy, work it out. Some marriages are worth keeping if there's a really good basis for it, no matter what's gone on, because at this stage of our lives there's so much history, so much family, so much . . . not just possessions, but mental possessions, like the time we did this, and when we did that, and all the wonderful history there. When you're in your declining years, your memories are so important, and your family and friends. Do you really want to throw that away and start a brand-new life with brand-new people?

**AK:** I think there's a desire to be revitalized or to reinvent oneself, however mythic, that propels people to seek someone new.

**LJ:** Well, a number of people that I know—three, actually—who have gone through this, the partner who took off for the new, better life, lived it for maybe ten years, and then was devastated that they didn't have the old life, because they realized what they left for isn't as valuable as what they built for thirty years. But it's gone now, it's just memories. And it's hard for me to imagine passing by the man I lived with for thirty years and just saying a pleasant "hello" in the supermarket.

**AK:** Do you ever cross paths?

**LJ:** I've never seen him. I mean, it's a small town so he probably knows what I'm doing and I probably know a little bit of what he's doing, but my life is rolling along and I have a very full life. I've had a lot of fun, actually. I've really enjoyed being single; after you pass through the shock, then it's like, "Well, I can do anything I want. I can go anywhere I want." One of the things I've been wanting to do for years and years is to go to South America and be a translator, and I went to Peru this year and I worked for two weeks as a translator with the Medical Missionaries, and I had a wonderful time.

**AK:** Your work now gives you the flexibility to do that?

**LJ:** Oh, sure, absolutely, because I won't have to do six dailies and a Sunday every week. I might do three dailies, I might do five, I might do one; it all depends on how well the classic material works into what I'm doing now. The stories are already written, and the backgrounds are already drawn. I don't have to devise another character.

**AK:** Rewriting history isn't an opportunity we have in life, only art.

**LJ:** No. Isn't it a great thing? I am so excited by this, because it's the best of all worlds. I get to fix my mistakes. You can't change the past, but you can perhaps tell the story a little more clearly.

**AK:** You talk about reaching a new generation with the strip, but it's a very different generation than existed in the seventies, pre-internet, pre-YouTube. How are you adjusting to that?

**LJ:** Well, I've just gone past a couple of strips that were really funny—they were both about a typewriter, and those are both gone. Not because I didn't think they were good. I just didn't think it would go. So it's not as if I'll change things. I just won't include them if they don't have any relationship to today.

**AK:** What has readers' reaction to your own marital split been?

**LJ:** Well, people want to know a lot about it, and it's nobody's business but mine, you know? And they're sad because it was a fantasy. And I was sad for them because I wanted to give them a real family behind the family in the strip that was together and communicated and could see through . . . see each other through all the ups and downs.

# Lynn Johnston and Kate Beaton "In Conversation"

RAINA TELGEMEIER / 2014

Courtesy of Toronto Public Library and Toronto Comics Arts Festival (May 9, 2014). Reprinted by permission.

**Raina Telgemeier:** Thanks, everybody! Wow! I'm used to being the person answering the questions, not asking them, so this is super exciting for me!

So, Lynn, let's start with you. Let's maybe set the scene just a little bit and, if you could, tell us what the industry was like before you started *For Better or For Worse* in 1979 and you were publishing small books that somehow became bestsellers and really, really popular with your audience. Let's just set the stage.

**Lynn Johnston:** When I first started going to the National Cartoonists Society events, I stood in a hallway next to Jim Davis, who had just started *Garfield*, and all of these seniors going by Mort Walker and a lot of the people that were working with *MAD* magazine and *New Yorker*. They went by kind of ignoring us and he said, "Yes, someday we'll be the old farts." And now I get to ignore all the young new people as I don't know what they do, I don't know their names! [*Everyone chuckles*]

But yeah, in '79, there was still a lot of potential for syndication and that was the thing. Cartoonists were hoping that they would get syndicated, and it's a lot of hard work. But as I was saying before we sat down this evening, our original contracts were twenty years long, so [if] you can hit the mark, you had twenty years guaranteed. So it was a great job. If you had over three hundred papers, you could make a very good living. One hundred fifty papers was a really good run. You have to sustain your characters; you have to sustain your work for three years before the audience buys into what you are doing. So it's kind of tough now with students, and you know, younger people getting into the business. And they don't realize what kind of pressure there is and how much they have to produce in a short period of time, and most burnout in three years. So I think that's why there are a lot of collaborations and comics are changing, It's not the panacea it was when I got involved. As my editor told me now, they might hire one cartoonist a year as opposed to maybe three or four in previous years. So things have changed and not necessarily for the better when it comes to syndication.

**RT:** And Kate, by contrast, you came to prominence during the mid-aughts with web comics, and you were also doing them sort of for fun, and they also just caught on and sort of became part of the internet zeitgeist. So can you sort of talk about your origins as well?

**KB:** Yeah, well, I never had to impress as in the syndicate or anything. I got into comics because I did them at my university paper, and then I was looking for an outlet after university where people would still read them because I missed having that audience and online was the answer. I met with some other cartoonists who were putting their work up and they said, "You should just make a website." So I did. And it wasn't a very good website, but it was enough to get the comics around. And it took off from there by word of mouth because it's kind of a meritocracy on the internet sometimes. So I lucked out. I came in at a time when comics had already established themselves online but there wasn't this sort of intense saturation of material that we now have, the BuzzFeed lists and the pirating of content from other places and people still went to your website to read your comic instead of feeding them off like at Tumblr, where there's a million other things competing for everyone's attention. So the mid-2000s were a good time to get into comics because there was an audience ready for it but there wasn't a million other things competing for their attention at the same time. So my content was one thing, but timing was another. So myself and my kind of peer group were kind of like wedged in that optimal moment.

**RT:** Lucky for all of us. So I'd like to ask you if you guys had role models growing up and particularly if you ever saw a woman doing something that you aspired to do, and whether that was important to you or not.

**LJ:** The women that I was aware were working for greeting card companies and animation studios and were hidden away. Some of them were magazine artists, and I didn't learn about some of these people until a long time after I started seeing their work. My role models really were Len Norris at the *Vancouver Sun*—he was their editorial cartoonist, and he was by far the best cartoonist on the planet as far as I was concerned. Because no matter what he gave you as a gag, there was so much more in the background and so much more going on, and I loved his style. He had been trained as an architect, so of course the illustrations were just superb. And of course, reading the comics all the time when comics were comics in the Saturday papers when you actually had a comics page and it really was big enough to read without a microscope. And then, you know, of course reading *Peanuts* and all those things in the paper. Yeah, my role models were people that I saw out there, and I think that's what all of us do if you do this type of work. You see what's out there and you emulate the people whose work you really admire. And Doug Wright, he was another person that I just loved; I just loved his work. And my father was a real comics fan, and he was the one who would point things out and say, "Look at this, no words and it's the best thing on the page." You know?

**KB:** I think that who you see is exactly what it is. Because, growing up especially, I was from such a small place that my role models were very local: a painter in my town who was the only artist, and people like Bruce McKinnon who did and sold those editorial comics for *The Halifax Herald*. And on the comics page—and this is where I would cite you, Lynn, definitely. I told you this before, but I believe that you look for a version of yourself when you think, *Can I do this or not?* And I used to watch animated movies and I'd be like, *Maybe I'll be an animator.* And I would stop the credits and count the names and there were no women, especially lead animators on main characters, there are just no women. And you're like, "Oh," like immediately something in your brain clicks and says, "No, that's gonna be hard." Or "Maybe it's not in the books for you." But you [Lynn] are a woman and you are a Canadian, and it was very easily read as Canadian: The characters drank milk out of bags. [*Everyone chuckles*] There were signifiers. And her specials were on CBC at Christmas and that kind of thing. And without even trying or without even realizing that, you just were an influence because your presence on the comics page said to people like me, "You can do this." And that's huge. It's huge. Because without you, there weren't that many women that you saw. And it's enormous. So—yes, right? [*Audience applauds*]

**RT:** So in 1985 Lynn won the Reuben Award, which is the American National Cartoonists Society's biggest honor, and she was both the first woman and the first Canadian to take this award home. What was that like for you, and did you have a feeling of how progressive it was at that time?

**LJ:** The most important thing about that day for me was going to Washington, meeting all the cartoonists, and having Charles Schulz come up to me. I hadn't met him before and he shook my hand, put his arm around me, and he whispered into my ear, "I voted for you." But the evening was a really stressful evening because Jim Davis, who did *Garfield*, was also up for the award. And there was an animosity between the Davis bunch and others . . . and I won, and I wasn't ready to win. I hadn't produced enough work. I didn't feel ready to win. And that night I felt as though I had won because nobody wanted Jim to win. And these things, they happen.

**KB:** He must have won later though, or some other time.

**LJ:** He eventually won.

**KB:** Yeah, yeah. . . .

**LJ:** But it was like, "Oh I guess we better give him the award." But it was stressful because I think you have to feel ready for something like that. You have to feel as though you have really accomplished enough that your peers. . . . I mean, I won before some of the people before from *MAD* magazine had won, and that's not right. Mort Drucker, everyone knows Mort Drucker. If you like *MAD* magazine, imagine—I won before Mort Drucker did. That's not right!

**KB:** It's funny because you can say that and we're all like, "These are all . . . it's fine that you won before. . . ." And you became great friends with Charles Schulz afterwards, yes?

**LJ:** Absolutely. Oh yes, absolutely. That was the best part. And, you know . . . the only time I felt the pressure of being a woman in the business was when I became the president of the association, and all the old boys' club were kind of expecting me to go make coffee for them and really, I had a gavel, and I made them shut up. [*Applause*] And one of them kept drawing nude cartoons of me until I drew a really good one of him. [*Laughter and applause*]

**KB:** She is not kidding! I've seen pictures of the old National Cartoonists Society, and they just have like secretaries on their lap and like bottles of wine and shit. It was like "What the hell is this?" It's insane.

**LJ:** Well, it was an old boys' club. It started out in a small place in New York.

**KB:** Like with cigars. . . .

**LJ:** Started out in New York.

**RT:** Well, that's within the industry. What about your readers? Did your readers ever say to you, "Well, you're a woman and you shouldn't be drawing a comic strip," or were they . . . ?

**LJ:** Never, no. Never! What about you, [Raina]?

**RT:** No. . . . I mean, Kate, you're also kind of no stranger to sexism and sexist reactions to your work. How do you handle it?

**KB:** It surprises you at first because you don't consider yourself anything but, like, "I draw comics and I put them online." And then you get reactions that surprise you. And it takes a while to acclimate to that, I suppose. And to learn what is worth responding to and what is worth ignoring. And the answer is that most are worth ignoring. But a few things come at you sideways when you begin and you're in your early twenties and you're like,

"What?" and you get your back up over it or you get upset—not without cause, because there's no reason for anybody to single anyone out based on any part of their person that way.

And for the most part, I mean, there's certain things that you can respond to. It's a difficult subject because it's all kind of case based. I don't deal with the same kind of things as someone in the DC [or] Marvel Universe does when they write about "I don't like the *New 52* treatment of whatever character." And then they have to do deal with just this, like, onslaught of sexist sludge that takes over. Because they had an opinion.

The indie comics world is really not so intense. It's there, but it's not. I mean, you [Raina] are part of the indie comics world as well. And there's lots more women, there's lots of girls. I meet so many girls who are coming into comics and so excited, and you know they're just going to take over in a couple of years. So you are just like, "Well, those guys' time is nearly done." [*Laughter*] And you hope for the best for the future of comics. It's like we have to deal with [things], including getting rid of sexist notions, racist notions, all that stuff. It's going to happen, because you see more and more coming in with a fight, but it's coming and eventually things will even out. So I don't know, it's a big topic.

**RT:** It is a big topic. And I always say just let the work speak for itself. And in your case, I think for both of you, it really does.

**KB:** Yeah, yeah, that's it exactly.

**LJ:** My husband did not like the way I treated John Patterson. [*Laughter*]

**RT:** Tell us more.

**LJ:** Well, he ran off with a woman.

**RT**: Was it the nose?

**LJ:** A woman he hired to run my company and that had been going on for years and years and years. And so a lot of the anxiety that was deep down inside, knowing that the marriage wasn't that solid, worked its way into the strip. So I often did show him in a rather, you know, critical light from time to time. I tried to make him loving and warm, and he was very funny. But there was an awful lot of, you know, meanness to John and the character in the strip, so....

**RT:** But you were mean to Elly as well.

**LJ:** Well, yeah, I was.

**KB:** Yeah, yeah.

**LJ:** I was mean to everybody perhaps. But yeah, he complained. Yes. He was my worst critic probably, next to me. My worst critic, yeah.

**RT:** This leads me right into asking you about using your real-life families, whether they are based loosely on your real family members or whether you are doing autobio about your parents and your relationship with them. And I think that really connects with readers, but how do you know where to draw the line?

**LJ:** I asked my family.

**RT:** You did?

**LJ:** Oh yeah, I did. And you've [*to Kate*] probably asked friends and family too. I know you did. [*To Raina*] You've asked friends and family.

**RT:** Sometimes! [*Laughter*] Sometimes after the fact: "Was this cool? Okay?"

**LJ:** Well, if it's a loving way of showing them. But most people want you to put their stories in the strip.

**KB:** Yeah, yeah. But to a point.

**LJ:** To a point, yeah. [*Laughter*] But they will tell you stuff hoping that you'll put it out there and it's really not . . .

**KB:** Oh yeah, yeah. But that's like every comedian, right? "Well, I know a joke." And [they're] like, "Oh . . . do you?" I don't have a problem. I have a problem with monetizing it, because my comics, unlike yours, are like my literal family. And people ask that I put them in a book, and I have a hard time exploiting that since it's done specifically. And because I'm from such a small place that if there was something available for people to buy, that they can go into where my mum works and they hold the comic and it feels like, "Umm. . . ." It would make them uncomfortable. Somehow my town is so small and hilarious that nobody really has a Twitter account, so I can tweet as much as I want. And no one really figures it out. But if there was a book, everyone would just have it, and then that would be like an invasion. Because it would be like coming into their personal lives and personal territory. But in the comics that I make I just try to replicate the love that I see. So I really enjoy connecting with readers in that sense, and [*to Lynn*] you probably did this. Like, so many people—even in anticipation of this panel, I saw people commenting about how they were excited to come because "the Pattersons were *my* family." And, you know, I grew up with them and they were like my siblings and. . . .

**RT:** I had a crush on Michael when I was ten. . . . [*Laughter*]

**LJ:** When Michael was engaged to Deanna, I got this desperate letter from a girl who said, "Wait, he's got to meet me first!" [*Laughter*]

**KB:** Oh no! . . . [*Smiles*]

**RT:** They were so real! Is there anything either one of you shared that was like oversharing that you regretted after the fact?

**KB:** Oh, everything I put on Twitter, probably. [*Laughter*] Just scrawling thoughts . . . sometimes I'd delete them later. I'm like, "Why did you say that?" You should sleep on something emotional that you're about to put on the internet. If you still want to say it the next day, maybe you can say it. There's like that immediate release of content. Less of my comic works, but more on the social media-type part of my job.

**LJ:** Well, for me, doing stories for a syndicate meant that if you wrote part of a story—because you're on this deadline all the time and you're desperate and sometimes you got to put out what you're doing, otherwise, you're going to miss your deadline. . . . If you send out half a story, and then you say, "Wait! I hate that!" you still have to finish it because it's already gone and it's out there and it's into the process. And there were times, yeah, when I wrote a story that I either didn't like that much or that was awfully personal. But in the end, the responses from other people were always that they'd had the same thing happened to them. So . . . *phew*. [*Wipes brow*]

**KB:** But especially with the deadline . . . having to come up with the content, you probably had a bad week, and then you'd still have to deliver and then live with it.

**LJ:** That's why I had everybody grow up and change, because it gave me a challenge. It gave me more incentive to be able to write stuff that was interesting to me. If it's not interesting to me, it's certainly not going to be interesting to anybody else. So. . . .

**KB:** And it gave it more depth too and life. Like, sometimes I read *Marvin* now and Marvin's still a baby? [*Laughter*] Why?

**LJ:** That's a lot of diapers.

**KB:** So many diapers. . . .

**RT:** Just based upon what you both said, writing personal comics really draws out the weirdos. But it can also be incredibly rewarding. So if you could each share an example of how writing from a personal place has brought out the best your readers.

**KB:** Oh [*long pause*] . . . um. . . . [*Laughter*] It's not like I'm going to say something bad. No. I have a wonderful readership, and I love it when people say the personal work is their favorite, and I make comics when I go home for Christmas—I chronicle the whole thing—and my family is great about it, and they don't complain. They should, but they don't. And some people write, you know, they're like, "I wasn't able to come home for the holidays and I get it vicariously through your comics and they are the best part of my holidays." And that's . . . what an amazing thing that is. Or when I made the Fort McMurray comics about working up in the oil sands. People who had worked there, who had felt the same thing and found it hard articulate to others. Because it is an otherworldly experience, it's very difficult to describe what it's like working in this environment of money and destruction, and you're there and you're participating in it. But it's not black and white by any means, what you see and what you experience. And to have people say that they felt comfort in reading those things and identify with it meant a lot because, of course, I left there and moved to a city where no one I knew had gone through it, and I felt completely crazy for a while, because it's a totally different experience. But yeah, just relating with people one on one like that is the best.

**LJ:** I'm surprised by how personal the letters are.

**KB:** Definitely.

**LJ:** I mean, they talk to you as if they've known you forever, they know that their story is safe with you.

**KB:** Yes, yeah.

**LJ:** Although my story's been out there and everybody is reading it; that they feel that their story is safe with you. And I did a story . . . the story about Lawrence coming out, and the letters that came back from that I still have, actually. I have all of them. And those were some of the finest letters I've ever read, and many of them were letters from people who had not spoken to their family or friends. . . .

**KB:** He was the first [out gay] comic character in syndicated strips right?

**LJ:** Actually, I think there was one in *Doonesbury*.

**KB:** Oh? Okay.

**LJ:** But he is very political and he tends to be in the political section of the editorial section of the newspaper.

**KB:** Definitely.

**LJ:** And mine is still in the comics section, so, you know, I was walking on a thin edge there for a while with some editors.

**KB:** If anybody didn't know that . . . in the early 1990s?

**LJ:** Yeah.

**KB:** Lynn had a teenage character come out as gay in her comics, and it was enormous and it caused a lot of talk and controversy but then a lot of obviously personal connection.

**LJ:** Super positive response.

**KB:** Wonderful.

**LJ:** Really, in the end. But I realized that there are people who you will never, ever have a conversation with because they will never agree to disagree. They are black and white and mostly black in terms of, you know, their darkness of their thought. And I realized why things don't change. . . .

**KB:** I remember when it happened. I was pretty young because it was '93 or something, right?

**LJ:** Uh-huh.

**KB:** But I remember it being reported outside of the comics world, which doesn't always happen. There's not a lot that happens on the comics page where someone is like, "Wow!"

**RT:** And then it was in the regular part of the newspaper.

**KB:** Yeah!

**LJ:** My editor said he thought I might lose about six papers, and at the time I had about fifteen hundred papers and I thought, *Well, if I lose six then it's worth it.* But I lost about forty-five papers. They were all printable, they were all in the States. *Halifax Herald*, mind you, dumped me right away. And I'm still not back in. . . .

**KB:** Are you kidding?

**LJ:** *Halifax Herald* wiped me off the slate. [*Audience laughs*]

**KB:** Shame.

**LJ:** But the funny thing is that at the time pretty well every major city had two papers, like the *Toronto Star*, *Toronto Sun*, *Vancouver Province*, *Vancouver Sun*. And so, once a newspaper dropped you, the other paper would pick you up. So we sold like fifty-five papers right off the bat! . . . It was like, "Yes!" But it was a really traumatic time, and I would lie awake saying, "What have I done?" It's one of those things where you send it off and say, "Oops, it's out and running now. What do I do?" But it's probably the one story I'm most proud of and the response, the letters that I got back from people were fabulous.

**RT:** Awesome. I was in high school when that strip came out too. And I ran to school and said to my school gay friends who were all still closeted, "Have you seen *For Better or For Worse*?"

**KB:** "It's Michael's best friend!"

**RT:** Awesome.

**LJ:** The fun thing now is that it's running again and anybody who was angry then can see Lawrence growing up with Michael as his best friend and next-door neighbor. So I'm thinking, *Yes! There ya go.*

**KB:** Yeah, yeah.

**LJ:** Kid next door.

**RT:** Do either of you feel a sense of responsibility to future cartoonists, to be a role model or spokesperson or . . .

**KB:** Yeah.

**RT:** Anything?

**KB:** You were talking about sexism before, and I said that a lot of the things . . . I ignore a lot that comes my way. But I do feel that that's a disservice to a generation of girls who are coming into comics without any idea that there are dark sides to it. . . . But there are still for women in almost every industry. You're like, "Wow, comics are really bad." Then the people in the tech industries are like, "No." [*Laughter*] "It's bad here." Or in the academic industries, they're like "No, it's here, the academics." Or anywhere, right? So it feels cowardly to not say anything all of the time, but you have to pick your battles, I suppose, and decide what you're going to comment on. Because it does no good to just be like, "That's somebody else's problem." Because then you meet these young readers at comic shows and they're just like, "I wanna be a cartoonist." And they're adorable and you're just like [*feigns tears running down her face*], "Oh, okay." [*Laughter*] "I want it to be beautiful for you." [*Laughter*]

**LJ:** I've tried to help other people by having them send me their work, and I've gone through it all and edited and worked with them and made suggestions, and some have been very, very close to being syndicated. And they give up! And I don't know what it is. I don't know what it is.

**RT:** It wasn't you; I can tell you that much.

**KB:** No, there's a culture definitely in this internet age of sort of instant gratification. You put something up and people are like "LOL." And you're like, "Job done." [*Laughter*] Good night! [*Laughter*]

And nobody's asking you to work three years on something and then maybe it'll work out. That just doesn't happen anymore. [*Laughter*] I could see why they burn out. . . . It's hard to see the long, long term in that sense.

When you see people whose comics come up on Tumblr and what gets the most notes and reblogs and whatever? It's probably not your best work. It's probably the one that references, like, Benedict Cumberbatch. [*Laughter*] And then some of them are like, "Oh, that's the good stuff." It's just Benedict Cumberbatch. [*Laughter*] It's not a mark of good quality, it's just internet stuff. And it's hard to discern what's worth it, I suppose. I definitely think there's so much information and static and noise coming in and the real addiction that you can get to an immediate response, that it's hard to see a long game. So [it's] difficult, but I understand.

**LJ:** Somebody asked me today or yesterday . . . if I was a young artist now with all of the internet potential there, would I still do what I'm doing? And I don't think so. I think I would run an advertising agency where I would make my money because I'm good at that. But I'm not very good at handling nastiness. And some of the people that send you messages— their anonymous messages are so horrible. And even though you know they're assholes, you just say, "Why am I doing this for you?" [*Chuckles*] "Where are the really nice people?"

**KB:** Oh yeah, yeah.

**LJ:** You want your hand held and your head patted once in a while, you know.

**KB:** What were you doing before you wrote *David, We're Having a Baby*?

**LJ:** *David, We're Pregnant!*? I was a medical artist.

**KB:** Yeah. Oh, great. Yeah.

**LJ:** Yeah, it was an interesting job. [*Laughter*]

**KB:** The end. [*Laughter*]

**LJ:** Well, I did a lot of cartoons for the university even though I was a medical artist and my job was to do guts and, you know, grafts. . . .

**KB:** Guts and grafts. [*Laughter*] That department.

**LJ:** I was really good at the plastic surgery art. I was interested in that.

**KB:** That's why you did a lot of comics at university. That's what I did. . . . Yeah.

**LJ:** Well, universities want comic art. They're doing posters and invitations to things, and this was a medical center, so they wanted comics for the kids to color in the intensive care. And so . . . if you can draw comics, they want you to draw comics. And eventually you're drawing comic guts, you know? And I did. And some of the students at McMaster's are still using my cartoons in epidemiology and biostatistics.

**RT:** Oh, that's great. [*Laughter*]

**LJ:** Boring, boring! But being statisticians, they did a check to see if the kids looking at the cartoons retained the information more than the kids looking at the black-and-white images and—

**KB:** And I bet they did.

**LJ:** —cartoons won, so. . . . [*Chuckles*]

**KB:** Comics are amazing mnemonic device. That's a fact.

**RT:** So you're both pretty funny cartoonists. You're the funniest cartoonists I've ever read. Can we talk about writing humor?. . .

**KB:** Sure.

**RT:** And I want to know whether jokes work best if they kinda come to you out of nowhere? Or if you spend time crafting your jokes?

**LJ:** Both.

**KB:** Both, yeah.

**LJ:** Oh yeah, both.

**KB:** Yeah. Well, how many of you [*to the audience*] have watched *Stripped*, the documentary? Oh yeah, quite a few. 'Cause you talk about having ideas and dry spells and then intense flashes of inspiration in that one. But yeah, it's not dependable at all. Especially on the deadlines and stuff, like if I'm in a bad mood, I'm just like, "No comics today." [*Laughter*] No syndicate is holding a gun to my head. And . . . I don't know . . . I'd like to think that I have some processes. I read and read and hope for the best, honestly.

**LJ:** I found [that] it's funny, because you're on a deadline and you have to have material right away, after a while, after you've been in the industry for about ten years, you trust yourself and you trust whatever it is that brings you the material. That it's going to come back, even though you have days when you're absolutely brain-dead and empty. And my process was to sit on my couch with a coffee and a lined pad and to write out the dailies, as if I was writing a script. And there were times when I couldn't even think of one, not one. But I knew that if I waited for twenty-four hours, I would be able to write two or three weeks, just sitting there. And I knew that it would come back, but it took a long time before I had the confidence to know that it would come back. And there were times when personal things happened that were horrible, but I knew that it was going to make the best cartoon in the world. And I couldn't wait. And one night, my husband and I . . . [*laughter*] my husband and I had moved into a new house, and we were used to a great big bathtub where we could light candles and sit down with a glass of wine and talk in this great big Jacuzzi tub. . . .

**KB:** In your bathtub? Oh!

**LJ:** Yeah. It was a Jacuzzi; it was a big one. Then we moved to this other house and we had a much smaller bathtub, and we lit up the candles, took out the wine. And as I settled down into the bath, he started to yell at me because my hair caught fire. [*Laughter*] Because a candle was right behind me. And he immediately shoved me down into the tub. . . . [*Laughter*] My feet are up in the air! So much for the romance of the evening, and I could not wait to get to that strip. [*Laughter and applause*]

**RT:** Oh, thank you for sharing that. [*Laughter*] Do you still love comics as much as you did when you first started?

**LJ:** Me?

**RT:** Both of you.

**LJ:** Both of us?

**KB:** Yeah. Yeah. It's funny 'cause neither of us were like die-hard comics fans, I feel like, coming into it. Like, enjoying, yeah, but I was never around too much comics. I came into like some weird sideways door. Then, when I got into it, I was like, "Oh wow, there's so much."

There was a shelf in my university library of graphic novels, and I read *Chester Brown*, and I read Craig Thompson, and the kind of ones that you would find at the Canadian libraries, I suppose. Just those two books. [*Laughter*] One was just called *Chester Brown*. Anyway. . . .

But that was amazing to me because I hadn't been part of any kind of comics culture. But then, I was running the comics page. . . . Yeah, I love comics just as much as that kind of burgeoning late teens, early twenties discovery of what they were. It was just an entire world that I had not been aware of, and there's always more and more. Yeah. I mean, how do you not love comics? That's why we're here.

**RT:** And, you're still making them.

**KB:** Yeah.

**RT:** So hopefully that means you're still into it.

**LJ:** Well, I grew up in a comic family. My father should have been in vaudeville. He was born too late. But he would show us how to pratfall and how to do crazy, loose-leg dances, and he used to get the Keystone Cop movies—

**KB:** I wanna see that.

**LJ:** —and run them forward and backwards to show us how the gags worked and say, "See, it doesn't just happen. Everything is choreographed and everything is timed." And he would run the pictures back and forth so we could see it. And he was the one who read me the comics in the, you know, Sunday funnies. He was the one who used to buy me the comic books. And the two of us watched the Disney films and we would laugh till we cried, till we literally cried. We would laugh so hard at Mickey Mouse and Goofy and Donald Duck and all that stuff. And he took me to all the movies and we would sit through them twice. And I grew up loving, loving, comic art and I wanted to be an animator so badly.

**KB:** Oh, I guess I was wrong about that then. . . .

**LJ:** But there was no animation school at the time. It was not something you could learn.

I went to Vancouver School of Art, and there was a little bit from the National Film Board. But really you had to apprentice. You had to go to a studio and beg for a job cleaning cells or something so that you could get in the door. And I got a job, literally working in the ink and paint department at Canawest Films in Vancouver. And they were a subsidiary of Hanna-Barbera, and we did some dreadful comics. Worst, worst, worst stuff on the planet. But the people were wonderful— the writers, the background people, the artists, all the people were wonderful. And I knew when I got involved in that that I belonged, because there was an aura in that room of cartoonists and comics people that just felt right. Up until then, I was swimming in the world, trying to figure out who are my people? My peeps, right? That's what you say now. [*Laughter*] "I belong here."

**KB:** That's funny, because I had the impression that you weren't involved in like a comic or art scene before you started with the. . . .

**LJ:** Oh yeah.

**KB:** Oh yeah. Wow. That's awesome. Good.

**LJ:** You bet. [*Laughter*] And comedians. I loved comedians. I mean, Bob Hope and Phyllis Diller and Carol Burnett and Bill Cosby and all those people. I not only watched them and enjoyed them, I wanted to be them, you know? I loved what they did.

**RT:** Can I ask you about Anthony's mustache? Is that a regret, or is that a solid choice . . . ?

**LJ:** Well, if characters are changing, you've got to do something . . . you know.

**KB:** Although now his mustache would be hip. . . .

**LJ:** You know, it's surprising the number of people who wrote to me and said how much they hated that mustache.

**RT:** Yeah. I had no problem with the mustache. A lot of my friends did, but it was controversial. [*Laughter*]

**LJ:** Oh, I'm going out with a guy right now—isn't that funny? I am sixty-seven, and I'm going out with somebody. But it's great. [*Applause*]

**RT:** She's still got it, folks!

**LJ:** And I want him to grow a mustache. [*Laughter*] It's one of those things that you just don't ask a guy to do. I'm waiting for Movember. . . . [*Laughter*]

**RT:** So what is it that keeps you coming back to the drawing board every day?

**KB:** Oh, I don't know. You've been doing it since you were. . . . I was talking about meeting a bunch of great guys who all knew Raina's work and were all like, "Oh my God, you know her?!" . . . [*Laughter*]

Anyway, so we were talking about being an artist and being in the studio, 'cause they were visiting our studio, and everyone was like, "Who likes to draw here?" And everyone was like, "He does." [*She points*] And it was this other kid who was like, "Yeah, that's me." [*Laughter*]

I was like [*points at imaginary person*], "I know you. I was you." You know, the one who could draw and was drawing and could be found. And that's what keeps you going back, 'cause that's what you always did. . . . John Glass and I were talking about that age of kids, which is really great. . . . Someone's an expert on certain things. He's like, "I like to draw cars," and I'm like, "Cool." And then he's like an expert on cars, but that's it. I was cats, so I'd be like, "I'll draw you a minx cat or a tabby cat, you name it." Anyway. Yeah.

**LJ:** I would keep drawing if I could see. And I'm having such problems seeing, and my hands shake. And it just drives me crazy because being young, you take seeing and your hands working for granted. It's there, it works, it's there. And now, it takes me forever to do one little drawing because I can't see. You know? It's just *pfft*.

**KB:** But you kept it up, basically, as much as you [could]. . . . You were still doing the line work and other people would do the solid inks, right?

**LJ:** At one point I had people inking backgrounds, but I did all the pencil work and I always did the characters. I never let anybody touch the characters. But I had a wonderful inker who did the backgrounds, and I've had a couple of wonderful people to work with. It was just a joy. Yeah.

**KB:** Yeah. Not without a fight then, eh?

**LJ:** Pardon me?

**KB:** I said, "Not going down without a fight, then?"

**LJ:** Well, no. But now I'm going to have to have . . . those cataract things done or whatever, and I don't want anyone to cut my eyeballs! [*Laughter*]

**RT:** But if they cut your eyeballs. . . . [*Laughter*] Do you think there is ever a chance we'll see something else from you, maybe a graphic novel? Oooh!

**LJ:** You know, I would rather tell stories than write stories now, 'cause I really like to story tell. But what I'm doing, and I know it sounds crazy, is that I'm doing fabric designs. I am drawing doodles of stuff that goes on and on and on and on, 'cause I can do it without thinking and without really drawing anything preliminary, but cats and dogs and fish and birds and Aztecs and . . .

**RT:** Out of the panels.

**LJ:** Pardon me?

**RT:** Out of the panels.

**LJ:** Just stuff. Just stuff. I can show you; I've got stuff. . . . Anyways, but that's fun because my daughter's working for me now, and she's the one that's carrying on with the business, and she's the one that's doing the books, and she's the one who can sculpt and sew and create. And so I'm just doing fabrics, and she's working with a seamstress who's going to make a clothing line, and all that kind of stuff. So we don't know where we're going, but one of the great things about having had such a good job is that I can afford to invest in something new, which is very exciting. But look after your eyes. Be grateful for all your healthy working parts.

**RT:** And Kate, do you have anything on the horizon that you can talk about?

**KB:** Yeah. Well, I've been working for a long time on a Scholastic book, a kid's book. And it's taken—

**RT:** That's the fat pony one?

**KB:** That is [it].

**RT:** Yay!

**KB:** It's about a princess who wants to be a warrior, and she asks for an awesome warrior horse, but she gets that instead, and she thinks that she's licked. They work it out in the end.

**LJ:** I would. . . . When you talk about graphic novel, I bow to your ability. The two of you are doing such a wonderful job with the work you're doing that I feel that what I've done, I've done, and I don't want to do. . . . I mean, the things that make you create are the things that you really want to do. You're living in that zone and you just have to get it out there, and you want other people to see what you see in your imagination. And that's the incentive to get that out there, but I've done that now, and I can't believe that I don't want to do it again. I can't believe that, because at one time that's all I wanted. And at one time, everything was a gag and I would write it down on any piece of paper that I had in my handbag. And now Jan Eliot who does *Stone Soup* is one of my dearest friends, and she called me the other day and said, "I'm absolutely drowning in misery, I can't think of anything," and I said, "Well, sorry, Jan, neither can I." At one time I would have been able to write her back with a dozen different ideas and now I can't. It's strange.

**KB:** Well, it's a really high gear way of living for a long time, and when you stop. . . .

**RT:** It's a momentum thing.

**KB:** Yeah, yeah, definitely. I took a break from comics for a while because I burned out, 'cause you can. Like anything. I feel like people who finished something like your graphic novel just . . . you see them near the end, and they're just like, "Oh. . . ." [*Chuckles*]

**LJ:** I'd say there is one thing that I really fantasize about, though, that if I was going to continue the strip from now into the future, I'd bump off the husband. And I know exactly how to do it. [*Laughter and applause*]

**RT:** Oh my God.

**LJ:** Yeah, I know exactly how to do it. And it would be very funny because there's no point in croaking unless it's funny, right? . . . [*Laughter*]

**RT:** Well, on that note. . . . [*Laughter*] If we could open it up to questions from the audience, we have a few minutes. Questions for Kate and Lynn? Or? And/or? Yes?

**Speaker 1:** Lynn, we're animation students, so I was wondering how the transition of having your comic strip turn into an animated series looked. And for Kate, I'm actually at Nova Scotia as well, so yeah, I can relate to the thing with just having the one artist in your town, and I was wondering if that had an effect on your strips or just going home, like your environment?

**KB:** Definitely. Do you want to go first?

**RT:** Let me just repeat the question for the benefit of those in the very back row. The first question is for Lynn, and it's about transitioning from comic strips to animation.

**LJ:** That was the most wonderful thing ever because you're working with such a fabulous team of people. The background artists, the writers—and you do work with writers; you can't just do it all yourself—the musicians. . . . It was just the best thing. And I remember when we did the very first

One of Johnston's favorite sound effects. FOR BETTER OR FOR WORSE © 2006 Lynn Johnston Productions. Dist. By ANDREWS MCMEEL SYNDICATION. Reprinted with permission. All rights reserved. FOR BETTER OR FOR WORSE © 1981 Lynn Johnston Productions. Dist. By ANDREWS MCMEEL SYNDICATION. Reprinted with permission. All rights reserved.

show, walking down the hallway at Atkinson Film-Arts, and these rooms are filled with young people drawing my characters, and in the background I can hear the soundtrack going back and forth as they're editing, and all of the storyboard is pasted up down the hallway, and I stood in the hallway and I said, "Lynn, if you don't stop right now and say this is the best time in your life, you're crazy." Because it really, really was. I loved working with all those talented, wonderful people. And the laughs we had. And people would go out of their way to get something right. Including one time we needed [a specific sound]—Farley is sniffing the ground underneath a fire hydrant, and when a cute dog goes by, he lifts his head up and hits his head on part of the fire hydrant. We needed that *punnnng* sound. One of the guys even went into the basement of the studio and bonked his head on a pipe to see if he could get the right sound.

[*Laughter*]

**KB:** I can't believe I'm going to tell you this, but you know when the Christmas specials come on and you live for the Christmas animated specials that come on then? Your [A] *Christmas Angel* was one of the *For Better or For Worse* comics or, uh, cartoons. And it was on something late and I was supposed to go to bed and I threw a tantrum.

**LJ:** Wow!

**KB:** And I was, like, way too old to throw a tantrum! [*Laughter*] I wanted to see it! Anyway, here we are. . . .

**RT:** Hey, did you get the second part of the question or do you need to . . .?

**KB:** You didn't say. I heard it but. . . . The question was about. . . .

**LJ:** Going home.

**KB:** Yeah, going home and the influence of having one artist. [Do] you want to repeat, if you can?

**S1:** I just think I can relate to the sentiment of being in a small Nova Scotian town that just had one artist, it wasn't very artistic. So I just wondered, going back to that after being thrown into this world, like, is it different? Like, how does it feel?

**KB:** Oh, they're all really proud, and that's great. I remember being in the guidance counselor's office and I was like, "I want to go into animation." And they were like, "Do you mean science?" I had no idea what to do. They're like, "You mean nursing? Teaching? Yes? Fishing?" [*Laughter*] No, but they are really proud, but they don't. . . . It's just a small place that they don't understand [what I do]. . . .

I remember [being] like, "I was in *The Comics Journal*," and they'd be like, "I have no idea." But I was in *Rolling Stone*. . . . *Rolling Stone* made like a list of like fifty comics and you could tell, I think, that when you look at that you're like, "Oh, some intern made that list." [*Laughter*] And it didn't register as a big deal for me, but I posted it to my mom's Facebook wall because she likes to be proud, but she won't ever be like, "This is what my daughter did." So you have to do it for her. [*Laughter*] So I was like, "Look at this, Mom!" And then everyone's like, "Oh my God, congratulations to both of you." [*Laughter*] . . . They just heard of that [magazine] before, that's why it's a big deal to them, but. . . . Oh yeah, I was in *The New Yorker*, and I told that to someone who was doing like a shuttle bus driving through my village, and I was like, "Yeah, *The New Yorker*." And he was like, "Ah, that must be some kind of like New York magazine, is it?" [*Laughter*] It is. [*Laughter*] You're not wrong. [*Laughter*]

Anyway, the painter. . . . His name is Peter Rankin, and he paints a lot of rural imagery- type stuff. And he was always very supportive because he picked me up from an early age, and we went to some art classes that he taught. And he was like, "You're good at this." And I was like [*excited inhale*]. And he sort of kept up with it and that's fantastic. And I catch up with him when I go home now. And it means a lot, because you don't take that kind of thing lightly. It's someone telling you that it's worth it when you're really young to do the thing that you love best. Because being an artist, there's all kinds of people are like, "Why?" It's not a good idea." And having people believe in you is a huge thing. So it's great. Where are you from?

**S1:** Bridgewater.

**KB:** Oh, right on. With the three churches. Yeah. [*Laughter*] Cool.

**RT:** All right. Another question? Oh, there's a microphone. Should we form a line behind the microphone?

**KB:** I thought that was part of the. . . .

**RT:** Yeah. That would be. . . . Okay cool.

**LJ:** Really, really useful.

**Speaker 2:** Hi. [*Very loud*]

**RT:** Wow, it works!

**S2:** Miss Johnston, your comics are legendary, wonderful, and I'm just so glad I get to thank you right now.

**LJ:** Thank you.

**S2:** And Miss Beaton, I've not read your work before, but I think after this, I most certainly will. Miss Johnston, my name is David. And what always struck me about your comics were that they were so much more detailed and better illustrated than all the other comics, including Jim Davis's stuff. [*Laughter*] Was it something you set out, said, "I want to be the most detailed," or was it just the world you had to create had to be that detailed?

**LJ:** It became more and more detailed as time went on. . . . And it started with the animation because they actually have to have floor plans of the houses. And they have to have an aerial view of the streets and the towns that you live in. If you were in animation, you know how detailed these things have to be. If somebody turns right from the kitchen to go to the living room, it has to be that way all the time. And so that started me with the detail. And I wanted to do it so that I could see it myself in every dimension and also show others how real it was to me.

**S2:** And in addition to that, your level of background detail, say, like compared to *Peanuts*, where essentially it's a white background, or *Garfield* where you have just one color in the back, you have quite a few. . . . You have a picture, also plants, also a glass of water. That verisimilitude is remarkable. Was that something conscious as well?

**LJ:** Well, that actually was a tip of the hat to Len Norris who was the *Vancouver Sun* illustrator. And also . . . well, I don't know, Doug Wright. There's a lot of people who put extra things in the background. . . . It's really a home, it's really a table with glassware on it and . . . yeah, I enjoyed that. Yeah. But thanks for noticing.

Actually, the people who helped me with the art, the inker, and I have a wonderful friend who does all the coloring, they hated comic book shops and drug stores and anything that had rows and rows and rows of things. They all had to be little colored in. You know, like at grocery stores, all that stuff, they hated that.

**S2:** I'm a doctor and I also hate drug stores, too. [*Laughter*]

**KB:** Thank you.

**Speaker 3 [young person]:** I have a question for Lynn. Out of all the comics that you did for *For Better or For Worse*, which one was your favorite? Like, the one that you liked the most out of all of them.

**LJ:** Well, there was only one that I ever framed of my own, and it was done right at the very beginning. And it's Elizabeth outside wearing her snowsuit, and the snow is coming down and she's saying, "Look at this, it's snowing. God made this happen just for me." Nothing really that you would write home about. But for some reason that one is the only one that I ever framed, but it's not by far my favorite. But thanks for asking it. I mean, if you have a favorite, then you shouldn't be in the business because it means you're never going to come up with anything else.

**S3:** Thank you.

**LJ:** Thank you.

**RT:** Thank you.

**Speaker 4 [young person]:** I wanted to know, it's a question for both of you, which was the name of the very first comic that you made?

**KB:** I used to make comics with my sister. And it was a weird process where we would draw the pictures and not write any words and then trade and see if the other one could figure it out.

Actually, it didn't have a name. The main characters had names. And we would work together on that and laugh our heads off. And it was probably the best time I ever had making comics. Yeah.

**LJ:** I used to draw comics when I was young. And the problem when you're young is that your brains go faster than your hands can go. And so in your head you will have finished the story, but your hands will only have drawn maybe three panels. And it's very, very difficult when you're young to do comics that other people can read the way you do. Because your mind is going so much faster. Just because that's the genius of being young and being able to imagine so clearly. . . . And it's really difficult. But I drew . . . I guess . . . we had budgie birds. And I drew budgie birds and people and budgies in clothes and budgies with feet and high heels, you know? They were weird. So my head was going somewhere and my hands were going somewhere else.

**RT:** Thank you.

**S4:** Thank you.

**Speaker 5:** I had a question for Ms. Beaton, which I hope doesn't sound stupid in light of the "You shouldn't have favorites" thing that Ms. Johnston said. But I noticed in *Hark! A Vagrant*, you write a lot of comics based on real historical events or real historical people.

**KB:** Yeah. Yeah.

**S5:** And I just wondered if you had a favorite, like, real event in history that is just so ridiculous, you were like, "I have to draw this right now."

**KB:** Yeah, but I can't draw it because it's already too ridiculous. [*Laughter*]

**LJ:** It's Rob Ford?

**KB:** We have to hear about that. No, no. [*Laughter*] It might be surpassed by Rob Ford, but no. When St. John's Newfoundland was a brand-new city and didn't have any people living in it, there was a ship full of convicts coming from Dublin or somewhere called the *Charming Nancy*. And it was bound for New England, which still . . . had penal colonies at the time. But there was an outbreak of typhoid or something on the ship. And the convicts were all sick, so the captain was like, "No, we're just going to dump them in Newfoundland instead. We're not going to tell anyone." [*Laughter*] They just dumped all of these convicts on a shore within walking distance of St. John's. And there's no phone. . . . St. John people were just eating their breakfast and all these convicts . . . [*laughter*] came out of the woodworks and were just drinking their liquor and causing havoc. And people were like, "Oh, it's winter, maybe you want a coat." But then [the convicts] would sell the coat for more liquor. [*Laughter*] . . . They tried to round up all the convicts, and all the women disappeared because there were not that many women in St. John's at the time.

**LJ:** You should do it.

**KB:** I know, I know. It was the first time that St. John's as a city had to get its stuff together and write to London and be like, "Excuse me, all these convicts are here." [*Laughter*] And London was like, "That doesn't sound like it's our problem." [*Laughter*] And then they figured it out eventually, but it's just an amazing story. And if I try to make it into a comic, it would just be . . . a thing that happened. So I haven't done it. It's pretty great.

**S5:** I see where you made about how it's already so ridiculous. How do you write that letter as a city? "Excuse me. . . ."

**KB:** Yeah, exactly.

**S5:** "You dropped a bunch of convicts on our front door."

**KB:** How do I parody that? You don't.

**S5:** Thank you.

**KB:** No problem.

**RT:** And this will be our last question.

**Speaker 6:** Pressure. Well, you both have a very distinctive illustrative thought style that is just kind of. . . . It's unforgettably your style. And I'm just wondering as an illustrator, who or what do you credit most with the development of that visual style? And do you ever feel that in the course of coming to the style that it is today, it ever changed really drastically? And if it did, was that a conscious decision or just something that came out of practice?

**KB:** I feel like if I have a personal style, it came into sort of relative isolation because I didn't have access to too many types of art or comics or things, I guess. . . . Like, I spoke with Jillian Tamaki about this once before, and there's kind of like a really good style that people seem to have these days, and it's amazing but it's all kind of the same style because they're all just sort of cliff-noting each other.

**LJ:** Like manga?

**KB:** No, no, more like a certain illustration type. And everybody's got the same Photoshop tricks and everybody's got the same sort of shorthand for expression and that kind of thing. And I drew by myself all the time, and that's kind of how I would attribute the style coming in. It's really hard to say where you get it from because everybody has influences. But I've often thought about that because that question of how you develop the style comes up as though it was a conscious choice. It was never really for me, but it has been for other people who say, "I'm going to change what I'm doing right now."

**LJ:** I think if you are young, you copy quite a bit.

**KB:** Yeah. Definitely.

**LJ:** Like I was influenced by *MAD* magazine and a lot of other stuff that I read and saw, but by the time you're putting work out there with your name on it, it has to be uniquely yours.

**KB:** Yeah. It's . . . um . . . copying, yeah.

**LJ:** Well, that's how you learn right at the very beginning.

**KB:** Yeah. Oh yeah, definitely.

**LJ:** Or you, you know, absorb what you love in other people's work and then it rolls around in your lottery balls and out comes your own set of numbers.

**KB:** Yeah.

**LJ:** Yeah.

**S6:** Thanks very much.

**RT:** Well, please thank me, or join me in thanking Kate and Lynn.

**KB:** No, thank you, Raina! [*Lynn laughs*]

**RT:** And thank you all for being here tonight.

# Cartoonist Lynn Johnston
# Answers the Proust Questionnaire

SHELAGH ROGERS / 2015

From *The Next Chapter, CBC News*, CBC/Radio Canada (2015). Reprinted by permission.

**Shelagh Rogers:** For more than thirty years, Lynn Johnston drew the lives of the Patterson family in her comic strip, *For Better or For Worse*. Lynn's illustration of suburban family life came out of her own experiences as a wife and mother, and her characters aged in real time over the life of the strip. Lynn retired a few years ago, but [the strip] lives on in reruns in some newspapers. *For Better or For Worse: The Comic Art of Lynn Johnston* is an anthology of the series, and it coincides with a touring exhibit of Lynn's work. Here is Lynn Johnston taking *The Next Chapter*'s version of the Proust Questionnaire. Tell me about your favorite character in fiction.

**Lynn Johnston:** Well, it has to go back to my childhood and I loved *Little Lulu,* and that's because her nemesis was a witch, and I always thought my mother was a witch. How embarrassing, but that's it.

**SR:** What do you value most in your friends?

**LJ:** Integrity . . . and listening . . . and caring. Because if a friend does not listen to you and hear what you're saying and return their concern or their interest, then I don't think it's a friendship at all. It's just . . . just someone.

**SR:** Your favorite painter?

**LJ:** Matisse. He slows me down and makes me calm. I love that. I think I like the color. The use of pastel, the little flickering shapes that he uses.

**SR:** Your favorite occupation?

**LJ:** Reading right now, reading and drawing funny things. I've always been able to draw, but I've never been able to draw things and enjoy drawing things seriously. I get the most fun out of drawing silly things and the sillier, the more joy I get of it. What I guess I really like about silly drawings is that you always want to feel smarter than something or someone else. So you draw a character with great big eyeballs and a huge nose and a great big mouth, and yeah! That person or animal is really dumber than me! And it, you know, kind of gives me a thrill.

**SR:** What do you regard as the lowest depth of misery?

**LJ:** Loneliness. When you feel as though you're all alone, that you're handling all kinds of trauma all by yourself, that there's no one to turn to.

**SR:** What is your principal defect?

**LJ:** Oh, dear me. I guess vanity? I don't like arrogance in myself and that I'm puffed up with importance when good things happen. I just want to stay aware of who I am and what I can do in relation to the world, to the world at large. I mean, so often, if you've achieved something and you get a lot of pats on the head, you think how wonderful you are. And then you get in an airplane and look down upon the world and see how everything's reduced down to the size of specks of sand and you say, "How important am I anyways? Keep it all in perspective."

**SR:** What is your greatest extravagance?

**LJ:** I give things away. I've over the years owned many, many things, whether it's clothing or toys or artwork or jewelry, and somebody says, "Gosh, that's a beautiful necklace." And I'll say, "Here, you know that you should have this necklace." And I enjoy giving things away. I give things away all the time. And then sometimes I say, "Wow, why did I do that? I really wanted to keep it." I think it comes from my father. My father used to give things away all the time, and I think he desperately wanted to be liked. And I guess by giving something away, it does mean that the other person might feel an obligation to give you something back.

**SR:** What's your greatest fear?

**LJ:** Losing people that I love. In fact, at one point, I prayed to God that if anything terrible happened to anybody in the family, please let it be me. And I discovered I had a neurological disorder, and for the longest time, it was terribly hard to deal with. And you know what? I was grateful. Because it happened to *me*. And I know that sounds corny, perhaps, but that's the way I felt. I thought it was a gift that I wasn't looking at one of my grandchildren saying, "Why couldn't it be me?" Because it was me.

**SR:** What's your greatest regret?

**LJ:** That I did not get to know my mother well, as an adult. We did not get along when I was very young. And it wasn't until I was maybe into my forties that we were able to converse comfortably, and then she died far too young. So I would have very much liked to have had more time with her. Because she was a marvelous person. She was bright and talented and just a brilliant writer, actually, and illustrator. So we had a lot in common, but we got off to a bad start.

**SR:** The cartoonist Lynn Johnston, answering the Proust Questionnaire. Her work has been gathered in an anthology called *For Better or For Worse: The Comic Art of Lynn Johnston*.

# Lynn Johnston—After the Strip

LISA LACO / 2016

From *Superior Morning with Lisa Laco, CBC News*, CBC/Radio Canada (2016).
Reprinted by permission.

**Lisa Laco:** You know for almost thirty years John, Elly, Elizabeth, Michael, and April Patterson were like our neighbors. The lives of the characters in Lynn Johnston's beloved comic strip, *For Better or For Worse*, often mirrored our own lives, for better or for worse. Lynn Johnston retired the strip gradually at the turn of the decade, but you can see some of her drawings right now at the Thunder Bay Art Gallery[, which is] hosting an exhibit called *For Better or For Worse: The Comic Art of Lynn Johnston*. And tonight the Pulitzer Prize–nominated artist will give a talk at the gallery "after the strip" here in our studio.

What a thrill to meet you. First of all, thank you for coming in.

**Lynn Johnston:** It was such a pleasure to be here. I have met so many wonderful people. The show is beautifully put together. I'm so honored.

**LL:** The Thunder Bay Art Gallery is truly a gem in our city, and you're working with a wonderful group of people.

**LJ:** It is; you're so lucky. I know, I know! It's one of those things where, geez, these are all potential best friends, and I have to leave.

**LL:** Okay, so when I said that in the beginning, "Pulitzer Prize–nominated," I completely forgot that. What was that like?

**LJ:** Well, it was interesting. I think one of the reasons why it didn't happen was because I don't do editorial comic art. And the Pulitzer tends to be something that is more political, more editorial. So there was controversy over it, but the nomination at the time meant a lot to me because the storyline was such a powerful one. Ultimately, I didn't think it would be. Canadians were really relaxed about the story of Lawrence coming out [as gay]. But the backlash was horrific from the United States. I got over two thousand letters. And although seventy percent were positive, the negative ones were so negative and so threatening that you know that you could never make peace with any of the people who put pen to paper there. And most of this came from the religious right. A lot came from Peoria, which was interesting because you'd say, "Why Peoria?"

And then you'd look at it and say, "Well, there's been a huge industrial breakdown there where people were being laid off work." There were all kinds of people that were very unhappy. So hey, why not just throw a whole lot of letters into the mail and get mad at something else? Right? So it was a tough time for somebody who wasn't used to death threats and hate mail and phone calls from eight in the morning till eleven at night.

**LL:** That busy?

**LJ:** Oh, it was really something. And my editor said, "You might lose a few papers." Well, I lost about forty-two papers, but fifty-two signed on right away. It was a really interesting time, and I thought it was an innocuous story simply written without a lot of detail. But yet, the best part of it was it opened up all kinds of dialogue between parents and kids. You know, a mother would write and say, "I haven't spoken to my daughter for six years and I called her this morning." Or a son who said, "I showed my dad the paper, and he said, 'I know.'" And just conversations between mostly moms and kids, dads, and kids, you know, people who had been estranged from their families or, you know, who had been threatened themselves and those letters, some of them I keep as genuine treasures.

**LL:** You know, it's interesting because you talk about that, and I remember the storyline at the time. And it was a really telling time in Canadian culture as well. I mean, people were just getting used to saying, like, you know, "I'm gay," or coming out. It was really seminal timing for you as well.

**LJ:** It was. And what happened was one of my very closest friends had been murdered. He was a comedy writer in Toronto, and he was gay. He used to do blackout comedy in gay bars, and I would go and watch, and he was hilarious. And he was murdered. And the attitude of the authorities at the time was "Well, you know, there's one more predator off the streets." But he was this tiny, elfin, joyous, funny man who wouldn't threaten anybody, and he was murdered for his bicycle, you know, with a knife. And so it broke my heart, and it broke the heart of his partner and his friends. And I thought, *Michael, this is for you because I've known you since we were both eleven years old. And you were the kid next door. You weren't a gay guy. You were Michael. You were funny.* We were in theater school together, you know, I mean, just all of this stuff. And so I did the story for him.

And I also did it for my brother-in-law, who was gay, who was so tired of his mother introducing him to "the right girl," right? And he got so frustrated when he said, "I'm never gonna marry a girl!" And I said, "I know!" So I asked him to help me write the story. And I said, "What's the one word you would say was the defining message when you were able to tell your mom and dad?" and he said it was a *relief*. He said, "Put that word in there—that it's a relief to be able to finally talk about who you are and who you've always been." And he said, "The way it goes is that the people who are angry with me, I say to them: 'You've changed. I've always been me. I haven't changed at all.'" And so all of these elements went into that story. It wasn't my story as much as it was done for Michael with my brother-in-law's voice, really.

**LL:** Was Elly always you?

**LJ:** More or less. It was the me I might have been. Certainly I always was interested in writing. So the way she drifted . . . you know, [she] could have been a writer, didn't finish her degree, ended up working in a bookstore and library. Yeah, that might have been me. It's tough. You have to write about stuff you know. Otherwise, it doesn't ring true.

**LL:** And what about your kids? I mean, because I know you have children. And these three brilliant children you had in the strip, I mean, Michael, April, Elizabeth. They were great kids.

**LJ:** Well, my son, Aaron Michael, and my daughter, Katherine Elizabeth. Katie was just on her way when I signed the twenty-year contract for the story, for the strip. And I was asked right away to come up with three weeks of work, right away before they even, you know, gave me a finished contract. And I had to rush to come up with characters and names and stuff. I had no idea! I had never developed a strip. And a lot of people submit something that they've been working on for years, but this to me landed on my desk like Monday and by Friday I had to have all this work out. So I was doing comics on packing boxes and sending them off to the syndicate thinking, *All I can do is the best I can do, and if I get this job, great, but if I don't, at least I gave it a shot.*

So they sent me the twenty-year contract. And I talked to Cathy Guisewite, who was another comic strip artist. She did a strip called *Cathy*. And she said, "Don't call the characters by their first names because you're too connected to it." So I changed the kids' names. And while the strip was developing, I thought that I would keep everything the same age like *Dennis the Menace* and *Peanuts*, but as my kids aged, the material changed the attitudes, the vocabulary, the things that were going on, life changed, and I couldn't not put that into the strip. But I let my children grow three years past the ages of the kids in the strip. and that way, they weren't parallel all the way down, and that three-year gap gave my kids a bit of a break.

**LL:** Did they mind?

**LJ:** Yeah. You know, they did find it difficult, but fortunately, we lived in small towns. We lived in Lynn Lake, which was like twelve hundred people, then we moved to North Bay, which was a very welcoming community. And, you know, you get to be known for who you are as a person in a smaller town, and it's not like being thrust into anonymity where people cover you with, you know, an M&M [candy coating] and they never get to know the real you and they assume you are something else. Like, how often do you get to know your doctor? You think your doctor lives on a planet. . . that you're not allowed to visit? Right? Often you think about doctors and, you know, politicians as people you could never communicate with but, geez, if you're welcome into their house . . . their bathroom flushes, and there's crud in the sink and . . . the dog is being thrown out the back door, and it's just like anybody else's house. So yeah, it was very healthy to be in a small town, and a small town also gives you resources. If I needed to go to a bookstore or the library or do research up at the jail, for example, or at the helicopter school. It was all there for me. And people knew what I did and who I was, and they'd say, "Yeah, come over on Thursday afternoon. We'll take you up for a flight." And it was that kind of camaraderie and close community that helped *For Better or For Worse* really be part of North Bay. I mean, the streets were North Bay, some of the characters were North Bay.

**LL:** There's a lot of people here in the city, or I've met a lot of people for the last little while who were into developing comic characters, and I think you might be working with some of them.

**LJ:** I met a number of people last night who were just so. . . . Thunder Bay—well, every community has its marvelous talent. And what we got together and talked about was where do you go from here and now that everything is changing, everything is becoming electronic, and you have to put your work out there, and not only do you have an incredible opportunity to send it to broadcast it everywhere, but you're also so vulnerable to theft and copying and to the attacks of, I call them, the fungus dwellers. You know, the basement mushroom people that have to send you horrible messages just put you down. Who are these people and what is the rest of their life like, you know? But, there they are, and they're quite depressing.

And so how does it work now? And that was what we talked last night till about nine o'clock, and they had their folios open, and they were such marvelous, talented, creative people, and they're all here in Thunder Bay. And the topic was, Where do we go from here? And it is the internet. It is sort of graphic novels. And you can take your time; some of the illustrations might take two weeks to do. It's not like the deadline-driven syndication work. And it's also all yours. It's one hundred percent yours, and you're not dealing with an editor who might say, "Chop this out" or "You can't do this or that." Yeah, it's a whole new world, and I'm sixty-nine. I'm going to be sixty-nine in May. So what do I know? I'm still back at "Gee whiz, there's going to be a color cover in the newspaper this week! Can you believe it? Color in the newspaper!"

**LL:** But the exhibit is called *After the Strip*. How's life been after the strip?

**LJ:** Well, I've sort of tried to reinvent myself. I've been working on fabric designs and I have been doing other comic strips to fit into the old strip to sort of make sure that it lines up. I've been doing writing for the website, but mostly I've been moving from North Bay to BC. . . . Man, it takes a lot of adjustment and time to unpack! And the stuff you lose and the stuff you don't need. Wow. Stuff!

**LL:** You know something, we hit a certain point in our lives where it is just all stuff.

**LJ:** It really is all stuff, and I laugh when I think about people who live in palaces and have gold toilet seats. The day you croak, you ain't taking nothing with you, honey.

**LL:** Do you like yourself? I mean, has life treated you well?

**LJ:** You know, I've had an up-and-down crazy life, but I wouldn't change a thing. I've had two marriages and two divorces. And many wonderful friends in my life. I've had a number of wonderful men friends since. And it's a life that has taken me all over the world. I never would have learned Spanish or learned to fly an airplane or seen the Arctic or lived in 70 [degrees] below [zero] and learned about trapping. I never would have lived on a farm and learned how to drive a combine and learned about what a prairie summer is all about. I mean, all the things that I've done because of the two men that I married, and I married them because they were funny! They were funny! They made me laugh. And despite the fact that, in the end, we didn't fit like the two cogs in the wheel that are supposed to last forever. It happens. But I wouldn't change a thing. I have two beautiful children. Each one of these men gave me laughs and two beautiful children. And none of us hate each other. There's no room in the planet for hate.

And life is good for me, you know. But the good days don't get identified if you don't have terrible days. You know, if you're not on the floor crying and wishing . . . that there was a vodka near you. [*Laughs*] And if you don't have a really terrible dinner once in a while. . . . I always think there's no such thing as heaven because we're always looking for something better, right? There's no such thing as perpetual bliss. I mean, yesterday's bliss might have been better because the food was good, [but] music is better today. If we could have had yesterday's bliss music with today's food or, you know, whatever. We're not happy with anything. So I think we have to make the best of everything here, and I think I have, and I think I still am.

**LL:** Thank you. It's been a real delight meeting you this morning. I wish we had more time. We could go on and on.

**LJ:** Oh, me too. And I love your office. What a great job you have.

**LL:** I'm really lucky.

# Interview: Lynn Johnston

**KURTIS FINDLAY / 2016**

From *The Pullbox Podcast* (July 11, 2016). Reprinted by permission.

**Kurtis Findlay:** I'm your host Kurtis Findlay. And today we have a very special guest. She is a very famous cartoonist. I'm sure you've all heard of the comic strip *For Better or For Worse*. I'd like to welcome Lynn Johnston to the show. Thank you for being here with me today.

**Lynn Johnston:** Well, thanks for inviting me. This is great.

**KF:** I'm going to get the fanboy part of the podcast out of the way right at the beginning here. I just want to say that you've been a big inspiration for me and my work for many years. I have a web comic about my children, and one of the reasons why I decided to do it that way is because I grew up reading the adventures of your family. I know your family, it's sort of semiautobiographical, but I wanted to kind of do the same thing. It's such a great keepsake and a good memory. Yeah.

**LJ:** It is.

**KF:** I am about the same [age], just a few years younger than Michael. So when I was reading it as a kid, he was just that much further ahead in life than I was. And I used to take the books out of the library and read them all the time, and I really identified with his character, in the way he had his outlook on life and that kind of stuff, his humor. . . . And so, in preparation for this podcast, I pulled all of my books out of storage and went through them all and read them again, and it was fascinating because now I identify with Elly and John.

**LJ:** The parents.

**KF:** The parents, right, because I have three kids of my own. And going through everything that they're going through, especially now that my kids are in school and all that, it's like, "Wow." It's such an interesting strip where you can have so many different people relating on different levels. Something like *Dilbert* doesn't get that sort of multigenerational readership.

**LJ:** Well, he has a different readership and his whole situation is different. His following is enormous. There is something for everyone in the comics.

**KF:** There sure is. And that's what's so great about it. And I feel like with *For Better or For Worse* there's something for everyone within that one comic strip, and that's what so great about it. I wanted to talk about—well, we're going to talk about a lot of things, hopefully. Let's start with what you were doing before *For Better or For Worse*. I'm a big animation fan. I love the history of animation, and I understand that you were in animation before you got into comics, is that right?

**LJ:** Yeah, I went to the Vancouver School of Art and in third year I dropped out to take a full-time job with Canawest Films. But it was KVOS TV, it was channel 12 out of Bellingham, but they had a satellite station in Vancouver, and they had taken on a lot of animated advertisements, things like that. Just little short animated clips. And I managed to get a contract with a Hanna-Barbera to do some dreadful Saturday morning stuff, just the worst.

**KF:** This was the 1970s?

**LJ:** 1960s, mid- to late '60s. So that was my very first art job. And I loved it because I belonged; they were my people. I just moved into that place, and I still know some of the artists right now, we were that close. The shows were awful. It was *Abbott and Costello* and *Shazam* and stuff like that. And the soundtracks were screaming. "Abbotttt!" We hated it! But you learn so much about timing and just the whole process of filming. And we were all the Ink and Paint Department. There were sixteen girls shoulder to shoulder. We were paid a dollar an hour. We weren't allowed to join a union. We had to sign a contract saying we wouldn't join a union. We were really badly treated. We worked twenty-four hours, so you would start at five in the morning or you would start at seven at night; it depended on where you were. You rotated through a twenty-four-hour cycle. Because they wanted it fast and they wanted it now. And they didn't care if it was good or not, and we were never praised, we were always criticized. But the fact that it was animation and there was no other way to learn the industry—we didn't care. We were there really just to learn and be a part of this scene. My friend Cecily, who was my neighbor in painting, her mom and dad were writers for Disney, and because Disney would never buy anything from a woman, her dad took credit for all the writing, and they couldn't believe how prolific he was! But his wife wrote half the stuff. And they wrote a lot of the Disney comic books for Scrooge McDuck and Gyro Gearloose and Donald and the kids, that kind of thing.

Cecily was married to a broadcaster, a radio guy. And I was married to a television camera man from CBC. And the four of us took off to Los Angeles, all hoping to get work. . . . Cecily and I were offered a job at Jay Ward Studios on Sunset Boulevard, which was great! I mean, Bullwinkle was revolving on a platform outside, and it was a funky old house. And we were given the opportunity to start now in backgrounds. They needed someone to start right now. So we're saying, "Yes, of course!" But the guys couldn't get a job because TV guys and radio guys were a dime a dozen in LA. And we said, "We don't care! Get a janitor's job! We don't care!" But those were the days when you followed your husband, and so four of us drove back, two very unhappy would-be animators.

**KF:** Yeah, right. So you didn't take the job after all?

**LJ:** No, I couldn't take the job, no. And they did *Super Chicken, George of the Jungle, Rocky and Bullwinkle*. I mean, the best of the best was happening in that studio. But as it turned out, ultimately it was a good thing that I didn't get the job. Well, I don't know. It might have been the best thing ever. But I'm saying it was a good thing because my husband and I headed off to Ontario where he could get a better job in television, which he did in Hamilton at CHCH [an independent television station]. And I managed to score a job at McMaster University in the medical department doing charts and graphs. And another guy who was a graphic artist was hired as well, and when they found out we were both really good artists, they put us through first-year medical school with the students.

And it was a brand-new medical school with a whole new philosophy. They wanted to have the students learning at their own pace through slide-tape presentations. So there was all of these little booths with slide-tape carousels and headphones, and we illustrated surgeries and different lectures and we illustrated textbooks and we actually did some animation and learned more about photography and specialized surgical work. Rotoscoping, all kinds of stuff there. So it just continued on.

**KF:** So this was not cartooning work, though. . . .

**LJ:** Yes.

**KF:** This was serious anatomy drawings and such. That's such a different ball game.

**LJ:** Yeah, but I loved it! I loved it! Because I want to know how the body works and I'm a questioner; I love science. I love to be shown things and to understand it, and often understanding comes through illustration. So I got to illustrate some fabulous surgery. A lot to do with the development of the fetus. And at the time I would work with fetuses pinned open on sort of black corkboards, and I would be working on these different slices of anatomy with these babies. But I'd never had a baby. So to me it was a really interesting little rubber character. But nowadays it would affect me deeply because there would be a spiritual connection to that.

**KF:** Right. Right. Yeah.

**LJ:** But I learned a lot. When you're working for a great big organization, they always need invitations and menus and posters and things like that. And so because I could cartoon, they would have me do that. And I finally was just doing comic art because a number of the doctors loved the way that it was fascinating for the students to see something that was cartooned and that they would listen to lecture if they saw something funny on the screen. So eventually they hired a couple more artists to do the serious medical stuff, and I just did cartoons. It was a crazy thing!

**KF:** There you go. And you didn't expect that to happen.

**LJ:** No, I didn't.

**KF:** So where did it go from there?

**LJ:** Well, I did a whole lot of cartoons for my obstetrician, who was the head of obstetrics and gynecology there at McMaster. And he was a specialist in difficult birth, but he took me as a patient because he liked me as a person, and I was doing lots of cartoons for him. I did a whole bunch of cartoons for the ceiling above his examining tables.

**KF:** So people would have something to look at that!

**LJ:** Yeah, that's right! And so that started my career with Universal Press Syndicate, surprisingly. Because he talked me into finding a publisher and like your first book here, just knocked my socks off that my art could be in a book and people would buy it. Isn't it exciting?

**KF:** So what book was that?

**LJ:** It was *David, We're Pregnant!* It was the very first little book, and it was just about pregnancy and how strange it is for the first time. Well, you know, you've got a family now. It's unlike any other experience ever, both physically and emotionally and everything. So this book sold very well, and I did two other books.

**KF:** I have one of them, I have *Hello Mom and Hello Dad.*

**LJ:** *Hi Mom! Hi Dad!* Yeah, that was the second one. And then *Do They Ever Grow Up?* is the third. And at the time I thought I continue as a medical artist and just do a book a year, and as it turns out life changed. I was divorced and I was a single mom. I changed from working for McMaster University to having my own graphic art studio in my house where I freelanced for doctors doing both medical art and cartoons, and I would go around to every ad agency with my baby on my back and my folio and beg for work. And I got everything from posters for the library—who were great, they would pay me thirty bucks right on cue—to magazine illustrations for *Atlantic* magazine, who didn't pay me for ninety days and even then still didn't pay me, those shmucks! [*Laughs*] Are you listening, *Atlantic* magazine? [*Laughs*]

**KF:** Yeah, right! Get on that! Is there interest now? [*Laughs*]

**LJ:** Yeah. So as an artist, you really do starve a lot, as do musicians and actors and anyone who works doing the thing that they really love and were born to do.

**KF:** So . . . how did that lead to the comic strip then if that was your introduction to Universal Press Syndicate?

**LJ:** Well, the three books were published in Canada, and the publishers in Canada were not hanging together. They were going out of business—two of them went right out of business, but not before they had sold the rights to a company in Minneapolis. And this guy had a small publishing company, but he could see the potential in these books. So he took the three books and sent them to Universal Press Syndicate with a letter saying, "If you don't syndicate her, I will." And he would have. He was a really forward-thinking guy. So I was very nervous. And I got a letter back from Universal Press Syndicate wanting twenty cartoons right away. They wanted three weeks' worth of work immediately. They gave me no time at all. And by then I was expecting baby number two, married again, on my way to Northern Manitoba, my husband was a flying dentist, and we were packing to leave when I got this letter wanting three weeks' worth of work. So on packing boxes I drew three weeks' worth of work starring us because I couldn't think of anything else that I could draw over and over again. And they sent me a twenty-year contract.

**KF:** Unreal.

**LJ:** Unreal, you bet. And what a great thing to get before leaving for a tiny northern mining town where I wouldn't be able to run my graphic art business or do animation or do anything like I was doing. I thought I might be able continue to do the books, but then we didn't have anything but Xerox. I think fax had just come in. And fax was very sketchy. You know. It was hard to really see what you got through at the other end. It came on a sort of warm, thin, coated paper.

**KF:** And this was the mid-'70s?

**LJ:** Yes.

**KF:** And so you were in this tiny town in Manitoba and you were starting to develop your comic strip then? The real, actual version of it?

**LJ:** Yeah. I asked if I could have a six-month lead time. So they gave me a development contract for six months so that I could learn to write dialogue because the first three little books were all little single-panel gags. Which are totally different, as you know. 'Cause when you do single panel, the gag is right there, and it has to come through in one shot.

**KF:** There's no set up.

**LJ:** No set up. Right.

**KF:** The staging is different. . . .

**LJ:** The timing is different. There's backgrounds. It's like a little storyboard. So it's a totally different set of skills, and I didn't have those. And they connected me with Cathy Guisewite, who did a strip called *Cathy*—

**KF:** Of course.

**LJ:** —which was a self-deprecating story about this little round girl. And Cathy herself was slender and gorgeous and quite different from the character she drew. And she was wonderful. She's one of the funniest people you could meet. She was on Johnny Carson three or four times. Hilarious, just a wonderful person. And her skills were as a writer. She had been in advertising for years. Her dad was in advertising. And the writing is the thing that really makes a comic strip work. I mean, you could have a very minimalist style of drawing, but if your writing is superb you can get away with almost stick figures. If your writing isn't good, your art fails terribly. And so I really needed to learn how to write.

And I had a great editor, really good editor with whom I got along well. And again, that's another rapport you have to build because you have a certain arrogance there and you say, "Well, what right do you have to edit my work?" But if you get a really good editor, they can only make you better and give you a sense of direction and really set the bar. So I had a great editor. His name was Lee Salem, and he's a great friend today. We write long letters back and forth, which to me is a joy. Because he and I are about the same age, but he's always seemed like somebody I wanted to work for or work hard for. And I think you need that. I think all of us need that. You need a mentor, someone whose expectations you want to live up to. Otherwise, you're just trying to please yourself and your audience. But the feedback from the audience isn't as important as the feedback from a really good editor, I think.

**KF:** So how did Cathy teach you?

**LJ:** She told me to write a script. She said, "Imagine as if you were writing a script for a sitcom and go from there." So I wrote everything out as a script. It looked just like a script. And I would sit on my couch with my back against a couple of pillows. I had my mandatory cup of coffee. And my knees were bent with a blank pad of paper on my knees, and I had a bag next to me in which was a pair of scissors and a whole lot of little white sticky tabs [so] that if I made mistake I could put a sticky tab over it and rewrite it. And I was very methodical and I never threw anything out. I took my time.

And after a while you learn to trust your skill. There are days when you can't think of a thing, not a thing, but as long as you focus on it, as long you fly around your imagination in the room that the characters live and you are one character after another, even the dog—you inhabit their body, and you think, *What would they be saying, what would they be doing?* And even if you can't think of a thing that day, guaranteed you'll come up with something the following day. So you have to trust your skill after a while. But at first it's terrifying because you've got that daily deadline. And you're going to turn out stuff you don't like. You're going to send it off and it's out there and it's ready to go into the paper and you might not like it, but that's the nature of the beast.

**KF:** So when you first started your comic strip, what was it like being a woman in this industry at that time? Because there weren't that many women cartoonists; Cathy is the only other one that comes to mind.

**LJ:** Right. Fortunately, the young men in the industry were welcoming and supportive, and a lot of the older cartoonists were as well. But there were a few hardcore old boys' club kind of guys who would love, at a meeting, to draw a picture of naked and then hand it to me. Well, of course, I would draw a picture of them naked and hand it back to them. But even if I sparred with them, they were still making Betty Boop jokes. And it's awfully hard to change these old guys, right? I met one on the street the other day, a British guy who was talking to me, and the way he was talking it was so insulting, but then I thought, *Jesus, guy, you can't help it; you're one of them!*

But the people our age—I mean anyone over twenty who is in the work field now—we're all equal. If you've got the talent. I mean, it's like music—if you got the chops, it doesn't matter who you are, what you look like, where you live, how you dress. If you got it, you're part of the group and all that matters is that you're doing a great job. So I was president of the National Cartoonists Society for a while. I really got involved. Got to know everybody. And I thrived in that. I was so lucky to meet all the people that were my heroes like from *MAD* magazine, Will Eisner, and all the people from DC and Marvel Comics, and Charles Shulz became a very close friend and all kinds of editorial people. I'm close to Mike Peters who does *Mother Goose and Grimm* and Jan Eliot who does *Stone Soup* and Hilary Price and just on and on and on. If I started naming the people . . . we would be here all night because I'm a part of an elite but loving and caring group of people. . . . I thought there would be a Hollywood welcome, "We hope you fail" kind of attitude. But it wasn't that at all; it was supportive and extremely welcoming.

**KF:** Oh, great. So that's quite a different shift, then, from how you were treated in animation. What a difference a decade or so makes.

That dog of course being the much-loved Farley, introduced in November 1980. FOR BETTER OR FOR WORSE © 1980 Lynn Johnston Productions. Dist. By ANDREWS MCMEEL SYNDICATION. Reprinted with permission. All rights reserved.

**LJ:** Well, we were factory workers, and the only time the boss, who was a greasy guy that would come in every so often, was if we were wearing mini-skirts at the time.

**KF:** Right.

**LJ:** And we would watch him kind of pant and slobber his way around the room and then leave again, and he had no idea what a joke he was, right?

**KF:** My wife and I are just starting to watch *Mad Men*, and you know, kind of figuring out the whole way things worked back then. And I don't know if that's an accurate portrayal or not.

**LJ:** It is, actually. It is. And some girls ask for it. And some guys are nicer than they appear. They play along with these games for the sake of the other guys; they don't want to look like someone who isn't part of the club. And it's the way it is.

**KF:** Wow. Let's see. . . . So tell me about your comic-strip family versus your real family. Why did you decide to make it so much like your own family?

**LJ:** Because they were there. They were—I shouldn't say targets, but they were my inspiration. But the characters in the strip, I tried not to draw them like my own kids. Michael looked a lot like my son Aaron. Katie had dark brown hair, and I gave Elizabeth blonde curly hair. You know, if I ever did anything that exactly happened in the house, I would ask them first if I could use the material. I had always asked them. And my husband probably got socked in the head more than anybody. I wasn't kind to him in a lot of ways, but he was very funny. And I often used word for word the things that'd he say. And he was great for the strip because he was such a funny guy with words. He was the one-liner king. So often if something happened, and I could use the material, it eased up on the situation because it was made fun of and turned into part of the comic art.

I kept the characters in the strip three years younger than my kids. I let my kids grow up a little bit. And that was partly by design but partly because when I first started I thought I was going to keep the characters the same age the whole time. But as kids grow, they get more interesting, actually. Their vocabulary changes and their relationships change with each other and with you. I couldn't let that material go. So I brought in a dog, which we didn't have, and produced another baby a few years later, and that was actually Cathy Guisewite's suggestion. She said, "If you want a baby in the strip and you've lost the baby since Elizabeth grew up, have another one!" And I said, "I can't do that because I'm not really having a baby!" And she said, "Lynn, it's a cartoon!" So what's funny is that Elly has this late pregnancy, and I actually gained the weight! I was so involved in this thing that I started to feel pregnant and think about it all the time. It was phenomenon for me that I was that close to the character that I would actually think about pregnancy as if it was really happening again.

So April actually looks like my daughter Kate as a child. But what was great about having the imaginary third child was that I didn't have to worry about embarrassing my own children or showing something that really happened that they wouldn't want me to show. April was free and clear. Her name was April because she was born on April 1 because she didn't exist. And friends in North Bay covered our lawn with storks in congratulations—

**KF:** Oh that's so funny.

**LJ:** —and threw a surprise party for me for the birth of this imaginary baby.

**KF:** What point would you say Michael and Elizabeth stopped being your own kids, or did they?

**LJ:** They were always my kids, but my own kids went in different directions. My son went into television and my daughter went to art school in Vancouver. She came out here to teach snowboarding and ended up helping a friend of mine, an artist friend, hang a show in Whistler and they got to talking and she had a folio and he said, "Wow, you should apply at the Emily Carr!" And she got in. So she's a grad from there, and she can do just about anything. She can do electronic sculpture, pottery, work in fabric, in leather, in metal, and just about anything. And so she's working for me. It's much easier right now for her with the two little kids to work at home, and so she manages the business. . . . She also wrote the last book that came out. So she has many skills. So once her kids are in school, she'll fly free and do something wonderful.

**KF:** One of my favorite characters, especially in the earlier years, is Lawrence.

**LJ:** Right.

**KF:** He's such a fascinating character because all this bad stuff happened to him in those early years, it seems like. . . . Because Michael is the character we all identify with, he goes along through life and not much happens to him—in the early years, at least. But then Lawrence is, like, a single mom, he moves away, and you throw a whole bunch of things of him. Now was that intentional to use him as the storytelling device rather than have those things happen to Michael?

**LJ:** No, it wasn't intentional. Because when you start—again, you're thrown into this—and once you start it's like being in a raft down the Colorado River. You're not going to get out till you get out to the other end. And I wanted different characters in the story to give it depth and interest. So Connie was supposed to be a nattering single woman who had a career, who would forever show up Elly by saying, "Well, I don't have children so I'm a free agent and I can date and I can wear these lovely clothes and go on trips and be a business person." And I thought she would be a foil for Elly, like the nemesis. I thought they would be enemies.

**KF:** That didn't happen at all.

**LJ:** It didn't happen. And I guess because I'm very realistic to say nobody's all bad. There's always a good side to somebody; even Hitler liked little kids and puppies. I don't know. I mean, there's always a good side to somebody, so I couldn't make her bad enough. I also wanted to draw characters that were not familiar to me. You tend to draw what you see in the mirror. And it's a challenge to draw somebody different. So I wanted a Black character in the strip. But because the strip is black and white, if you put a screen on a character's face, you can't really see their facial expressions, and this was before color was in the dailies. So I couldn't have [a] genuinely Black [character]. So I had him darker skinned with the black curly hair, but he was still, you know, a brown kid, right? So where does he fit in? Does he have a family? What was his family like? I don't know. He was floating around. Connie was floating around. Annie was floating around, but she again as a neighbor who had marriage problems and had two kids and lived over the fence. They're Catholic. So they didn't go to the same school as Michael and Elizabeth, and was I going to get into the Catholic, non-Catholic debate? I don't know! But I like to challenge myself. So I left that in my mental library. And eventually I had to start connecting these people and figure out where did they live and how did they relate, and that didn't happen for maybe two years.

And Connie no longer was a negative. She was a suddenly a person with a heart and soul and a life, and darn if Lawrence didn't appear to be part of her life. So then you have to fabricate a story: Why would she have a brown child? Well, she was married to a man who was South American, a Black South American man. But I was involved with the Medical Missionaries for a while and I had gone down to South America and experienced some of that lifestyle. And so that to me seemed like a perfect way for her, as having a nursing background, to meet somebody down there and have a relationship, and, hoping to marry, come back expecting this man's child, which is what she did.

**KF:** Right. And you didn't tell that story until Lawrence was an adult.

**LJ:** Right.

**KF:** So did you have that in your mind for a while? Or did you think of that . . . ?

**LJ:** It took me a long time to come up with that. Because your mind is racing around every other character, including the dog. Who's doing what? Is this funny? You do a little vignette and it can't last longer than two weeks. Otherwise, your audience gets bored. You still have to have a gag a day. You still have to have some kind of punch line every day for the person who doesn't read it Monday and Tuesday and Friday. Their Wednesday still has to have some merit. You can't just hope they can follow the storyline. So they had to be simple, easygoing stories and each day had to have some sort of punch line, and then I would wrap it up and go onto something else. So in my creative days, when I'm on the couch with this pad on my lap, I'd be floating around saying, "What's happening in the neighborhood now? Who have I not brought into the mix lately?" And then you've got to punctuate a story with unrelated gags that are about school, clothing, or about weather outside, just so that it doesn't become a boring endless story that you have to really work to make interesting. And then you can't have a beginning, middle, and an end because its endless. So I had little vignettes. And I think the story about Lawrence was the longest story I ever wrote because you needed the time to develop it, but by then the readership was comfortable with these vignettes and also comfortable the characters.

It takes three years for the readers to care about your characters because they have less than thirty seconds a day to read your work. I mean, how long does it take to read a comic strip? Maybe three seconds? One-two-three, I'm done, right? Because we all read fast, we all absorb fast, and you're onto the next thing. So less than thirty seconds, maybe three seconds a day to trap your audience into reading it the following day. And so after three years, they'll say, "Oh yeah, Lawrence is the kid Mike hangs out with. He's in the same class at school along with Gordon." Just like you'd say Charlie Brown would never kick the football and Lucy's always the fussbudget and Linus is always going to be pensive and thoughtful, and you get to know the characters. But it takes three years. Which is a long time, and a lot of new young cartoonists burn out after three years because it's a lot of work.

**KF:** It is a lot of work! Especially with the amount of characters you shove into your strip.

**LJ:** Yeah, that was something. But we all have a lot of people in our lives.

**KF:** Yeah, yeah. And the juggling act that you mentioned. . . . So when you are in your heyday, let's say once you got to the late eighties, once you established this neighborhood of characters, how did you keep track of all of them?

**LJ:** I didn't, obviously. The people who were real scholars of the strip would say, "Hey, this character was named this the last time we saw her and she looked like this." I mean, I did lose track. I lost track of all kinds of things and I made a lot of mistakes. And it wasn't until we did animation that I really had to really keep track and have everything. . . . And I also had a wonderful gal, because websites happened, and with websites come a real searchable archive, and people could go back and say, "Hey, look at this! The kitchen was in this direction last time, and you've changed it."

**KF:** It's amazing people pay that close attention to these things.

**LJ:** They do, they do! And you can't get away stuff, you really can't. And it's okay, it's wonderful to know that someone is that interested in your work to be that . . . observant.

**KF:** I'm fascinated in the aging aspect of it. And as I was going through your old books—

because I was kind of reading them at an accelerated pace—these characters gradually age so nicely. . . . How did you decide to age your kids, or the people, not just the kids, but the adults as well? When did you decide to add those bags under Elly's eyes and those little details that make them older?

**LJ:** Well, . . . you say it was gradual, but it was actually in fits and starts. It would be nice to have characters that don't change, everything's the same. [*Sings*] "Da, ta, da, da, da, da." You just carry on and you say, "Oops, five years has gone by. Maybe there should be. . . ." Elly never changed her hairstyle because she was too much of a constant character. But Elizabeth and some of the other characters needed to change, and the dog had to get old. I'd get to a point where I'd think, *Oh, I've got to make a change*, and then I would check my charts to see how tall everyone would be—the teenagers, how tall they would be compared to their parents. And I had growth charts, and every so often I would check the growth charts, and it's surprising how tall a two-year-old is. When you're drawing something freehand without checking measurements, you just draw them far too small. Because in your head you think, *Two years* *old, but I've got a two-year-old, and gosh, he's tall.* My grandson is much bigger in reality than you'd think of him being as a two-year-old. So I had to be very cognizant of the heights of everyone. Of course the adults stay the same, but their looks change a little bit.

**KF:** Yeah, I remember I was reading . . . the story where Elizabeth cuts her hair really short, and then from that point it's like a few years, I think, up until Michael's wedding or something like that, [and] her hair gets longer and longer and longer. And I think that takes some sort of forethought in order to grow it out like that.

**LJ:** Yeah. Well, I have seen other comic strips where people have changed the hair and then suddenly the hair is long again because they didn't like the way the character looked. And I thought, *I don't want to do that because if its reality based to some extent, it better reflect that in aging, and hair, and that sort of thing.* And I know Elly had a permanent for a while. Her hair was very curly, but I couldn't just change. It had to grow out.

**KF:** Yeah, it's amazing you can keep track of all those little details.

**LJ:** Well, I had to. I had to for myself, but also for the readers. And I had great editors who would have said to me, "You know what, you've got to watch this, change that, check this." They did their job; they were great.

**KF:** So how far in advance did you plan your stories? . . . The example I want to give is the grandparents. Elly's parents realize that they need to sell their huge house and move into something smaller. So they talk about it, and then it's like a couple months later they sell the place, and then a couple months after that they clear it out and move, or something like that. So how far ahead are you thinking when you're thinking of these storylines?

**LJ:** Well, when you know someone's going to move, you—

**KF:** Jot it on a calendar?

**LJ:** Yes! In fact, I did keep it on a calendar. But you also think ahead. And I was always thinking eight weeks ahead. You had to be ahead of the publication date of the dailies six weeks and the color Sundays eight weeks. Nowadays it's a matter of hours, I guess, but in those days all the work went to Buffalo for coloring, and it had to go as far as Guam and Australia.

**KF:** What? Really!

**LJ:** Yeah! Places like that. And so it was impossible to get it there if your art wasn't turned in on time and they would fine you one hundred bucks everyday you were late.

**KF:** Oh man.

**LJ:** And there were people who factored that into their month. "Oh well, I'm going to lose hundred or two hundred bucks because I'm late." But I was fined once. And I realized, boy, you can't be that close to your deadline. It just doesn't work emotionally. I mean, what if you got sick? What if you broke a finger? What if you wanted to go on a holiday, God forbid?

**KF:** I heard Charles Shulz worked a full year in advance. Is that true?

**LJ:** I don't know. I really don't know. I know that at one time he did get way, way, way ahead because one time he wanted to go on a holiday, and another time he had heart surgery and he knew he was going into heart surgery, so he did work ahead. But he was a tireless worker. He wrote it all himself, he drew it all himself, he pushed himself like very few other artists ever did. . . . He had nothing but disdain for people who were late on their deadlines.

**KF:** How did you meet Charles Schulz?

**LJ:** Well, he came to the Reuben Awards, which is the Oscars of the industry. The year that I won for 1985, I won in 1986. It's a statue that is about a little more than a foot high. It's very heavy. It was designed by Rube Goldberg in New York years ago. I won. I was nominated along with Jim Davis, who does *Garfield*. And that year I won, and Schulz was there at the event. It was in Washington, DC. He came up to me in a crowded hallway and he said, "I voted for you." And I was just shocked. Cathy Guisewite introduced me. They'd known each other for a while. And after that, I got to know him quite well. He'd phone me and would tell me that he liked my work. And he became somebody I worked for almost as well. "If Sparky likes this, then, you know, that's okay." His nickname was Sparky. It took me a while to get used to that because it's kind of a goofy name. But anybody who called him Charles didn't know him well, and he would sort of smirk as if to say, "Well, he thinks he knows me, but he doesn't."

**KF:** Tell me a little bit about your animated specials. You did one initially, *The Bestest Present*, in 1985.

**LJ:** Right.

**KF:** What was your role in that production? How involved were you?

**LJ:** It all started with a script. And do you know Gordon Pinsent, who is an actor?

**KF:** No.

**LJ:** He's a Canadian actor, and he's a wonderful character actor. And he's a guy who's a little bit older than I am. He's got the most incredible voice. If you hear it in an advertisement, you'd immediately know it's him, or even as an actor behind the scenes on an animated show or something. He's just one of these guys. Anyways, he's a prolific writer. And one day I saw him in a restaurant minding his own business, reading the paper, having breakfast, and I said, "Mr. Pinsent, how do you write a play?" And he looked up at me wearily and said, "Just do it." Right. So I thought, *Yeah, I guess that's what you do.* So I went home and I wrote this play, and it was *The Bestest Present*. And I looked up the name of animation studios in Canada, found one in Ottawa, sent it off there. And I got a phone call at about nine o'clock at night from Bill Stevens, who ran this little studio. It was Crawley Films. Crawley was a big deal in Ontario. Everybody knew Crawley Films. And Bill had bought into the company and owned the animation part of it. And he called me from home and said, "I'm reading this story and I love it and I want to send you a contract. When can we start?" And I thought, *Wow, this is too good to be true!* And it was . . . it was true, and it was good. And the first show was a great little show because it took a full year to do. I flew down to Ottawa as often as I could. By then we were living in North Bay. We were moving to North Bay in 1985, I think. So I was able to go back and forth. We had an airplane, so we would fly back and forth.

And I worked on that show from beginning to end. The whole storyboard. All of the character development. Again, I was plunged right into animation, which I loved. But this time it was other people animating my work. And one day when we were right in the middle of it, I walked down the hallway—it was a real old building, it was part of a church. And I walked down the hallway, on one side where kids, I thought, eighteen and twenty at drafting, anima- tion tables, working. There were people in the sound department running the soundtrack back and forth, and back and forth, getting all the frames in the correct [order]. Whatever they do . . . they were doing it. And there were storyboards were plastered all over the walls. And I stood there and I shut my eyes and said, "If you don't stop and say, 'Isn't this one of the most wonderful days of your life?,' you're missing an opportunity." And that Polaroid shot is in my head today. Yeah, it was great. And the show turned out to be a really nice little show. I was very proud of it. And of course, there's things wrong with it. If you see the train rolling around the display in the department store, the front wheels are missing. [*Laughs*]

**KF:** Oh no! I love those little animation oddities. Yeah. That's great. So from there you did several more specials. Holiday themed usually, right?

**LJ:** Well, this company ran into trouble, as animation studios often do because it's a very costly business. And sometimes people are in it for love and they are not business people and things happen. So the first show was pro- duced by this company, Atkinson Film-Arts, and it died. The company died. So then I was approached by Lacewood Productions, also in Ottawa, and I did six shows with them, and they ran into all kinds of trouble and had to let all their animators go. And then there were a couple of other companies that were interested, and I signed up with a third company. And I just wasn't happy doing a huge run of stories, one right after the other, because you can't help but lose control of everything, everything.

**KF:** This was the television series?

**LJ:** Yes. I just wasn't happy. It was fast and the stories weren't good and there were so many bad mistakes. And I was supposed to be checking every storyboard and working on the storyboards to make sure that continuity was there. And while I was working on the storyboard, the damn thing would be overseas somewhere and they're finishing it off. . . . I felt lied to. You know, why am I working twenty [hours] . . . ? I mean, I was working full time on the strip. So I'm up at four in the morning correcting storyboards, when they're not even gonna look at those storyboards, they're animating it already. And there's so many mistakes were made. It was just silly. You know, why not do a few shows and do them really well? But as the animators joked, "They don't want it good. They want it now." And I wasn't willing to work under that kind of pressure. And also, I didn't want to turn out crap. It was really not good work. And yet your name is on it. And everybody thinks you did the whole thing. "Oh, why couldn't she write a better story? Why couldn't she draw a better background?"

They say, "Fix it in post." You've heard that, right? There's only so much you can fix in post. They tried. What I did love was working with all the talent. The artists, the writers, the background people, the camera people. I mean, the team of people there were just bar none. They always are. Animation studios are packed with talent and wonderful people—hardworking, willing to work around the clock, willing to work till they fall off their chair at their desk. But it's the people that own the companies that are ruthless and they don't care often about quality. Unless, you know, you're with Disney or Pixar or a company that will do one good show a year or ever so many years. But they can afford that.

**KF:** Yeah, so this company farmed up the animation to a few different places, right?

**LJ:** Yeah. Oh yeah.

**KF:** Was that where you found the disconnect was, when it went to animation?

**LJ:** Oh yeah.

**KF:** And that show lasted for two seasons, I think, right? You did two seasons. And did you pull the plug on it?

**LJ:** Yes, I did. Yeah. I didn't want it to go into syndication. And I think you need twenty-six shows. I think we had twenty-three, and they wanted three more. And I didn't want to do the three more. No, I just stopped it. I just I have too much pride. And maybe there was money to be made there. I don't know. I don't know. And it's nice to be with the big guys and be syndicated in the States and all that stuff. But I had so much control over the comic strip and no control over this.

**KF:** Yeah, that's got to be frustrating.

**LJ:** It was worse than frustrating. It was terribly sad. Because all the money and the time that went into it. It should be better.

**KF:** Yeah. I looked those some of those cartoons up on YouTube. And yeah, you're right, they don't compare to those original specials at all. It's quite interesting seeing where it went and hearing your thoughts on it. And . . . I'm glad to hear you say that you were not proud of them.

**LJ:** No. They were awful. And Charles Schulz had the same problem that when his show went to Saturday morning shows, every day. He hated it so badly. He was miserable because it was awful work and somebody else had to write it and somebody else had to draw it and somebody else had to . . . you know. . . .

**KF:** That's kind of the nature of turning your property in to a franchise, though, I think.

**LJ:** It's okay if the other people at the other end really care. But if all they want is "We don't want it good, we want it now. . . ."

**KF:** Which is most TV execs.

**LJ:** Well, yeah. But I'm no slouch, and none of the people on the team are slouches. We are all super hard workers, but they pushed us beyond the ability to even get anything good out. And plus, they were farming it out to overseas people who didn't know the strip, didn't know the characters. Didn't try to get them on model. Didn't know how to animate. So key animation is the hand is up at the top, then the hand is down below, and then somebody [else] does the four or five images in between. Well, the key animation might be okay, but everything in between was garbage.

**KF:** I noticed that—like pans were all, I think, on twos.[1] It was so choppy.

**LJ:** It was horrible.

**KF:** It was really a lot of cost-saving techniques there.

**LJ:** Yeah. I mean, there's one scene where Michael is supposed to be selling hot dogs on the street corner, and they had no money to have cars go by. So every time he did a close up of Michael talking to somebody, you'd hear cars honking and people walking and stuff. And they tried. I mean, you got to hand it to these guys, they are clever. The post guys were clever, but they couldn't save it. It was horrible. It was horrible.

**KF:** Oh, wow. And so you haven't done anything since?

**LJ:** No. No.

**KF:** Probably for that reason?

**LJ:** Absolutely. Yeah, I have never. . . . You know, we've all been angry in our lives, right? We've all been angry to the point of tears, to the point of wanting to break something you really like. I have never been so angry and so unhappy as I was with those shows, the last shows. And I felt so ignored and so insulted. Because it could have been good with just a little effort. 'Cause every artist on the show would have given, and did give, their best. You know, you can't fault the artists or the writers. They were really good writers. But you can only write so fast. And if they take an unfinished script and then try to finish it as it's being animated. . . .

**KF:** Yikes, yeah, that's not gonna work.

**LJ:** No! So it was horrible!

**KF:** But at least your comic strip lived on after that. And it's probably another ten years or so I think now.

**LJ:** Well, I can't believe that I was able to do all that work.

**KF:** Yeah. So did you have any assistants working with you?

**LJ:** I did. Yeah, I did. I had a couple of artists working with me. I hired a wonderful girl from California for a while, and she had been working on *Dennis the Menace* and really wanted to move back east. Her mom and dad were in Buffalo. She wanted to move back east. So I hired her, and she was terrific. She brought her husband and her kids. And her husband wasn't happy in Northern Ontario. He really wasn't happy. So they moved down to Buffalo. . . . By then I knew the value of a really good graphic artist, so I hired a girl who lived in North Bay, and she was absolutely fabulous. I couldn't have asked for a better artist. And it worked out that I would draw everything in pencil and I would ink just the characters, and Laura would ink everything else. And that's how things became more and more detailed because she was such a good artist that I could draw every leaf on the tree and draw every brick in the building.

**KF:** So this is probably the late nineties?

**LJ:** Yeah, yeah.

**KF:** Okay. And then you started playing with shading, using different patterns. . . .

**LJ:** Right. Right. Well, of course computer technology was enhanced all along the way. We went from not having really anything to full color and beyond. And so a friend of Laura's was a wonderful colorist, so we hired her too. I had some of the best artwork out there because I wanted it and hired people to do that for me, and it was magic to stand behind somebody and watch them fully color something and have it come to 3D life almost by touching buttons and moving a mouse. Just great.

**KF:** Did that all translate well when it went to actually went to print?

**LJ:** Oh yes, it did. Well, we had to be aware—we always had some papers printed in black and white.

**KF:** Even the Sundays?

**LJ:** Yes. Some papers, especially international papers.

**KF:** Would they print the color version in black and white? Or would you send them the lined version?

**LJ:** The color version they would do in black and white.

**KF:** Oh. Okay.

**LJ:** So *The Japan Times*, for example, is an English-language newspaper, but it just printed in black and white for a while. It might be in color now, but at the time, we had to think, *If we color it, they might take that color image.* And you have to think of everything in terms of grayscale, so you couldn't have a navy blue jacket next to a dark red house.

**KF:** They'd be the same color.

**LJ:** They'd be the same color. So we had to always be aware of the gray tones. And that was a skill in its own.

**KF:** Really. I imagine so. When you finished the strip or when you finish the main story, and you decided to end after Elizabeth's wedding, you went back and your strip became a series of kind of reprints and then you also did originals with younger kids.

**LJ:** Yes. Yes.

**KF:** Why did you decide to do that?

**LJ:** Well, like what you said, "When I first opened your book, I said, 'Oh, I don't really like those.'" Those are ones I did right early on and I wasn't too happy with them, but we put those in the book anyways. Okay?

**KF:** Yeah.

**LJ:** And when you're done, you always look at that and say, "You know what? That beginning was a little rough." But that's how you are when you start any project, right? Until you get used to it and become a professional at it, your beginnings are always pretty evident. So if they were going to rerun my work from the beginning, I wanted to go back to the beginning and change a lot of the stuff because I simply wasn't happy with it. Also, there was character development missing. There were story arcs that were just out of nowhere that needed some kind of beginning, you know. I mean, I really wanted to fix it and to make it better. Simply because I'm such a perfectionist, I guess. I don't think of myself as a perfectionist. I just want it right. And so I wanted to go back and I added a lot of new material and I probably extended it about a year with new material simply because I wanted to fix it. And if you fix one thing, maybe that means you have to fix something else along the way. It was a good decision to make for two reasons. One, editors who were not comfortable running the strip a second time wanted that new material and continued the strip, which was great of them to do that. I mean, I'm very, very lucky to have that. But it also gave me a chance to make the beginning better, [and] how often do you get to do that?

**KF:** Yeah, definitely. And you feel like you accomplished that?

**LJ:** I did. I did.

**KF:** So when you decided to stop that, did most papers just continue on reprinting the rest of stories?

**LJ:** Yeah, most papers did. Some dropped it, which is understandable. Some amalgamated with other papers. Some papers went out of business. I mean, that happens. But right now, I would say I'm about fourteen hundred papers still, perhaps in around there.

**KF:** What was your height?

**LJ:** Over two thousand papers. But of course it sounds like a lot, but some papers just took the dailies. Some papers just took the Sundays. And some took both. They would count everything as a market, so it's sort of doubled, you know, with some just taking the dailies and some just taking the Sundays.

**KF:** But you'll take it. Numbers are everything, right?

**LJ:** Numbers are everything. So all in all, there were over two thousand papers carrying *For Better or For Worse*. And it went into many international papers, but they were always English-language papers. . . . There were about six that were not. I think it was translated into a few languages. But the problem was that that it really I used a lot of puns and wordplay.

**KF:** I always wondered if puns translate into Chinese.

**LJ:** It doesn't. No, it doesn't. And even into French it doesn't translate. "Paying through the nose," for example, is a great visual for a gag. But I think in Quebec, it's "someone's hand's in my pocket." Right? And so all of these puns just would not translate. In Denmark they had a cartoonist translating the comics, and he just loved trying to bring puns into it. He was a real master. And I had someone do some translation for me who was also a cartoonist. And she did a great job in French. But that's rare to have a translator who can translate puns and wordplay.

**KF:** So would they just translate it and let the joke fall flat?

**LJ:** In some cases they had no choice. In some cases they changed it altogether because it would still work for the storyline, but because I didn't speak Danish I wouldn't have known if it worked! [*Laughs*]

**KF:** Right! Okay, so I want to also ask you about your fabrics. Because that's kind of what you're doing now. Tell us a little bit about that, what you're up to these days.

**LJ:** Well, it all started with an invitation—well, I was given a star on the Walk of Fame in Toronto.

**KF:** Yes. Nice.

**LJ:** I was going to be on the stage with Shania Twain and Andrea Martin and some other really neat people. And I thought, *Well, what do you wear to something like that?* And I wanted it to be funny and fun because I'm a cartoonist. And I wanted to breeze onto the stage wearing something funny, but I couldn't find any fabric that I liked. And I looked and looked. And I had a friend who actually was a designer and would have made a dress for me had I found the right fabric. And by the time it was getting close to the event, I was desperate—well, not desperate, but I was wondering what the hell I'm going to wear. So I got this idea and I went to a local wedding dress shop and I bought a wedding dress and I drew over the skirt with cartoon faces. I can show it to you, it's upstairs.

**KF:** Sure, I'd love to see it.

**LJ:** I wore that and it was a huge hit! Everybody thought, you know, "Where did you get that dress?" and "Did you do that?" "Oh my God, that's incredible!" And it got a lot of comments, and it was very elegant but really funny. So I wore it a few times to different events and then we sort of retired it to a hanger upstairs. And one day my daughter said, "You know, that fabric squeezy paint that you buy at Walmart is going to deteriorate someday, we better digitize that image." So she took this huge dress, opened the thing right up, and photographed it many times and was able to digitize it into a pattern, through a program, that she and my graphic artist—I have a graphic artist who's just a great guy, he has been working with us for many years in North Bay—and he was able to take a program and turn it into a pattern and multiply it in all directions so it was an unending [design]. . . . I think it is called "wallpapering."

**KF:** Okay. Yeah.

**LJ:** So we learned an awful lot about how to do a design, but we were, again, reinventing the wheel. And a friend of mine who is a cartoonist but is also a fabric designer—she mostly does quilting fabrics—so we brought her in to North Bay from Newfoundland, and she did a weeklong training session for my daughter, myself, [and] my designer. And taught us how to properly repeat a fabric pattern. So then I started to draw patterns, which really are a 12 × 12-inch design, which you add maybe twelve different characters to. And then when you wallpaper the design, you plug those little extras into the holes that are created as you're making the pattern. And then you reduce it down on the screen and you can see where the colors don't work and where dark areas might be lightened because you don't want your eyes to be drawn to one specific spot.

**KF:** Right.

**LJ:** Yeah. And so that's what we've been up to. And she and I, Deborah Payton is her name, we just came back from a big fabric show in New York, where all the designers go, and it's a combined fabric design and paper design [show]. So you're going from people who are making quilts and children's clothes and bedding and all that to an area where they are doing wallpaper and greeting cards and wrapping paper and things like that. It's very exciting. And there's lectures on licensing and marketing and legal issues and trends and color forecasts and things like that. So it was a marvelous event to go to and inspired us to perhaps get a booth next year.

**KF:** Oh yeah?

**LJ:** Yeah.

**KF:** And you have products some products for sale on your website?

**LJ:** Well, we do. But we're kind of holding back a little bit because as we got into the fabric designs, we decided to move and we packed up two households, two big households, threw everything into a giant truck and landed in North Vancouver, and we're still unpacking. As you saw today. I just finished unpacking more stuff today. And it's awful. . . . I'm such a nitpicker that until I get my own environment tidied up, it's awfully hard for me to sit down and relax and do cartoons. So fortunately, I don't have to.

**KF:** Right.

**LJ:** But I will push myself into the deadlines again, as soon as soon as the fall comes around because I need a deadline. I need I need that commitment. I can't just say to myself, like somebody perhaps doing a graphic novel, "I will have this finished by the end of May." I mean. . . .

**KF:** It's arbitrary.

**LJ:** That's an overwhelming amount of self-discipline. And I thought of myself as self-disciplined, but by golly, that whip is cracked if you've got a contract and you're working for a client, you need to produce. I would like that again, but not so stringent.

**KF:** I can say that I'll fine you a hundred bucks every time you're late if you want! [*Laughs*]

**LJ:** Then you'd have to be following what I did and be on my case! [*Laughs*]

**KF:** Well, okay!

**LJ:** And you got enough to do!

**KF:** True! One final question here. What what's on the horizon for *For Better or For Worse*, if anything?

**LJ:** Well, there will be another contract review because everything's still contract. And it'll be interesting to see where they want to go with it, whether they want to continue with it, and the number of papers. . . . I think is if there are a significant number of papers, the syndicate will want to continue. So it'll be interesting to see what happens when we renegotiate the contract, which is great.

I'm going to head into the fabrics. . . . We've just got one book out there. I don't know, honestly. I'm very happy with the work I did. If somebody sees it and wants to do something else with it that would be great. But I have no plans. I have no marketing people. I have no agent. I have no nothing. I'm very happy to be getting an income from the work that I did, so that's a luxury. And allows me to play around with these fabrics and do birthday cards for friends and the occasional goofy painting, which I do.

**KF:** Right. Well, thank you for spending this time with us. I completely enjoyed this interview, and I hope our listeners are enjoying it as well.

**LJ:** Well, it's great to know you are enthused enough about my work to ask questions about it because right now I consider myself an old fart. I'm sixty-nine. I'm going to be seventy in a year, and I just can't believe it because in my head I'm still nineteen. [*Laughs*] So it's great to talk to young people and have them like my work. That's a wonderful, wonderful compliment.

**KF:** Oh great! Our listenership are young people, and I am hoping that they will have fond memories of this and find this interesting as well.

**LJ:** Great. Me too.

**KF:** Thank you very much!

Note

1. This refers to the camera moving back and forth between the two characters.

# An Interview with Lynn Johnston, Creator of the Classic *For Better or For Worse*

JASON SACKS / 2019

From *Classic Comics Cavalcade* podcast (September 11, 2019). Reprinted by permission.

**Jason Sacks:** Hi, I'm Jason Sacks. Welcome to *Classic Comics Cavalcade*. This week, my guest is Lynn Johnston, the creator of the classic comic strip, *For Better or For Worse*, certainly, one of my favorite strips and a strip that really chronicles the life of an extended family over that same period of time. Unlike most comic strips, the characters in *For Better or For Worse* grew, changed, got older, had interesting complex lives and life experiences. And yet the series never lost its naturalistic feel or its amazingly sweet sense of humor. You'll hear a lot of that from Lynn in the following hour. She was an absolute delight to speak to, one of the nicest people I've had the chance to chat with, as well as just a wonderful creative force. This is just one of my favorite interviews I've ever had a chance to do, and I hope you enjoy it as well. . . .

Congratulations on the anniversary. It's about the fortieth anniversary of this strip. Is that right?

**Lynn Johnston:** It is. It is, September this month. The strip started September of 1979. It just seems—well, it was a lifetime ago.

**Sacks:** Several people's lifetimes ago, I guess.

**Johnston:** Yeah, yeah. Yes, I was in my thirties when I signed a contract. . . . I've been looking through boxes of photographs and see me as I was then, and Cathy Guisewite and Jim Unger and Tom Wilson and all the wonderful people that I met when I first started working for Universal Press. Just a lifetime ago, two lifetimes ago, and so many of these people are gone now, which is sobering.

**Sacks:** It is, well, yeah. Unfortunately, that's a journey we all go through in life.

**Johnston:** Well, how old are you, may I ask?

134

**Sacks:** Oh, of course you may, I'm fifty-three.

**Johnston:** Ah, you have a very youthful voice.

**Sacks:** I appreciate that. Yeah, so I've gone through a lot of the same transitions in life, you know. Of course, losing your parents is always the toughest thing to deal with.

**Johnston:** Yes, yes, it is. I lost mine at the age of . . . both my parents were both seventy-two when they died, one right after the other. And I'm seventy-two now, so once I get past this year, it's free sailing.

**Sacks:** That's it. Well, you're in your bonus time now anyway, right? You just moved back to North Van[couver]. I heard in your interview with Kurtis [Findlay] that you're getting to reconnect with some old friends?

**Johnston:** Oh gosh, yes, I hang out with people that I went to elementary school with. And the funny thing is that we all in our hearts look the same, even though, you know, it's difficult to see past the lines and the gray hair now. But the only time we really look old is in photographs when we're close to each other when we're sitting across the table and having a coffee together. You know, the years don't exist; you're still on the Ridgeway [Elementary] School playground and still the same age as we were when we first met, right? You can fantasize anything when you're talking to an old friend, but it's photographs when it's a static image that you look at and say, "Who the hell is that?"

**Sacks:** Right, I do that all the time. "Wait, that's who I am? That's just not right."

**Johnston:** Right. You know, I remember in my twenties making jokes about old farts—

you know, wrinkle city, menopause manor, watching some old biddy walk across the street with a walker—and now that's pretty close to me, right? And the amazing thing is you don't realize this when you're young, but when you are that old person with your glaucoma glasses, you know, you really don't feel any different in your heart than you were when you were thirteen, fifteen, eighteen, twenty. I think my best years certainly, physically and mentally, were between, say, thirty-five and fifty-five. I think I did my best work then. And so I have tremendous respect for people in their twenties who are doing phenomenal work because that's when you had the energy and before you have your family, that's when you have the time. And people in their twenties are producing the most amazing work.

**Sacks:** What's something you've read recently that you really enjoy or took in that you enjoy?

**Johnston:** Well, I recently saw a fabulous young performer. Actually, it was last night on YouTube. And he's got to be in his twenties, and if I'd known you were going to ask I would have gone back and looked into it. He can just play everything and the music over the past ten years has been so abysmally awful that I have run out of restaurants, bars, clothing stores, because I couldn't stand the *thud, thud, thud* and the same four cords and the same whining women. I just am so hopeful now that there's going to be music in our lives again.

**Sacks:** I just think every generation does things their own different way. And, you know, frankly, a lot of the music I listened to when I was in my twenties—that was the early 1980s—

there's not a lot of great music that came out of that era, or I'm kind of rediscovering some of the great music, I suppose. . . .

**Johnston:** I'm looking back at the Eagles. And even the Beatles when their later work was just fabulous. Where's the craftsmanship in the music now? Get away from the electronic repetitive crud. It's just, you know, it's too easy. And who's going to be humming along to some of the stuff we hear now? Nobody in thirty years. They're still going to be playing the Eagles and the Beatles and just going back in time to when music really had some heart, soul and guts, and talent. Pardon me, I'm on a rant! [*Laughs*]

**Sacks:** You're entitled. At a certain point, we all get in our rants.

**Johnston:** Steely Dan, there's another. Steely Dan, holy smokes. What a group! Anyways, I digress. Sorry!

**Sacks:** Now you got me thinking about music and the song ages in my head for Steely Dan and just how unique and remarkable that stuff was. Wow.

**Johnston:** Oh yeah, you bet!

**Sacks:** So you touched a bit on joining the comic strip fraternity, I suppose, as a pretentious way of saying it. You had the most remarkable way of kind of getting discovered and getting your contract.

**Johnston:** Yeah, I think it was unusual in that most people apply. They send in their folios and they wait for rejection slips, which inevitably come, from what I hear from a lot of people. But my work was sent to them, as Cathy Guisewite's was as well. Cathy's mother sent Cathy's work to Universal Press. And I had worked with a publisher in Minneapolis who sent mine. I had done three little books of cartoons, and he sent those to Universal Press. And then there's just sheer terror of being offered a contract when you have really nothing to go with. No characters developed, no storyline, no ideas for a comic strip—just a contract.

**Sacks:** So yeah, so you had just done three little books that were like single-panel cartoons about parenthood. At the time your kids were really young, and somehow you reached a syndicate, or a friend sent it to the

syndicate, and they very quickly offered you a twenty-year contract to produce a strip. And then you somehow persuade them to give you six months
to formulate the strip.

**Johnston:** Pretty much, yeah, when they were interested in my work.
They wanted three weeks of dailies right away as fast as I could do them, and
that was a panic. I was married again, had another baby, and was moving to
Northern Manitoba to an isolated mining town. As far north in Manitoba,
Canada, as you can go. If you can visualize the North American continent, you
see where James Bay comes below Hudson Bay, that little teardrop of a bay
there. We were on the same level as on the Saskatchewan–Manitoba border.
And you really couldn't get there unless you were flying. It was really an Arctic
community. So we were moving up there as I got this request for three weeks
of daily comics as soon as I could get them out. And I was literally doing these
on packing boxes. I had no drafting table or anything. I was sitting with my
feet spread, expecting my second baby, and drawing on packing boxes. And I
really didn't know whether I'd hear from these people again. I was confident
that what I sent was the best I could do, which is all you can do, right? And
they sent me a twenty-year contract just as we were wrapping up and moving.

**Sacks:** That's just so amazing.

**Johnston:** It is. It is. Yeah. . . .

**Sacks:** You're obviously a very sociable person. Personal contact means a
lot to you. You move to this tiny town in the middle of nowhere. That must
have been tough. You grew up in Vancouver, right?

**Johnston:** I grew up in North Vancouver, which is just across the pond
from the main city. So you really are in the heart of the beast here. And I
moved to Hamilton, Ontario, which is another fairly big city, and when I met
my second husband I loved the thought of the adventure of going north. I had
settled into my little house in Dundas and already had a child, and he was in
dental school. And his plan was to learn to fly, buy a small aircraft, and work as
a flying dentist up in Northern Canada somewhere, anywhere. He just wanted
to provide a service to the First Nations communities up there. And there are
so many isolated communities that get very little medical attention. So it was
a really worthy cause, and I love to fly. And so I met him up at the airport.

Actually, I was looking in the window of small aircrafts thinking, *Who owns
these?* and *I would love to learn to fly.* And he came in, landed, walked across
the tarmac. We got a conversation going, and he said, "Do you want to fly to
the next airport for a hamburger?" And I had my baby on my hip and it was a
windy day in March, and I said, "Well, sure." I had met him before, you know.
He was acquaintance from years beforehand. He had worked at CHCH TV

with my first husband. And he was a familiar face, and I thought, *Well, what the heck, why not?* He got his pilot's license [and] off we went, and for me it was magic. A magic carpet that took you up into the sky, and son of a gun. So we started to go together and I would go with him when he was taking his float license. And I even learned to fly when we were together there. He would turn over the controls to me. And I love flying over these steel mills because you get this rush of hot air and the aircraft would bounce up high into the sky. I mean, it was just a joy.

So we married after he finished dental school, and we bought aircraft, and we moved up to Lynn Lake, Manitoba, just as this contract was happening, and as it turns out, it was probably the best gift I could ever have been given to be spirited away to some small isolated village when the success happened. And it happened all too fast. And I'm pretty theatrical, and I love stand-up comedy and performance and all of that stuff. I always imagined doing more in terms of theater. . . . Anyways, I was too theatrical to be having success like that in a big city. Because you're accessible then. If you're in a tiny, tiny little mining town, nobody's going to fly the number of hours it takes to get up to Lynn Lake, Manitoba, to see somebody who's drawing cartoons.

So I was, first of all, isolated from publicity, which was very healthy for me. And the other thing was, when you're in a small town, you get to know everybody, and there's no such thing as class. You know, because we're all in the same fishbowl. And you become a nicer person. But you also become aware of everybody's circumstances, and so you know the guy that's sleeping in the doorway of the drugstore and you know the girl whose husband was killed in a plane crash and you know the woman at the front counter at the grocery store and the guy that owns the grocery store and the woman who lives upstairs the grocery store and the woman who's a newspaper editor with the newspaper with too many graph sheets that comes out once a week. I mean, it was being closeted in society and being privileged to know a lot of people in very close circumstances. So that really is helpful to somebody who's a writer; you get to see other people's points of view.

And when I started this strip, I expected none of the characters to change in age; everybody's going to stay the same. And there was going to be some black and white. Elly was going to be a woman who really resented being a housewife and jealous of her neighbor who was a successful nursing staff member at a big hospital who was going up the ladder there and she was gonna be Elly's nemesis. But living in a small town teaches you that there's no all bad in anybody. I mean, we're all a mix of good and bad and fine and dandy and down dirty. . . . So there's no such thing as the ultimate villain and the ultimate heroine. Everybody became human very quickly in the strip. After a year, everybody started to have personalities that were quite realistic, and everybody started to grow. The children started to grow, and circumstances changed, and it developed as a story rather than a comic strip.

**Sacks:** It just seemed to naturally evolve as I started reading them. And there's so many moments where you have a person who starts out as just a bad, nasty character [who] turns out to be something very different. Just earlier today, I was reading some of the stories around Jeremy Jones.

**Johnston:** Oh yeah, Jeremy.

**Sacks:** Who's oh-so-mean to April at the beginning, just a bully in school. And then he turns as you get to know him better and just reveals other sides of himself.

**Johnston:** Yes, you find out. In fact, I've done a number of workshops in elementary schools and things like that. And I talked to the kids about the characters that I want them to design and I said, "Think about *Aliens*. Think about that creepy thing that pulls itself out of the works in the bowels of the spaceship to terrorize and eat everybody and drool all over. Well, what's he gonna be doing on a Saturday night when he's home alone? Does he have his feet up? Does he have a beer? What did he watch on TV? Is he married? Or is it a he? Is it a she, you know? What happens when it gets a boil on his butt and can't work for a day? I mean, what's going on in the background of this guy?" And so everyone laughs and says, "Yeah, I never thought about that! What does Godzilla do on his day off, right?" And so that's the way the characters were for me. What's the other side of this character? It can't be all bad.

**Sacks:** Mm-hmm. Yeah, there's a quote from you on the site: "I know all the people so well. I know where their houses are, what their furniture's like, where they work, I know their voices, their mannerisms, their thoughts are open to me." Which is just so interesting. Like you really did see them as real people.

**Johnston:** Well, I think anybody who writes, a novelist, must certainly live in every body of every character, knowing their innermost thoughts and feelings, right? And I know when you're an actor and you're given a role, you have to study that character. So that you can play that character realistically. In fact, I know that there are people who find it awfully hard to get out of that character once the movie is over. They spend months as a villain or months as somebody who has maybe a blindness or other horrific thing that they have to portray in a movie and afterward, they have to come out of that person and be them again.

**Sacks:** But you're doing that for ninety people or something. That's like a Russian novel.

**Johnston:** [*Laughs*] One character inside another? Well, it's really only just maybe ten people. And toward the end, there were just really too many characters, which is another really good reason for stopping when I did. Too many characters. And too many realistic situations. I just pushed myself into being someone who told short stories. And suddenly I was no longer drawing the funny stuff. I couldn't stretch the faces. Everybody had a perfectly believable skeletal structure inside so I couldn't elongate arms or enlarge eyeballs and do all those wonderful things that smack you in the head with goofiness, right? I've lost that.

**Sacks:** Do you like the earlier strips, where the cartooning's so loose? It is remarkably loose compared to the newer ones.

**Johnston:** Right, absolutely. The stuff that I did, say, in the middle ten years or so are the best, just because there was confidence to the writing, I think there was humor to it, but also the characters were elastic. And the backgrounds weren't so detailed. I didn't dwell so much on every brick on the house and every branch on the tree. But I kept wanting to get better and better and better, do better, draw better. And when you do that you sometimes perfect yourself into a state where it's just too, I don't know, too perfect. And nothing is perfect. Everything has to be fluid and loose and fleeting. You know, I really drew myself into a box.

**Sacks:** You almost felt like you got too precise, too clean in a way.

**Johnston:** Exactly. That's the best way to put it. It was too precise. Yeah, it was engineered.

**Sacks:** I guess. Yeah. I mean, it's interesting because so many artists . . . strive for the perfect line or the perfect rendering. But I think with humor especially, well, it's hard to categorize the work you did also. As you said, especially towards the end it almost veered into short stories.

**Johnston:** Yeah. Yeah. And also I was pressuring myself to do some relevant stories too. . . . I mean, the initial Elizabeth and Michael and April were all adults and teens. And there are significant stories in this time of your life. And so significant stories don't necessarily lend themselves to great humor. And in the end, it's an entertainment medium, right? Comic art—you turn to it for some relief from what's going on in the news, and I was starting to create stuff that was in the news, bullying and feminist issues and the death of the parents and things like that. . . . There were times when I did do some serious stories that happened to run at very serious times, like the story of the death of Farley happened at the same time as the Oklahoma bombing. So it was a real tragedy.

And then Michael and Deanna get married and the wedding takes place at the time when the twin towers came down. And so you look at it and you say,

Some moments from the death of Farley storyline. FOR BETTER OR FOR WORSE © 1995 Lynn Johnston Productions. Dist. By ANDREWS MCMEEL SYNDICATION. Reprinted with permission. All rights reserved.

"Well, if I'm going to do a serious story, what's going to run in the headlines the day that the story runs?" And if people turn to the comics page for relief from the news, you can't *not* fulfill that hope. I mean, there were times when the serious stories were quick, but I was seeing that you couldn't run them for longer than two weeks because people would be exhausted and they['d say,] "Come on, let's get back to the laughs again."

**Sacks:** Yeah, it's different. Part of the mechanism of being in a daily newspaper strip where you need to have something to bring people back every day and some level of predictability.

**Johnston:** Right. And I found that I could write more confidently if I was writing little vignettes like "And then what happened?" Something makes you laugh, the dog does something, or the kids do something. But then what happens? What is the comeuppance to that? So that's how the little story started. But they started as these simple little funny vignettes. You know, somebody does something at school and lies about it. The next day and the next day, there's the comeuppance, but then the serious stories started to happen.

**Sacks:** Well, you have a mix in a lot of your stories of sadness and happiness. So Elizabeth and Anthony get married at the same time that the grandma is dying. April has that horrible thing where she goes down to the river and nearly gets washed away. The dog saves her, and the dog passes away. Deanna's auto accident brings her close to Michael. And there's really a recurring motif where tragedy leads to happiness or vice versa. I guess it keeps us on an even keel.

**Johnston:** I kept up with the title *For Better or For Worse*, right? Sometimes it's better, sometimes it's worse. And I was charged with producing a strip right at the very beginning, when I signed that huge contract, of doing something that was not all roses from the woman's point of view and a family. A lot of the family strips were done by guys who I assumed were given the freedom to work in the studio, and then when they came out, dinner was on the table, and the wife was wiping her hands on her apron and saying, "How was your day, dear?" And you can't really write and draw serious family stories about laundry and kids and garbage and dog paw prints or whatever happens, you know. From that side of the drafting table, you have to be cleanin' out the trash with your own two hands. Yeah, so I was able to do what I was asked to do. And because of the wonderful company I worked for, I was given tremendous treatment. I was not edited very closely at all after the first year. They let me just fly. And I was able to do pretty well anything I wanted to do. They trusted me with that. And there were times when an idea was rejected, but then that has to happen. And you learn that everything that's rejected by your editor, you say, "Well, in the end, I appreciate the fact that you didn't let me send that out there because I probably wouldn't have been happy with it once it ran."

**Sacks:** What's an example of that? Something that you were persuaded not to do?

**Johnston:** Well, there was some ideas that I had about child abuse and about infidelity. . . . There was an imaginary neighborhood, of course, and Anne next door, her husband was not only a junk collector and their whole yard was full of junk that he picked up and he was getting to be a hoarder, but he was also unfaithful to his wife. And Annie knew about it but wasn't able to pinpoint what her anxiety was. And, you know, eventually, she's going to find out. I alluded to all this without getting into it. After a while of talking it over with my editor thinking, *That would be a long-term investigation with a lot of pretty sensitive, intimate stuff going on.* And really, at the time that I started this idea, the kids were still young and in school, and life was still, you know, the easygoing ups and downs of the Patterson family, and should I really delve into this? And the crazy thing was that in my own life that was actually going on, so maybe deep down inside I knew that this was territory I better not touch. Because you don't break up a marriage until you know for sure that something is going on. But you can suspect. And you're guilty for suspecting, and it's very easy to believe what you're told because you don't want to believe the truth. So in not doing these stories, perhaps I was covering my own, I don't know, delicate, sensitive background, you know. Not wanting people to know that much.

**Sacks:** Was the strip kind of a respite, a relief for you during those times when you could just escape into a different world?

**Johnston:** Well, you have total control in the comic strip. I mean, call it creative, which is rather a large word. You know, you're "the creator of the comic strip." But it's a world that you do create, and you have total control. You know. Who's gonna do what, who's gonna say what? You are the dog, you are the kids, you are the grandparents, you are every character and you know, you can choreograph what's going to happen. Who's gonna die, who's gonna get married and to whom? And so real life is quite the opposite, of course. It's serendipity all the way. You know, you have to hope for the best. . . . You have to hope for the best.

**Sacks:** Yeah, life is just a series of accidents in a lot of ways, right?

**Johnston:** Yeah. And open doors. Yeah. And wonderful opportunities. And, I mean, with every bad thing, good things happen. Right? And that's why *For Better or For Worse*, it was up and down. I was having lunch with a friend the other day, and it was a horrible lunch. . . . We were eating this food, and it was just, "I can't believe I ordered this." And we chuffed our way through it. But the laugh was that every bad lunch, it makes a good lunch one hundred percent better, right? You'd say, "Wow, compared to yesterday!" And that's why I don't think there's anything like heaven. I mean, because if everything is perfect, we get so bored. You know? The same old music and the same great food and the same great sex and the same great relationships and you look perfect. How boring! Let's stir things up! Let's tell God off tomorrow and see what happens! [*Laughs*]

**Sacks:** You got me thinking about great old music. There's a Talking Heads song called "Heaven." It's about exactly that, which I just loved, and the song stuck with me for years.

**Johnston:** I'm not the only one who thinks that way, I know.

**Sacks:** "Heaven is a place where nothing ever happens" is the chorus. . . . So how far in advance did you plan the character arcs? Because there's so many cases where people meet early on and then end up reconnecting in some ways, you know?

The whole story with Lilliput's, for example, it's always in the background, and it becomes a prominent thing. When you first brought it in, did you have any idea, for example, that Elly would be buying the store and running a store for a few years?

**Johnston:** No, no. A lot of it was just as life really happens. It just flowed into the storyline. It just worked. And people criticize me for having Elizabeth married her childhood sweetheart and Michael actually married the girl that he met at university and had known in elementary school and everything is full circle. But in reality, my own life has been that way. Right now, I'm partnered with a wonderful man that I met in grade five. I've moved back to my own little hometown and living on the same street I grew up—not planned. I was looking for a place to buy and I was driving down the street and there was a big for sale sign on a place opposite my old house, and I went in and bought it. It was just right for me. And, you know, it's in North Vancouver between the bridges. I can overlook the shipyards and hear the sound of the foghorns in the morning. I mean, it's home. I can walk to my old elementary school. And Paul and I met at our fiftieth high school reunion. And I've done exactly what the characters in *For Better or For Worse* did. I reconnected with someone I knew in elementary school.

**Sacks:** Wow, that's funny. Life imitates art, huh?

**Johnston:** It does. It does. Yeah.

**Sacks:** Well, 'cause I think it's really one of the strong points of this strip. So like April and her friend Becky—or "Rebeccah" when she becomes a star, a musical star—their relationship is so founded in reality. I mean, they met in the first day of preschool, and so they have this friendship that can survive anything. And I think that's so much like real life.

**Johnston:** Well, you look at a lot of these businesses, these big successful businesses—a lot of these have been started by people who met in school. I think even Facebook was started by people who met in school. . . . And bands, band members. I mean, I think, again, the Eagles probably were people who knew each other as teenagers. And so a lot of things that are successful later in life, the seed of it began in high school.

**Sacks:** I'm sure you were drawing all your life too. This love for you became a career that kind of carried you through everything.

**Johnston:** It was the one thing that gave me confidence because I was not happy at home. I'd look in the mirror and I think, *What an ugly kid*. And I was a fighter, a scrapper, and it wasn't until high school when I was editor of the school annual that I really realized that I fit into an art career and a graphic art publishing career 'cause the teachers can see that potential in me. But I didn't have a lot of friends through school. So the fact that I could draw was . . . I think of it as my Dumbo's feather, you know? It's like that glass of wine you carry around at a cocktail party. You don't know anybody and you don't want to be bothered with your stupid small talk. "Hi, how are you?" "How long have you known so-and-so?" Blah, blah, blah. You've got your obligatory Dumbo's feather of a cocktail in your hand. If you put that down, you might as well go back to your room in the hotel because you don't belong. And so that ability always in the background, knowing that I can draw, was my glass of wine at a cocktail party; even if you think I'm a schmuck, at least I can draw.

**Sacks:** Yeah, "at least I can do the one thing." So very few people actually make careers out of the things that they would aspire to do when they were young, though.

**Johnston:** It's hard, it's hard.

**Sacks:** I'll often have conversations with people about that very subject. So I write. I'm a writer. I write comic histories. I have several books out through TwoMorrows Publishing about the history of American comic books, which is why I ended up doing my classic comics podcast and I talk to friends at work or whatever, and I'm literally the only one who's doing the work that he wanted to do when he was fifteen or sixteen. And I feel privileged to be in that position in my life.

**Johnston:** Privileged, but at the same time, you're a real hard worker and you're focused and you're dedicated and, you know, you have a goal, and you respect your work, and you have confidence in what you're doing. And I think sometimes that drives you forward. And if you're good at what you do, you can succeed. I mean, there are times when you're good at what you do and it has to be a hobby, but occasionally, and you're an example of it, you can succeed and make a career of what you love to do most. And the danger of that is, "Oh, my goodness, I don't have a hobby, what am I going to do?" And your work becomes your hobby. And I know that when I had my twenty-year contract turned into thirty years, you're working all the time. You're always on record whenever you're traveling. If you're a writer, you're remembering the smell and the scent, the breeze and crunch of the rocks under your feet on the shore. And all of these senses, you're absorbing and you're recording all the time if you're a writer and an artist and a cartoonist. And so you know your job is with you all the time, but you still have to have that work ethic and that energy and that focus to make a career of it.

**Sacks:** One of the things you talked about with Kurtis was it took you a few years before you really had that confidence. I think you were talking about sitting on the couch and just coming up with your ideas, and some days it would flow, and some days it wouldn't. And knowing that over time it'll just even itself out.

**Johnston:** That's right. You have to trust that that will come back. And at first, it's frightening when you can't think of anything, but you have to trust that it will happen. And there can be a day where you're ready to write, you want to write. You've got all your stuff; you've got your coffee, your notepad. You've got your lunch, whatever it is, and you sit down to write. And nothing happens. And you have to sit there and daydream about the characters and who they are. And it's like a symphony where you're directing. You know, now it's the horns, and now it's the violins.

I mean, am I going to be the dog today? Am I going to be Michael? Am I going to be Elizabeth? And who have I not highlighted in the past? And where are the storylines leading me? And who do I need to focus on now? And all of those thoughts have to be there for you on the day when you cannot think of any dialogue. There's no punch line. There's nothing funny. And you just have to sit there and force yourself to be all of the characters, one at a time. In order to be the dog, you have to feel what it's like to shake off a coat full of water, right? You know, you just have to be the characters. And then the next day or the day after, that you'll write two weeks' worth of stuff without a hitch. And I don't know where that magic comes from. I really don't. And it's one of the things that we often talk about, or at least when I first got into the industry, the other young new people in the industry, they'd all come together and say, "How do you write? Where did the ideas come from?" We don't know. Jim Davis used to say "Schenectady." You know, "Where do your ideas come from?" "Schenectady!"

You'd get interviewed so many times when you're newly successful, right? Jim Davis, he does *Garfield*, right? He decided that he would like to have a suit and hat, and every section of the suit and hat would have the answers to all these most often asked questions. You'd give out those. The brim of your hat, it would say, "Since I was a child," you know? "Well, I use draft 4b paper." You know? . . .

**Sacks:** "Yes, I do love lasagna."

**Johnston:** Yeah, the favorite answer was "Six weeks dailies, eight weeks Sunday" for "How far in advance [do you complete comics?]" So he'd pull open his lapel, "Six weeks dailies eight weeks Sunday." And we laughed about it, but it's a curio that if somebody's interviewing you wants to know, we wanted to know too! Where do the ideas come from? We have no idea.

**Sacks:** Well, there's a few different ways that people approach the idea. Some people keep a notepad and are continually referring back to it. Some people will get butcher paper, maybe now Microsoft Project or something, and literally plan everything out. It sounds like you allowed yourself to improvise a lot.

**Johnston:** I did, but I did keep notes. In fact, this was the time when we all had check books in our purses, right? We wrote checks for groceries and checks for our insurance and things like that. And you always had a checkbook in your car or your purse. And my checkbook was filled with gag ideas. I mean, there's no possible way I could throw out the stubs of my checks or the back part of a folder as it would be full of gag ideas.

**Sacks:** Did you ever get complaints from your kids about being present in the moment? "Mom, stop thinking about everything else but us!"

**Johnston:** . . . Both of my kids are very funny. And my son would walk up to me holding a piece of cake in his hand and icing on his face, just making sure I could see, and he'd say, "Can I have some cake before dinner?" And I would say, "No," but he's standing there eating it. They would do things to me. And I remember one time he came in and asked me a few questions and I said, "Uh-huh, uh-huh." He said, "Can I take the scissors to the sheers, like, cut the curtains in the living room?" And I said, "Uh-huh, uh-huh," and he said, "You're not listening to me, are you?" So I mean, yeah, it was tough for the kids, it really was. That and traveling. Because you know—being a writer, you know what it's like. The work that you do is inside and kind of solitary. And you just look forward to getting out there and being away from it. And for me, because I was on record all the time, if I was on an airplane, I might have three hours where I had no choice but to relax, read a book, have a drink, you know. I loved those times.

And it was not easy for my family. Even though I had wonderful sitters. My mother- and father-in-law, always we lived within a five-minute walk from them even when we moved to North Bay from this little mining town. My parents-in-law moved too. And we bought houses next to each other, and my kids were always over at Ruth and Tom's house. So we had an extended family that covered everything. And yet it was tough for the kids when I took off and played. I remember my son watching me leave with a suitcase, and he put his hands on his hips and said, "Are you turning into Lynn Johnston *again*?" You know? And I was. In fact, if I could play the role of Lynn Johnston. I did a stand-up thing at an event, and there was a cocktail party afterward, I was Lynn Johnston. I didn't need my little obligatory glass of wine or cocktail. I could walk around and say the same things and the same platitudes and respond to the same questions, and, you know, I would be the puppet that I was as Lynn Johnston. But if I was suddenly in a room full of strangers, I needed that glass of wine. I had no Dumbo's feather. And yeah, in a way, I kind of enjoyed that notoriety. I enjoyed being Lynn Johnston, and there are times when you have to curb that arrogance when standing in line for a hamburger and say, "Well, I should be at the front of the line!" [*Laughs*] Really, you know, you gotta wash the old pits like everybody else! Right? [*Laughs*]

**Sacks:** But you also needed to be out hanging out with your peers and going to the parties and stuff. It's all part of the lifestyle, also a part of keeping yourself balanced. I mean, it sounds like you had some great times at the National Cartoonists Society.

**Johnston:** Oh yeah, tremendous rewards in the hard work. I mean, the hard work was balanced with wonderful rewards. I mean, I got to meet all of my heroes. You know, people who work for *MAD* magazine and Will Eisner and Charles Shulz. And, oh, you know, people, [like] Frank and Ollie from Disney, two of the Grand Old Men. I mean, I got to know them and borrowed the cars and stayed in the guest room. What a joy!

Phyllis Diller, I got to know Phyllis. And she was one of the most important of my connections. Just a fabulous person to know. And when I went to her house she showed me her joke drawers. She had a bureau upstairs and each drawer—I mean, it was a big bureau—and each drawer you pulled out and there were these 4 × 5-inch, 3 × 5-inch cards with jokes on them. And thousands of jokes. Literally thousands of them in alphabetical order and in subject matter order. When she opened the drawers to this massive bureau, she said, "I wrote these all myself. This is my work." And I thought, *Yeah, over the years, all of us who are in this business of writing have thousands of lines.* I mean, if you looked at all the gags in comic art, it would show, you know, endless bureaus of thought and comedy. I was so impressed by her. She was somebody that really gave me a tremendous sense of unique belonging. Belonging to a very interesting and accomplished bunch of people. Yeah.

**Sacks:** . . . I know almost nothing about her, aside from obviously what I've seen on television over the years. It sounds like she really achieved the fame that she had hoped to have but worked extremely hard every day to accept it.

**Johnston:** Oh yeah. Oh yeah. She was very proud of the fact that she wrote all her own material. . . . She worked with Bob Hope a great deal. And the two of them traveled a lot to the USO events overseas and things like that. But he had writers working for him, and he would often do his monologues and they were memorized. But she not only could write her own material, but she was also very spontaneously funny, which a lot of comedians are not. If you watch *Comedians in Cars Having Coffee* with Jerry Seinfeld, some of those encounters are boring as hell. Others are hilarious because some of these people have the ability to riff and stand on a line, and you're giving them a line, and they create something that goes with it, and they're just naturally funny. Other comedians are not. It's hard work, you know. And it's writing and memorizing. It's a curious business, this making people laugh.

**Sacks:** Right! So that gets back to you wanting to be a stand-up comic, in some ways. You could play that game a little bit, and then you could go back to your normal life, being with a family. You got to balance it.

**Johnston:** As a stand-up comic, there is no normal life. I think it's probably the hardest job on the planet; I really do. That, and being a chef at a snotty restaurant! [*Laughs*] You're on your feet all day and everybody expects you to be wonderful and talented and give them what they want one hundred percent of the time, you know. You're feeding people when you're a stand-up comic. And they're not just happy with what you give them today. They want more and more and funnier and funnier because laughter is a drug, right? It's a drug. And so you want to suck that laughter out of comedians and performers. You want that as an audience. And there are times when your audience, you hate them because they want too much. If you're a musician, you can play the same song over and over again if the audience demands that, but if you're a comedian, they want new gags; they want funny stuff. And that's where YouTube is just such a terrible thing for comedians because people can see your material right there on YouTube and when you come to their town to do the show, they'll sit back in their chair and say, "Oh, I've heard that one before." How can you, how can you feed this insatiable mob? You cannot. And so that's where drugs come in. And that's where suicide comes in. That's where this devastation comes in. I think stand-up comedy is the hardest thing. So for those of us who are writers like yourself and myself and we can work in the privacy of our studio at home and put our work out there. And when you do put it out there, you fix the mistakes, you think. It's the best you could do that day. But if you're on the stage, you know you're within pelting distance of the first tomato, right? And, you know, they can reach you! So it's a tough one. For that, I had tremendous respect for Phyllis as well, because she, you know, she and Carol Burnett and all of these people, they just put their lives and their health on the line.

**Sacks:** And every moment, they could just be stumbling. Right. Yeah, anyone who was in the kind of written arts has the chance to revise and clean up their work. . . . Along those lines, you got me thinking about you going back and kind of revised some of your earliest strips. You were a little too loose, I think, for some of them? And then you ended up kind of feeling like that was a fool's errand to go cleaning up your early work? Am I getting that story right?

**Johnston:** For the first three years it was kind of a staggering walk until I could get up and sort of have a full gait that was comfortable. So that staggering first three years I really had not settled who the characters were or how these eventual storylines were going to evolve. So I went back to the roots of it and I cleaned up a lot of stuff so that the later stuff made sense. Then I took out some things that didn't make sense. Connie—this other neighbor who Elly was going to be very jealous of—was taking flying lessons when I first started the strip because I was taking flying lessons and I thought, *This is magic. This is incredible. What an experience!* And I wanted to share that. But I only mentioned that Connie was taking flying lessons and never went back to it. Partly because it was such a huge subject to cover and she was an auxiliary character; and the other was that I had to establish everybody else and what their lives were like. So I couldn't rush into that. So I think we chopped that right out. That's just one example of some of the things that I changed.

**Sacks:** So you changed a few, but you were the mostly we're happy with it? I mean, you obviously got a chance to reread and comment on everything in the first volume of the collection. How'd that feel to you, rereading it after these years?

**Johnston:** Well, I see that even though I thought I was hiding a lot of our private family truth in the fantasy and the comedy of it, I see that I was telling an awful lot of family truth right there. And you can't help it. You really can't. You write and draw what you know. And even if the names and places are changed to protect the innocent, it's still something you know.

**Sacks:** Well, sure, and the parents were analogs for you. I mean, your husband was a dentist and John's a dentist.

**Johnston:** Right.

**Sacks:** I mean, just even there the parallels are pretty obvious. There's a little couple of jokes about the pretty hygienist that you threw in there, which I'm sure are coming from real life.

**Johnston:** Well, that eventually came to haunt me, right. Eventually what happened was that a pretty hygienist became more than just a pretty hygienist. . . . And that happened at a time when I was thinking of wrapping up the strip at the end anyway. So that is one of the things that made me look at the comics and decide that I'm going to climb out of this fantasy world and live my own life and be real.

**Sacks:** Yeah well, you certainly had a great career of it. Interesting sort of fame you get from being a comic strip artist. You're one of the few artists who my parents would recognize her name, you and Charles Schulz and a few others. And yet we certainly had no idea what you look like except for the few rare times that you would appear on TV. So this is an odd sort of fame.

**Johnston:** Well, it's a healthy fame. It's much healthier, I think, than any other famous, quote-unquote, thing, because you can escape from the publicity, which, again, is a drug. It's wonderful when people ask your opinion, to be interviewed. I mean, you're asking me questions about my life, you know. I could just walk out of here and be nasty to everyone. [*Laughs*] "Don't you know who I am?" Right?

**Sacks:** True.

**Johnston:** So that kind of drug is dangerous as well. It does not do you or your family any good at all. So for the strip to be running a second time is a joy and a gift. And it gives me a chance to stand back and look at it again. I'm hearing from readers who were children when the strip came out. And now they're parents saying, "I'm looking at this from a totally different point of view. I had no idea how my mother felt, and now I do." And so we continue to work with the comics. As you see them now, they're running again. Some changes have been made with adding seat belts in cars, and we recently had to remove the words *Bill Cosby* from one of those punch lines.

**Sacks:** Yeah, sadly.

**Johnston:** So we're making a few minor, minor changes, but the strip is running as it ran. And I just can't believe how wonderful it is to see the work running a second time. But, I mean, I will read a book that I enjoyed a second time, so I'm grateful that people are happy to read it again.

**Sacks:** I definitely got a different perspective on it now than when I was reading it as a kid. I kind of fell away from reading your work when I moved out of the house and I stopped getting the newspaper. So it was a real education to get back—not education; a real pleasure to get back and catch up with these characters. And yeah, get different perspectives on their lives.

**Johnston:** You must read an awful lot of comic art, an awful lot of graphic novels, an awful lot of dialogue. You must just be immersed in it.

**Sacks:** Yeah, well, if you could see a photo of my office, I've got big bookshelves behind me filled with comics. Although I'm going through a phase where I'm reading classic science fiction these days. Different sort of entertainment, I suppose.

**Johnston:** That stuff scares me, science fiction. Because it's all coming true.

**Sacks:** Yeah. Yeah. In good ways and in bad ways. And it's remarkable how much prescient work there is about our current political situation.

**Johnston:** Yes, yes. It's all a very interesting story, isn't it? You can't make this stuff up, as they say.

**Sacks:** Oh my God. I don't want to go too far down that rabbit hole because I'll get depressed! [*Lynn laughs*] You may be retired, but you're still busy. You're working on your fabric business?

**Johnston:** We've been doing fabric design for the past four or five years, and we have not yet released them. We've just recently signed a contract with a licensing agency. And we're doing some really interesting stuff. It's not *For Better or For Worse*. We're using Farley the dog in quite a bit in some of the patterns, but these are, you know, cartoon characters, and they're funny, but they look more like paisley. And when you get close to them, you can see that they're zoo animals—

**Sacks:** Oh neat!

**Johnston:** —or cats or fish, or funny dogs or funny birds, cats, dogs, all mixed up together. And each one of these patterns that I do goes to a quilt designer who is just a genius. I love her to bits. And . . . she can create thirty patterns out of one design. So we have a tremendous number of colored and uncolored . . . I mean, the magic of Photoshop allows you to do everything from black lines and full color to monochromatic to whatever you want. So every pattern can be any size, any color. You can isolate one character from the pattern and make a pattern out of that.

So the new technology, as much as we sometimes hate it, has given us infinite freedom. It's like looking at the stars at night and wondering how far the universe goes. When it comes to these patterns, we can take a simple pattern and turn it into hundreds of other ideas. So we're exploring that, and my job is the staff artist. That's all I want to do is draw. And we're working on a bunch of other things. Of course, I occasionally do spot art for the strip and other publications as they come out. But for the most part, it's all completely new. And I'm also painting and trying to get myself to leave that black line alone to get into color and how one color pushes against another and leave a lump on the canvas and not smooth it out and try to make it perfect. I want imperfection again! [*Laughs*]

**Sacks:** Is it abstract art or representational?

**Johnston:** It's a bit of both. What I do is I take photographs of things I find the colors really intriguing and colors that I wouldn't normally put together. You know, roses and greens. If you take a photograph of a hillside covered with fireweed, for example, fireweed changes colors; it's pastel pink and deep rosy red and it's brown and scarlet and then it'll be on a bed of lichen, which is pastel green. I wouldn't put those colors together, but in nature, they're there. So I take these photographs and then I use the photographs to create realistic paintings but with a fantasy look to them. They're realistic colors, realistic designs, but it's different. Someday I'll do a show. Someday, you'll see what I'm working on. Right now, it's all experimental. And it goes along with the fabric designs, which are black lines and illustrative. And alongside it, you'll see these big canvases of color, which are something totally new. Anyways, yeah, it's a great life if your body works and you're healthy.

**Sacks:** Yeah, well, I hope you're doing okay.

**Johnston:** I'm seventy-two, and I'm doing okay! I don't think I've ever been happier. That's the key to longevity, to stay happy and healthy if you can.

**Sacks:** Yeah, that's it. That's the secret to life in general. And stay connected to your friends.

**Johnston:** Yes. Yes. I have a wealth of good friends.

**Sacks:** Well, it's been a tremendous pleasure talking to you today.

**Johnston:** Well, thank you so much for the call! And I really do hope that you come up and visit! I have your info written down here. I'm thrilled that Kurtis put us together. I love what you're doing because if it wasn't for yourself and people like Kurtis, a lot of us who, you know, blunder along drawing pictures for a living and our work would be lost to the wind, really. Giving stuff away and selling stuff and letting it slip out into the garbage. I mean, the fact that you all are so approving and interested in what we do has given it all such credibility, really.

**Sacks:** Well, thank you. We wouldn't feel that way if there wasn't worth, if wasn't worth celebrating and remembering. Like I mentioned, going back and rereading a lot of the old strips on your website has just been a tremendous pleasure.

**Johnston:** Well, thank you.

# *Blockhead*: Lynn Johnston Parts 1 and 2

## GEOFF GROGAN / 2020

From *Blockhead: Cartoonists Talk Comics* podcast (Part 1: March 12, 2020, Part 2: March 20, 2020). Reprinted by permission.

### PART 1

**Geoff Grogan:** Hello again, welcome to another edition of *Blockhead*. Today is a very special day, and we got an episode lined up for you. Yes indeed. This is the one I've been talking about for it seems like months now, but only it's only been a few weeks. But I've been anticipating it; I hope you have been too. Today we have a true cartooning legend with us. We have Lynn Johnston of the beloved comic strip *For Better or For Worse* to celebrate the forty-first anniversary of *For Better or For Worse*. We sit down with Lynn to talk about her life, her career, *For Better or For Worse*, how it developed, cartooning in general, Charles Schulz, comics—everything under the sun that we could think of, we touch base on in this conversation, and it's just terrific.

And I have to tell you, Lynn was just so forthcoming and so nice, and it was a real pleasure to have the opportunity to talk to her. And I have to say this was just one of the special moments in this podcast for me, so I think you're gonna enjoy it. If you're a fan of comics, if you're a fan of comic strips and cartooning over the last fifty or sixty years, and you care about comics history, then I know you must be a Lynn Johnston fan. So sit back and get ready.

Hello, Lynn Johnston! Welcome to *Blockhead*.

**Johnston:** Hello, thanks for calling.

**Grogan:** Sure. I mean, I'm thrilled to call. This is just a big, exciting moment for me to be able to reach out and talk to you, who is one of the greatest cartoonists the last fifty years. I mean, it's amazing. And it's fun and it's exciting. And I'm sitting on pins and needles here because I'm so excited to talk to you.

**Johnston:** Well, get up, get up! It's great. It's great to hear you say those lovely things because anytime I talk to anybody under, say, thirty, they have no idea what *For Better or For Worse* was; they know *Peanuts*, though.

**Grogan:** I guess, but still, *For Better or For Worse* is still in, what? Two thousand papers or something like that?

**Johnston:** It was twelve hundred, I think.

**Grogan:** Twelve hundred. Okay, that's just not because the strip is shrinking, but rather because the newspaper business is.

**Johnston:** It is, yeah.

**Grogan:** And yeah, it's interesting what you mentioned about folks under thirty. They just don't read newspapers like we did growing up, and I'm . . . a baby boomer, late-end baby boomer, so newspapers were a big part of my upbringing and a part of my everyday routine through adulthood. Up until even today, but I read them online. And you know, it's a changing world out there in terms of how people get their information, and it's impacted the comic strip industry. But *For Better or For Worse* is still out there and still available. And it's a stellar achievement. And last year was its fortieth anniversary, and you had a big retrospective.

**Johnston:** Yes, and we're very lucky to have a wonderful collection of books coming out through IDW in San Diego. They do classic comic strips just as they originally appeared in the paper. So everything you see in these fabulous books, there's going to be nine of them altogether, and they're huge. They're big, big collections. And they are the original colors, the original size, and it's really a lovely thing to be able to have.

**Grogan:** I have seen those books, and although my collections are all—I don't want to date myself, but they're all the older ones—I have seen those books. They are beautiful. IDW does a wonderful job reproducing your work and reproducing classic comic strips in general. It's a golden era for the reprinting of and collecting of classic comic strips.

**Johnston:** Well, I'm thrilled that that's the case because if it wasn't for the people who love the work and collect it and keep it in hermetically sealed files in the Library of Congress and other places—I mean, we don't take care of our work. And for the longest time, I had really no record except for what my web designer kept and what my father-in-law and all kept; he cut everything out and put it in scrapbooks. If it wasn't for the scrapbooks, we would have missed a lot of original art.

**Grogan:** Oh, yeah. And I'm sure cartoonists are notorious for not saving their work or for tossing it aside.

**Johnston:** Yeah, when you think about all the drawings, and where do you put it? Where to you put it?

**Grogan:** You gotta rent a storage container or facility just to store it because it's like ten thousand strips you've drawn, isn't it?

**Johnston:** About that, sure.

**Grogan:** Wow. Unbelievable. The strip ran for thirty years with all new material correct from 1979?

**Johnston:** Yes. Yeah.

**Grogan:** And then it went into reruns. So still thirty years of comic strips. It's unbelievable. Thirty years and 365 days a year. I'm not a math whiz. So I can't do the [math].

**Johnston:** Well, everybody who does a daily syndicated comic strip, that's their life. That's what you do. So everybody who's still working who started when I did, I mean, imagine the drawers and cabinets and plus the online filing.

**Grogan:** It's a ton of work that's out there and, you know, it's wonderful. There are institutions now that are trying to collect that material here in the US. Billy Ireland museum.

**Johnston:** Right.

**Grogan:** It's a great resource for collecting old comic strips and original artwork. And of course, the Shulz Museum has all of, not all of—

**Johnston:** Yeah. Yeah.

**Grogan:** —but a great chunk of Charles Shulz's work. And your work, your original work, was just in a retrospective exhibition. I guess it's traveling now. What was it at, the Art Gallery of Sudbury?

**Johnston:** It was in the Washington at the Canadian Embassy. It's just being packed up from there and sent back. Yeah.

**Grogan:** Oh, that's fantastic. I didn't realize it had gone to Washington.

**Johnston:** It's there. It's just finished now, packed up and sent back now.

**Grogan:** How did that retrospective come together? What was the impetus behind it, and who originated the idea, and how did it all come together?

**Johnston:** Well, it usually starts with one enthusiastic person who thinks it's a good idea. And that was somebody at the Sudbury Gallery in Canada. And it was really a year-long project because you have to write a catalog to go with it and then have merchandise and other stuff. And it was a well-received show, and it traveled around Ontario, and then it went out to eastern Canada. And then, just as we were packing it up from there, they requested it down in Washington, which was lovely. So it's down there now, just coming back.

**Grogan:** Right, there was original artwork, right? There was a lot of original art.

**Johnston:** Some of it was original, and some of it was, you know, there are wonderful copies now. Fabulous copies. And so some of the storylines like the death of Farley and Lawrence's coming-out story, they're in different archives. One is, I think, in the San Francisco Museum, and one of them is at the Ohio State [University], and then some are with the Canadian Archives as well. Some are not really that available, and it's much easier to copy it than to try and wrench it from the archives people who, with their gloved hands, hold on real tight! Who won't let anything go. [*Laughs*]

**Grogan:** Yeah, they don't want to let it go. You said it took about a year to put together. How were you involved in the choices for the material that was going to be the exhibition and storylines? Or were those pretty obvious things that were going to be focused?

**Johnston:** We do let them do the choosing, the people of the Sudbury Gallery, and there were things that they wanted to show. And also, it was a retrospective of work that I did when I was a little kid and the work that I'm doing now, which is surface designs, fabric designs for any kind of surface . . . because I don't want to stop working. And so we're working with T-shirt companies and ties and all kinds of other things just for fun. You know, just to get some new patterns, new ideas, new designs out there. So that's what we're messing around with right now.

And I paint on the side for fun.

**Grogan:** Oh, that's great, and some of that is available to be seen in this wonderful book—I think it's the catalog from the show—*The Comic Art of Lynn Johnston*, which is available pretty much anywhere and on Amazon, if people are interested. And there's a really generous selection of your wonderful fabric designs and your forays into painting and a number of different things that are all brand new. It's all pretty exciting.

**Johnston:** Sort of new. Yeah. Yeah. Sort of new. So you have to keep working. You have to keep going, and there's no possible way I could sustain a comic strip now. It's a huge amount of work. People tend to think, *Well, you just do a drawing a day and send it in*. But that's not the case. They don't accept anything less than a week's worth at a time. And the week's worth has to be good, you know, in order to make it good and well drawn and well thought out. I mean, it does take time, and you really have to work hard at it. You're working on planes and in hotel rooms and on holiday weekends. And yeah, it's a lot of work.

**Grogan:** It never stops. It's constant. I mean, I don't want to call it a grind, but it is a constant pressure, and that's great creatively. On the one hand, all of that pushing you to create. The cost of creation just makes you that much better. And certainly, you can see the evolution of your style artistically over the course of thirty years; it changes dramatically from the beginning.

**Johnston:** Everybody's style changes. Look at anybody's original bit. Young *Garfield*—look at the original Garfield. He looks nothing like today. And the original Charlie Brown looks nothing like Charlie Brown today. We all grow and change, and you can't help that because you want to improve. Once you get the job, you're just a fledgling, and once you learn how to handle those pens and you get the right paper, then you just want to get better and better at what you're doing. And it becomes your signature. You know, when you write your signature, it's never the same twice, but it's always identifiable as your signature because of the way you draw it. And so the comic art characters become part of your signature, and it just comes out of your pen the way it comes out. But it takes years of practice to get it to look the way it does when you're at the top of your game.

**Grogan:** Yeah, it's wonderful to see, comparing the early work that you did and those first strips, and you were trying to get a lot of information into the strips in those early ones. And you got tons of information into the strip in the later ones. And it's really interesting to see the distinction between how you approached all that information in the early years versus later. . . . I love the early style. Absolutely. It's wonderful. But it's interesting to see how in the later style, you become so much more of a designer in a way, in relationship to the earlier work, which is very intuitive and very free-flowing, and in the later work there's this understanding of how much is going to be legible in the newspaper. How much is going to be legible when you're looking at an illustration, how much is the reader going to pick up on it. There's just this enormous amount of control and skill that's evident.

**Johnston:** Well, two things. One, when I first started, it was going to be a gag a day, just a gag a day. But that didn't work out because I kept saying to myself, "And then what happened?" You do a gag, and one person barks at the other, and then you say, "But then there's always a comeuppance." If the kid yells at the mom, well, obviously the mom's gonna say, "That's not acceptable." And you've got another storyline starting. So after about the first two years, I started doing storylines, and that changed my writing style.

But the other thing that changed my drawing style was hiring another graphic artist to work with me. That was a lifesaver. She was a really talented girl, and she could use the pens that I used. I drew everything out in pencil, but the only thing I actually inked myself was the characters. I wouldn't let anybody touch those. But she inked everything else and erased the panel because every time I erase something, I don't know, I get a coffee ring on it, or I sneeze, or the ink goes with my eraser, and there you got a big Wite-Out patch to fix. And I loved it when Laura would just erase everything for me, and she was very clean, and a wonderfully talented artist. So that helped immeasurably.

**Grogan:** Well, yeah, absolutely. . . . This is cartooning stuff now, but we have a lot of cartoonists who listen to the show. So there's a wonderfully organic line that you have all the way through the strip, particularly in the figures. And I love that kind of flowing quality that you had. I mean, one of the things that I noticed when the strip first came out—and I was like eighteen or nineteen, I think, when the strip first came out, so I was reading it pretty much early on—and immediately I gravitated to it because it was new visuals on the comics page. But also, it was really clear that you loved to draw and you could really draw in a really beautiful way. There were a number of fairly well-drawn comic strips on the comics page in those days, and then there were a number of them that weren't quite so. But yours stood out because it had a very contemporary feeling, as well as being a very kind of flowing, fluid feeling, which it maintained all the way through the strip.

**Johnston:** It's funny that you would say it had a contemporary look because what I was using was the old flexible nib pen that you used in the 1930s, I guess. People would write with these old metal flexible nib pens. My mother was a calligrapher, actually; her dad was a stamp collector and dealer in forgeries. So they had these incredible displays, and all of the history of the stamps had to be written by calligraphy in the day. So my mother was a wonderful calligrapher, and she had all of these fine-tipped pens, one of which was a C6 Speedball pen, which I love. . . . It's not so long ago, but when I started school, we were using dip pens, and you'd have an inkwell in your desk, and of course, little kids are forever making use of that, right?

**Grogan:** Sure.

**Johnston:** But you did learn to use a quill-tip pen, which gives you that variable line, either a fine, fine hair or else a big wide line. When I'm drawing— and I'm pretty sure other people feel the same way, especially if you're using something that widens when you press on it—[I find that] you really breathe life into your characters with that line. You can push and pull on the line as if you were actually touching the character. So whenever I did the pencil line, I called it "ghosting," and when I drew the ink line over it, it was bringing the characters to life. And anytime I've ever done a workshop or worked with students at all, I talk about the ghost line and then the lifeline that comes when you actually touch that character with the ink and make it permanent.

**Grogan:** Oh, that's what brings it to life. Absolutely. And it's the variation in that line. As you said, that really imbues the sense of the artist's touch and also just a sense of vitality. Because that flat straight line, you know, just feels so dull and kind of dead, but when you bring that beautiful variation into the work, it really just sings. And that's great. So do you still work with those kinds of pens? You still work with the same pen?

**Johnston:** Yeah, I do.

**Grogan:** You do?

**Johnston:** Because I love the line, but because I'm seventy-two, and that's a pain in the neck because stuff starts working when you're older—you know, all the stuff that you took for granted, everything from your voice to your balance to your vision to whatever—there's changes. And my hands shake now, which drives me crazy. And I also have a growth in my right eye, so my depth perception is out. And you just say, "Damn body, damn!" [*Laughs*]

**Grogan:** Yeah, yeah. Joseph Campbell used to say you have to identify with the mind and just let the body go.

**Johnston:** Well, yeah, and don't look in the mirror. Don't look! Yeah, so I'm finding that the dip pen for me is a little bit of a problem now because my hands shake. . . . There's some wonderful products now [like] Staedler; there's wonderful products from Japan, Germany that are coming out that give you a really solid black line that you can erase or use Wite-Out over, it's lightfast, all of that. And I'm starting to use that more and more, and I use it on a tracing vellum, which is almost like a plastic. It's paper, but it's a drafting vellum. I draw in pencil on a piece of scrap—you know, a cheap piece of paper—and then over top of that I put this drafting vellum, so that if I make a mistake I can just either throw the vellum out or I can Wite-Out. But my original drawing is always there. And I know that people who work on computers have all kinds of ways of fixing things, but I'm not a tablet person. I never will be now because the learning curve is huge. But yeah, I work on vellum now with some really nice felt-tip pens.

**Grogan:** I've done that before, and so I'm familiar with the texture that vellum has when you put . . . there's a nice flowing quality. Yeah, it's really nice to where the ink goes down and whatnot, and it holds; it doesn't bleed—

**Johnston:** Right.

**Grogan:** —and you would think it would, and it doesn't, which is kind of cool. And I think that's something that a lot of folks who've done. I think have seen some stuff by Bill Watterson and others who have used similar materials in the past. I was gonna ask you . . . whether you've ever used the iPad or something like that, simply because there is the Apple pen. I was always reluctant to try it, but the Apple pen has great responsive quality, which is kind of nice. It didn't have it for the longest time, but now it does.

So now, at this point in your career, you're trying new things that actually you sort of tried a little bit when you had that time when you were in art school before you went out into the working world and took on a variety of different jobs. So it's kind of nice, in a way, to go back and resuscitate some of that interest in a variety of different mediums, and that must be very gratifying.

**Johnston:** It is. It's quite different. When I was in art school, I took the advertising program, and it was a fine arts college, and we were called the hacks. So anything that we did was considered, you know, commercial; we were the only ones that made a living in the end. You know, typically, in art school, your instructors, especially in advertising, might be twenty-five years out of date. So, you know, color was just starting to come into the newspapers; boy, I sound like a fossil. But color was just starting to come out in the newspapers, and only the front page was colored because it was so expensive and it was often misregistered so you get these halos of the red and blue and the initial printing colors. It was hard for them to register these first-page color printing systems. But in art school, we were saying, "Why are we doing everything in black and white and gray and using frisket paper and all this antiquated stuff when everything is color now?" We were desperate for color, so many of us quit and went into the workforce without graduating from art school because they just didn't have what we needed. I mean, you're wasting your time, right? So I got a job in an animation studio and decided that was where I wanted to go. And this was in Vancouver, Canada, and the animation studio was farming stuff; they were bringing stuff in from Hanna-Barbera and some of the other Saturday morning shows. And there was no art school for animators. So you had to apprentice just by working dog jobs in an animation studio, which is what I started to do. And that just changed my life. I decided that where I wanted to be was in animation.

**Grogan:** Ah, and that didn't quite work out, although there are animated versions of the comic strip. But you didn't stay in animation long, although I do understand that you did have at least some intermittent contact or brief contact with the Jay Ward Studios, who did [*Rocky and*] *Bullwinkle*.

**Johnston:** That's right. Well, a friend of mine was from Los Angeles, and she and I were working together; she had moved to Vancouver and was working in this studio with me, and the two of us were married to radio and TV guys, the Boss rock jocks type people. And off we went to Los Angeles to visit her family; they wrote for Disney. And we just went down to visit, and she and I took our folios, and her mom and dad said, "You guys have got to go in and do some searching around because it looks like you'd be great to work in animation down here where it's really happening." So both of us were offered a job at Jay Ward Studios.

They wanted us to start right away in backgrounds because we were both good artists, and our background art was good, and our storyboard art was good. But our husbands would not allow us to take the jobs because they would divorce us, right? Because they were in radio and TV. And radio and TV guys in Los Angeles . . . they're not gonna hire Canadians when they have their own folk coming out of technical schools ready to take up a microphone or a camera, right? So, sadly, we drove back to Canada with our husbands, the two of us in the back seat in tears that we couldn't work for *Super Chicken*, *George of the Jungle*, *Rocky and Bullwinkle*. It was just heartbreaking for us.

So we went we came back to Canada, and then I ended up moving with my husband to Ontario, Canada, because it was more work in television for him. And that's when I got a job at McMaster University as a medical artist. I applied for the job. I saw an ad in the paper, and I spent all night drawing guts and skeletons and muscles and whatever I could draw from *Gray's Anatomy* and *Grant's* [*Atlas of*] *Anatomy*. And I took my folio in and got the job, and they put me through first-year medical school with a couple of other very good artists, and they trained us their own way. They didn't hire medical illustrators from Toronto because that's a very specialized job. They wanted people that they wanted to hire and train. So that's what I did. And for about seven years, I worked as a medical illustrator or medical artist for McMaster University, and I used all my animation skills. It was very, very helpful.

**Grogan:** Wow! How did animation skills come into play in doing medical research?

**Johnston:** Well, one thing that I remember particularly was a biopsy needle. A biopsy needle is a strange split needle inside a tube. If you're doing a biopsy of the kidney, for example, you locate the position of the kidney and then you put the first tube in to touch the kidney. And the second tube is a split needle, and you have to push that down through the initial tube, and it goes into the kidney, and then you take the first tube, push it over top, and then you pull the whole thing out, which gives you a little tiny worm of kidney in the second needle inside. But to try to explain that or show somebody what it looks like, it's impossible. Even if you take someone into a clinic and do a biopsy on, say, a pig that's not alive, you know. You can do all kinds of things. But it's a drawing that will absolutely clearly show somebody how this works. So I was able to animate a kidney biopsy, for example. But I did heart surgery and all kinds of stuff. And there's all kinds of plastic surgical techniques that you really can't see in photographs because everything is red and yellow and the tissue is all different colors. So a drawing is so clear and so easy for a student to follow. They know exactly what they're looking at.

**Grogan:** Oh my gosh, I'd never thought of that before, but obviously, yeah, you need clarity. And that kind of clarity in image making is going to play a role in your comic work later on, because you've got to be able to communicate clearly with relatively simple drawings because they're going to be reduced so much.

**Johnston:** What it really helps with was anatomy. Like, I know my anatomy, I really do. And so when I took a sculpture course at one time, the sculptor had us begin with the skull, and then we added all the muscles on and then we added the flesh on the side, just to show you what the anatomy of the head was before you were actually going to try and do a portrait of somebody in clay. But I can do that in my head for the body because I had to work as a medical artist for so long and do so many illustrations of skeletal structure and muscular insertion, and you know, it's just such a useful thing to have if you're going to be drawing bodies of any kind, whether it's animal or human. You really need to know what the body, what the skeleton and what the muscular system is like underneath that surface, or you really cannot draw that well. It's essential. Unless, of course, you're drawing cartoons that are really cartoons, like big heads and little bodies and things like that, then you don't need that. But for me, I wanted it to be as realistic as possible.

And I used the *Archie* cartoons. They were very helpful. Not only were they beautifully drawn, but they would give you perspectives that were hard to draw and things like, what does it look like when two people hold hands? Unless you photograph two people holding hands from the back and the front, how do the fingers curl around one after the other, right? And *Archie* was great for clothing. I mean, they would research the clothing of the day, and everybody's wearing up to date. Especially Veronica and Betty, they're wearing the absolute fashion of the day, and I found that really helpful for resource material.

**Grogan:** Oh yeah. And those were beautifully drawn comics, as you said. One artist who always stands out to me is Harry Lucey. I don't know if you know his name, but he's one of those guys you saw in *Archie Comics*. You know, you identify him and say, "That's the good artist." He's really great, [and] Dan DeCarlo. I mean, both of them were just fabulous. I think what happens when you're looking at those comics is folks just sort of take them for granted. You know, they're beautifully produced, they're consistent, and they have all these wonderful qualities that we just sort of get used to and accept as being mass-produced, and we don't think about the people behind them, but they were masters.

**Johnston:** They were.

**Grogan:** Yeah, absolutely. Because there's a cartoony quality, but there's also a natural quality. Now, I haven't read *Archie* in a while, but I think they're going for a different, almost not naturalistic, but almost hyper superhero style. It's a little different. But I prefer those guys.

**Johnston:** You want something that the audience can live up to. I never liked superhero characters because, for me, they weren't believable, and especially the women were always these Barbie doll-looking characters and at first, it was, "Save me, Superman! Save me!" And I thought, *Oh, save yourself, you wimp!* I just couldn't identify with all these perfect people, but I love *Little Lulu* and *Dottie*, and I didn't like *Nancy* as a strip, but I loved those sloppy rounded characters because that was me. You know, that was something I could identify with. So I like realistic. I like stuff that is possible.

**Grogan:** Yeah. Oh yeah, absolutely. And that's one of the underlying qualities to *For Better or For Worse* that runs through the entire strip, and . . . I don't want to leave aside everything about your career trajectory yet, but I do want to comment on this. One of the wonderful things about this strip that I think is a minor miracle of a kind is that it's you found a way of weaving in everyday life, everyday occurrences, that feel very much a part of our lives as readers, and things that we're familiar with and we experience in one form or another. And yet you found the gentle humor in all of it. And I mean, some of its very touching, some of it's filled with pathos and brings tears to our eyes, but then other parts of it are just. . . . You find the humor in all of it, and every day it makes you want to read the next strip and the next strip and the next strip. There's just this wonderful balancing act that happens within *For Better or For Worse* that I think is really rare. And because it is so seamless, it's easy again, like *Archie Comics*; it's easy to take for granted because you do it so well.

**Johnston:** Well, thank you. Gee. I'm floating here!

**Grogan:** Well, I have to tell you, when I read *For Better or For Worse*—and in preparation to talk to you, you know, I went back and read a lot of stuff—I have to say it both makes me laugh and also almost brings me to tears while I'm reading it. Even the strips that are not necessarily sad, because it reminds me so much of things or feelings in general that happened in my own family, in my own life. And I think that readers all over the place have the same kind of relationship with the comic strip and I think that's just, like I said, a miracle to kind of be able to put all of these tendencies together, to come up with a strip that really reads as so universal.

**Johnston:** Well, it's kind of like *Seinfeld*, where it was a strip about nothing, right? *Seinfeld* was a show about nothing. And really everybody connected so gloriously with *Seinfeld*. For example, something like people who talk too slowly. [*Laughs*] I mean, just little things like that or things that you talk about with your friends over a beer, right? "Oh, that person drives me crazy because they're always saying, 'You know.'" Well, that could become a whole show in *Seinfeld*. It's something we all identify with. And I guess whenever I did a strip that was a little personal or a little goofy, I knew somebody out there would have that happen to them. And one that comes to mind is John Patterson in the comic strip drops a frozen turkey on his foot and he breaks his foot. . . . Because I went to buy one of these big twenty-pound turkeys one time, and as I picked it up out of the freezer with one of those little plastic handles, I thought, *If this handle breaks and it falls on my foot, I'd kill myself here.* So I did the strip knowing that somebody else there would have had this happen.

And as soon as the strip ran, I got a letter from a guy who said, "I did that. I dropped a frozen turkey on my foot." And he said, "I couldn't get any sympathy because it was funny. Everybody laughed, [but] I was in terrible pain." So I sent him the strip. That was my plan. The first person who called me, who wrote to me that they dropped the turkey on their foot, would get that original strip. And I had a nice dialogue with the guy afterward, you know. It connected me to all kinds of people.

**Grogan:** Yeah, it's funny because you mentioned something like that because we have a couple of dogs, and the dogs are driving my wife and I crazy because they want to go in and out all the time, particularly when we're in this one room where there's a sliding glass door, and they want to go in and out all the time. And I just read this strip the other day where Eddie and Dixie want to go in and out all the time, in and out, in and out, in and out. And it was perfect because it's exactly the experience that we're having, and *For Better or For Worse* does that so well it picks up on so many of these little moments as well as the big ones.

**Johnston:** I no longer have a pet.

**Grogan:** Ah, really.

**Johnston:** Because of these moments. [*Laughs*]

**Grogan:** Well, yeah, and I can understand that, at a certain point it gets cumbersome to be caring [for a pet].

**Johnston:** They were owning me.

**Grogan:** Yeah, and exactly. They will do that. They train you the way they want you to be trained. [*Laughs*] Ah, well. Getting back to your career, then. Now, it's interesting, the road to syndication for you was really pretty unique in a way. I mean, it grew out of visits to your obstetrician.

**Johnston:** Oh yeah, there was nothing on the ceiling above the examining table. He was one of the people that I did cartoons for. His name is Murray Enkin, and he was the pioneer in Canada for natural childbirth, for family childbirth, where the husband and children could come in and watch. And it was a whole new method. He really believed that midwives should be part of this. And so he had me do a whole lot of cartoons about childbirth and all the different exercises you take with the Lamaze methods of childbirth, things like that. So after seeing him as a physician and saying, "You know, you'd better put something on the ceiling over the examining tables," he said, "Well, you're the cartoonist, I challenge you to do some cartoons." So after my son was born, there were about eighty cartoons. And shortly after that, my husband left with the voluptuous script assistant. And I was on my own with a baby boy. So I was thinking the world had come to an end, and I was freelancing as a medical artist for McMaster and doing odd jobs and working in. . . . I started a little graphic art studio in my house, and it was doing quite well, actually. I had clients.

The trouble with your own business is that often people don't need you. You're desperate for that thirty bucks that's coming from Nova Scotia, and the dog magazine won't pay you. Argh! Anyway, when I got a call from my doctor to come over and have dinner, I was shocked. I mean, who gets an invitation from their obstetrician to go to their house? So when I got to the house, his wife opened the door and there he was, sitting in the middle of his living room with a bottle of champagne and all my cartoons around him in the order that I had done them. And he said, "Kid, you got a book," and he popped open the champagne. And he helped me get a publisher. And that first little book sold very well. So I did two more, all on raising little kids, and I thought, *This is what I'm gonna do. I'm gonna do freelance advertising, and I'll do a book a year, and that'll be me.* And I ended up getting a publisher in Minneapolis, who sent the books to the Universal Press Syndicate with a note saying "If you don't syndicate her, I will." And I got a twenty-year contract from Universal Press.

**Grogan:** Wow. On the basis of those books?

**Johnston:** Yeah.

**Grogan:** That's fantastic. What a story that is. And actually, you had some trouble getting paid for the books, didn't you?

**Johnston:** Oh, gosh. Yes. I mean, you go from publisher to publisher if you're doing these little press runs. And the first publisher was being funded by the Canada Council. And he got money from the Canada Council and put a pool in his backyard. [*Geoff laughs*] Yeah, and after a number of years, he owed me $20,000 for that first book, and rather than go to all the trouble of going to court and all that stuff, I just got the rights to the book back for that $20,000. . . . As an artist, especially as a young unknown artist—and as musicians and singers and dancers and artists of all kinds—you get taken advantage of because it's a skill that people think, *Oh, well, it comes to you for free, so that should come to me for free.* But you're not going to not pay your electrician, or you're not going to not pay your drywaller. . . . So it's subsistence living at the best, and I was very lucky to get this contract with Universal Press. And in the end, it was a good company to work for. It was a great company to work for. I'm very, very lucky. I got into it at a time when comics were still a big deal in the newspapers. And the newspapers were solid. Yeah, I was very lucky to get the job when I did.

**Grogan:** Well, the books that came out originally with those cartoons about pregnancy and about raising toddlers and whatnot—I'm not sure that folks, you know, particularly younger people, will be aware, but there was a period of time when just the word *pregnant* was something that people didn't say out loud in front of other people.

**Johnston:** No. . . .

**Grogan:** On television Rob and Laura Petrie slept in different beds, and no one talked about where little Ritchie came from. All of that was disguised, and there was this kind of veneer or cloak, this invisibility cloak, you know, over the whole process. And so when you were doing that, it was really unique to find comic material about what a woman goes through when she's pregnant and what happens in her life and particularly from a woman's point of view as well.

**Johnston:** There was a series of little books that came out, I think from Britain, and it was called *Eggbert and Eggberta.* And it was showing a baby in the womb and all the thoughts that a baby has, and it was considered really, really a serious breach. That's a funny word for this, but it was considered bad form. And anybody that owned these little books certainly kept them under brown paper wrapper. And all it was was a little baby in a shape that looked like a balloon around it. And he was thinking, and one I can remember was this little baby is squeezed, and he's saying, "Mom's wearing a girdle again." And things like that. And there's another one where the baby is looking through the opening of the balloon saying, "Peekaboo, I see you," as if the doctor is looking at it during birth or something. It was considered very, very bad taste this *Eggbert and Eggberta,* But I had seen those books and thought they were kind of cool. And I guess I'd been in my teens or something when the kids would pass them around, like, "Hey, did you see what I found?"

**Grogan:** But your books were very different in the sense that they were about the experiences you were having and the experiences other women were having at those times. I mean, it was from your point of view instead of from the child's point of view.

**Johnston:** Absolutely. And I tried to show all kinds of different people, different backgrounds, different types of people, and with their different attitudes. Some people are really looking forward to getting pregnant and excited about it, some people are shocked and weren't expecting it. Some people are expecting twins and aren't prepared. And so I tried to show all different ethnicities and different age groups and different situations so that it wasn't just one character and one person's experience. That was because I was still working as a medical artist, and I was still working for Dr. Enkin and doing all kinds of drawings for him.

**Grogan:** And you were seeing folks with all kinds of different backgrounds and experiences.

**Johnston:** Right.

**Grogan:** Yeah. . . . It's interesting. It's not the path you would normally think would lead to syndication, but in a way, if you hadn't worked in the hospital and you hadn't had the obstetrician you did, you may not have ended up with a syndication contract. You may have ended up doing something entirely different. Your graphic studio might have taken off, whatever, but it's kind of interesting that pathway that led you to the place that you needed to be.

**Johnston:** Well, I think everybody's got a story. Everybody has a story. There's always somebody who gives you a hand or offers advice or opens the door for you. And yeah, I've had some wonderful, wonderful people in my life who've helped me not only have the courage to do something, but once I got into it, to steer me along,

**Grogan:** And that's what happened once you got picked up by Universal and Lee Salem and the folks there started to work with you on a regular basis, help you put the strip together and formulate the strip. How did that process go? You're sort of thrown into it.

**Johnston:** Well, for the first six months, I asked if I could just practice. Some people who really want a career in syndicated comics, they work for a long time, sometimes a lifetime, perfecting their characters and storylines and ideas, and they submit something that's already got a form to it, but I had nothing. I just had my own family that I could maybe draw, if I was lucky, over and over again. And so I asked for this six-month development period. So I had to develop my contract, and I worked with Lee, and this was really before computers so you did everything on fax. Fax machine was an absolutely wonderful invention at the time. So I could send my pencil sketches to Lee by fax and he would call me, and we'd go over everything on the phone, and that was wonderful. I appreciated that so much. So after a while, I was confident that I could begin and then, it's like a raft going down the Colorado River. No paddles—you just hope to make it to the other end because you're not getting out! [*Laughs*] There's no place to stop!

**Grogan:** You had a twenty-year contract, so there was no way. So what kinds of things did Lee suggest about the strip and the characters, gags, and whatnot?

**Johnston:** Legibility, subject matter, economy of words. You need to write almost as if you're a poet so that your reader doesn't get hung up on words that are not necessarily suitable. You want to be able to get from the first panel to the end as easily and as smoothly as possible without stopping anywhere to say, "Wait a minute, I'm confused." And so it's a writing style, and it really is almost like poetry. So that the words flow from beginning to end, and that your gag line is well timed. It's timing as well. And Lee was an extremely good editor. So I really enjoyed his help. And, of course, he would tell me what was acceptable and what wasn't acceptable. You know, there are times when you think something's funny and nobody else does. And one of my very best editors was my mother-in-law, who never even got an elephant joke. And if she didn't get an idea, and I was like, "Look it's obvious. See, look, this is what happened. And here's the punch line . . . ," and she would say, "Yeah, but. . . ." And I knew that well, there's a huge percentage of my reader-ship that isn't going to get it. So Ruth was my best editor. I would take all my stuff to her first.

**Grogan:** Was that mostly in the early days, or did that last throughout your tenure on the strip?

**Johnston:** As long as Ruth was alive, she was one of my best editors. Because really, if somebody looks at something and says, "I don't get it," you really have to look at it again and say, "Yeah, if you don't get it, then others aren't going to get it either." I mean, there's a huge ego involved in something like this. If you get that job, your ego is just flat-out fat, right? So you think that you know it all and that whatever you do, other people should get it because you're so clever, but often cleverness is not enough. You have to be very clear, very obvious in what you're doing.

**Grogan:** You know, what's really astonishing is that you were coming from an art background primarily. You'd grown up as an artist, and all of a sudden, now you're in this field where writing is like ninety percent of what makes a successful syndicated cartoonist.

**Johnston:** Yeah, that's true. Yeah, if you don't have the writing, you don't have the art.

**Grogan:** Right. And the writing is really what carries it along. Because, you know, a variety of art styles can work within the world of comics, and it's always lovely to see beautiful art and whatnot. But if the writing is not there, then it falls flat. And the writing was really as you developed, the writing became more and more complex, more and more multilayered, you know.

**Johnston:** Yeah, it's a skill that you really do have to have. It takes a while to learn.

**Grogan:** Uh-huh. Yeah.

**Johnston:** Once you're there, it's really rewarding because you can edit yourself and you do know if something's going to work or if something is not going to work.

**Grogan:** As you were developing as a writer, you are going from this fairly small nuclear family to a multi-family epic in a way. How did you develop the skills? Was it just sort of a gradual growth? Because . . . it went from being strip being really about Elly and the children and John, and then everybody's growing up, and it becomes about their friends and it becomes more and more complex as time goes on, and then multigenerational. It's really quite extraordinary. That must have been a challenge.

**Johnston:** It had to happen. Because I get bored very quickly with things that aren't moving along. And so anytime I introduced a new character or change the ages of the character, it added more of a challenge to me, which added more interest to me, and I figured, if I'm bored with this, everybody else is going to be bored with this. So I might really have added too many characters, but if you think about your own life and you own family and all of the auxiliary friends and neighbors and teachers and the guy that sells you your groceries. Really, there are so many, each one of us has literally thousands of connections, if you think about it. So by the time I ended up the strip, I had well over a hundred characters that were there, whether it was friends, teachers, even the bus driver, all these different characters, which I had to learn how to draw and have a voice for—so it's an acting job as well.

**Grogan:** Where were the inspirations for these characters? Were they people who you encountered in life?

**Johnston:** Sure. Oh yeah. In fact, I think you really do need to imagine a certain individual if you're doing a character, whether you're acting or drawing a character. You really do need to think about somebody who would have that body language or that style of speech. The one character that really comes to mind is Aunt Fiona, who showed up after the character April is born. And she comes ostensibly to help, and she turns out to be the biggest nuisance in the world.

Well, she was based on my Aunt Margaret, who owned a pool hall and who was an alcoholic. She was funny, funny, funny. She kept a shotgun in her bathroom in case her ex-husband ever showed up, honest to God. "So Margaret," I said, "The room, the bathroom is so small you can't get the damn thing up to your shoulder properly." She says, "I don't care, honey. If he shows up, shoot him in the head, or I'll shoot him in the nuts. I don't care. One way or the other, he's going down!" [*Geoff laughs*] A shotgun in the bathroom. I mean funny, funny.

And it was a pool hall, and I loved the pool hall. And it was it had a really seedy, dirty little kitchen, and she made the hot dogs and burgers and fries for her customers and all the cues were bent. Holy smokes, what a place! And I was hoping that I could really show the pool hall, but she was too wonderful a character, and it would have just taken the strip away in another direction. So I had to just allude to the fact that she had a pool hall, and that was it. So yeah, eventually, there was too much material. It went on and on and on.

**Grogan:** And that could have been a strip unto itself.

**Johnston:** I mean, it would have been great. It would have been great. Because I had Margaret to think about, you know, and Margaret was a hoot. She was an absolute hoot.

**Grogan:** Oh my gosh. Were there any storylines at that point that were outright rejected by the syndicate?

**Johnston:** Ah. . . . There were a couple of situations that we didn't do because they were going to be either too close to home or kind of depressing, and I didn't want to do depressing stuff. And some things are unresolvable. The character next door, Annie, her husband, was a hoarder, and he was a womanizer, and she knew that he was unfaithful to her. And it was a big problem for her, but I never got into that story, although it was very clear in my mind. But I never got into it. And that was partly from talking to Lee and partly from just on my own, thinking that just might not be a great idea.

**Grogan:** Yeah. I mean, sometimes you can open up a door and that door can lead you down a path that just doesn't feel right, somehow or another.

**Johnston:** Yeah. Yeah. So that's the case. Yeah.


## PART 2

**Grogan:** One of the things about your work—well, the physical aspect of your work—you're in Vancouver. You've been in Canada all these years, and your syndicate is located in Kansas City. Did you ever have any trouble sending your strips from wherever you were living at the time? I know you lived in Ontario and then you moved west again. But did you ever have any glitches where strips got lost in the mail?

**Johnston:** Sure. Yeah, when we were sending hard copy, yeah. I had a whole pile of stuff lost; at one point I had to redo a full week of strips. I was grateful that it was just one week that was lost. But we'd have tracking numbers and everything, and you'd just assume that it's an art fan that might have just wandered off with your week's work. But if that was the case, it was never published, so it was probably never of any value.

**Grogan:** Oh my.

**Johnston:** Quickly, there was a system of being able to send everything by electronic mail. And so it was great for all of us.

**Grogan:** Yeah, I guess that sort of took hold in the mid-1990s. Right? Somewhere around there where you were able to start sending digital files.

**Johnston:** Yeah, it changed everything.

**Grogan:** Yeah, absolutely. Sure. Certainly, the convenience level and the timing level. But, boy, when you lost that week of strips, then you had to hustle to get everything together in a week again—you must have been losing your mind.

**Johnston:** Yeah, it was pretty tough. But then at the same time, every time you send out a package, you say to yourself, "I hope this gets there," and you have to be slightly prepared for not getting there. And when I did lose that week, I was living almost in the Arctic. It was as far north as you could drive in Manitoba, Canada, in a little tiny mining town. So the artwork had to go by Grey Goose Bus Line down to Winnipeg, and then on FedEx or Purolator from Winnipeg to Kansas City. So wherever it was lost, it was within that hop. I used to joke about sending stuff out by dog team, but it was pretty close.

**Grogan:** Oh my gosh, when you were working, you said you lost a week. So, fortunately, it was just a week. Usually, you sent out packages that were larger than that, I'm guessing—like four or five weeks?

**Johnston:** Oh no, no, you can't produce that much. Producing two weeks is a huge effort. Producing one week is sort of typical but it takes a couple of days to write two weeks. It takes a couple of days to draw it up. And then it takes some time to get it inked. And then you've got to get it out there. So it takes time to get the work out. It's not fast, it's not easy. And I guess at the time we had more space so there was more artwork. Maybe today people are just drawing stick figures and hope that the dialogue will get them through, but at the time we cared about the art and the backgrounds and what the reader was seeing.

**Grogan:** As time went on in *For Better or For Worse*, I think—as you note in *The Comic Art of Lynn Johnston*, the new book that's out—the work became more detailed and you became much more exacting in terms of what you were drawing for.

**Johnston:** Right.

**Grogan:** You would draw all the cans on the shelf in the grocery store or something like that. It must have taken you much longer than to prepare a week as time went on. Was that the case?

**Johnston:** No, no. I'm fast. I'm very quick, and I get my work done quickly. It's just that the inking is tiresome, and it takes time. And my assistant, you know, it took her time. She was quick as well. But it's not an easy job. I keep wanting to tell people that. People assume that it's an easy job, but the thought process that goes into it is really exhausting. There are times when you cannot think of one thing, nothing. But you still have to dedicate your writing day to thinking whatever you can think. And you'll sit there and nothing will come—at least, that happened to me. For a full forty-eight hours there might be nothing, and then the next day you'll think of two to three weeks, and you'll say, "Where were you yesterday? Where were you the day before?" This magic bubble that descends and gifts itself to you with this stuff. You know, there's this magic stuff that is not there from time to time. So you might lose three days of your week just trying to think of something. So it's not an easy job. It isn't.

**Grogan:** Yeah, especially when you think about the number of years you put in. I mean, thirty years working on the comic strip like that. As I was saying to a cartoonist a couple of weeks ago, it's one thing to do it for five years. It's another thing to do it for thirty years, and the idea is to keep pushing that creative mechanism within you, whatever it is. Then your creativity is responsive to your environment, right? To what's going on in your life, to what you ate that day, or whether you've got a headache or not.

**Johnston:** You get used to it. It's like any job that you get good at. I mean, if you're making leather straps, you're gonna get pretty good at those leather straps by the time you've done it for ten years, right? And so you're going to be a perfectionist, and you're going to make it a better leather strap. And by the time you've done it for thirty years, people come to you and ask, "How do you do this thing?" So it's like any other job that you've done for a long time: you get a rhythm to it, you get a sense of what you can do. You know who can help you with it, and you're dedicated to a deadline, a timeline. So that's helpful, but it's also it's like a big foot in your back at all times.

What happened to me was that I perfected the characters to the point where they were no longer easy to stretch and morph into comics. They were now very realistic. Once you give a character lips, it's no longer a cartoon. You can't yawn with the jaw to the floor anymore. It's got to be human. And I was talking about knowing my anatomy well from being a medical artist; well, eventually, I just turned everything real and was so focused on anatomy that I really lost the comic characters altogether. But I was also losing my babies and puppies and all the things that made the strip fun and funny. I had too many characters, and I really was ready to let it go. Also, my marriage was a wreck. I was having all kinds of trouble. And I kept thinking, *When the strip is finished, everything will be okay.* So I really thought that by ending the strip and now becoming secondary and hidden away and no longer "Lynn Johnston" that things would work for me, for our marriage, but that was not the case.

**Grogan:** I'm sorry. I'm sorry to hear that. The strip had autobiographical qualities to it. So as you're going through that, I suppose it must have been difficult to write it.

**Johnston:** Well, you do get into a zone of fantasy. And this was my fantasy world over which I had one hundred percent control, which was kind of nice, right? People come and go and people change jobs and people are threatened and people cry, and I'm God! I make it happen on the page. But in your own life, of course, this is nothing you personally can control. So in a way, it was kind of nice to fall into the fantasy world of everything I had control over. And we're actually pretty nice people in this family. We didn't destroy each other over this marriage breakdown. And I was able to, even after the divorce, continue for a while as I added new material to the old strips as it was being rerun. I didn't want it to run exactly as it had run because I didn't think it was good enough. So once they said to me that they would like to run it a second time, I wanted to fix the first three years, which I did! Yeah, I added lots of new material, and it was really kind of exciting and kind of fun, and I kept it alive, but I also had to write about a marriage that was working when mine really had broken down.

**Grogan:** Yeah, and I don't want to touch on a sore spot, but it must have been a sense of melancholy in reliving some of what you were going through as you're reworking the strip and dealing with Elly and John.

**Johnston:** Sure.

**Grogan:** I can imagine that would have been a very personal thing.

**Johnston:** But it was also helpful.

**Grogan:** Healing maybe in a way, too?

**Johnston:** Hmmm. Yeah, well, you know, you're in love with the person you marry, right? And the marriage lasts for as long as the two of you can make it work. And at first, everything's fine, right? So I was able to go back to the "everything's fine" stage.

**Grogan:** It's great that there's a record of it in the comic strip in a way. In *For Better or For Worse*, one of the things I just love about it is how organic it is and how natural it feels and every aspect of it, the development of the characters in the life and everything. . . . I suppose that has to do with the fact that the characters age in time. But it's also in the way that you write them, in the way that you care for them. I really get the sense as I read the strip that you really love the Pattersons. You really loved Elly and John and Michael and April and Elizabeth. I mean, there's this sense of that warmth that you have for the characters too. And I think that's one of the things that makes it feel so universal to the reader and brings us in and makes it so tangible to us as readers.

**Johnston:** It really was based on real stuff, real people. It really was. Friends from my past and friends in the neighborhood and my family and my extended family. Yeah. Because you can't write about what you don't know. I mean, I never would have been able to write about working on a farm if I hadn't worked on my sister and brother-in-law's farm, and that was fabulous education. I mean, boy, what respect I have for farmers! And even in the worst of times, there's some wonderful humor that keeps everybody going out there on the farm. And yeah, I really had some great adventures that helped to connect me to real-life situations. And it was far more interesting if I changed the characters' locations, introduced new neighbors, brought in family members that were new, and I had to learn how to draw them over and over again. I mean, I really got bored fast. So I entertained myself by switching things up often.

**Grogan:** Yes, yeah. It's also that's the way life is, you know.

**Johnston:** Yeah.

**Grogan:** And that's the way *For Better or For Worse* feels. The changes feel natural, they don't feel imposed. And I think that's one of the things it's hard to do. It's really easy to contrive a situation and put your characters into that, but it reads as contrived, and that never happened in *For Better or For Worse*. It always feels very natural and organic, as though it's happening as life happens, and I think that's kind of a magic quality. That's not easily put in a bottle or onto the comics page

**Johnston:** Well, there are many characters that don't change. They work with writers, and that's a fabulous relationship. I mean, if you can work with a good writer that loves your characters, it really is a love affair. You know the characters well enough to know what they would and wouldn't do. So I have no qualms at all about working with writers if you have characters that stay the same because after a while you really do need some input. I think the only person I know—there are probably many more, but I know that Charles Schulz never worked with writers. He was always very proud of the fact that he came up with all his own material all the time.

**Grogan:** Yeah, in fact, from what I've read, he rejected ideas that came from family members or from letters or from other people. They'd say, "Here's an idea that's a good one." He might think it was a good idea, but he wouldn't touch it, because he didn't come up with it.

**Johnston:** In fact, I have a story for you. We used to call each other every so often; we were quite good friends. And he called me one day and said, "I can't think of a single thing. My brain is blank. I got my deadline. And how are you today?" That kind of thing. And he said, "I'm up and down and up and down. I'm on the bungee cord of life." And I said, "Sparky, that's a daily right there, a bungee cord of life." And he said, "Well, you came up with that." I said, "No, I didn't. You did!" Anyways, he said, "I'm not going to use that."

And a while later, he called me up again on one of these things. "Well, I can't think of anything today," and I said, "What about the bungee cord of life?" and he said, "Well, you came up with that!" I said, "Absolutely not!" And I gave him the conversation over again. So he used it. And he sent me the original with a note that I thought that was great fun. But it certainly made it clear to me that he didn't use anybody else's ideas. I had to convince him it was his.

**Grogan:** Oh my gosh, yeah, that is something for sure. Because he had that sense of pride. So tell me, what was your relationship with Charles Schulz like?

**Johnston:** Well, everybody needs a mentor. Everybody needs somebody whose approval they work for. And he was my approval guy. I mean, I also wanted to work for the approval of Lee, who was my editor, and Sue, who was my other editor at the syndicate, but I always used to secretly say to myself, "I hope Sparky likes this one," right? I did work for his approval. I really wanted him to call me up and say, "That was a good one." He always liked the ones that I did with the dog.

**Grogan:** Wow. And I guess the story that is out in the world I've heard before is that he was very upset when Farley passed away.

**Johnston:** [*Laughs*] Well, to the point where he said to me, "If you kill off that dog, I'm gonna have Snoopy hit by a truck, and he's going to be in hospital, and everybody will care about Snoopy and nobody will care about your dumb story!" And he was quite angry. And so I didn't tell him when I was going to do this because I knew he would bark at me. So I wrote the story. And I cleared it with my editors. And I sent it out, and it ran. And he was kind of blindsided by it. And he called me up, and he said, "That stupid little girl! That stupid April! What in the world was she doing? Going down to the creek? Where were her parents? That stupid little girl!" And I was shocked that he would see it as a window into the real world. And I knew that it was a story, but when he said April was to blame, that stupid little girl. I was shocked. I was surprised. It was a different response altogether than I expected.

**Grogan:** And did he eventually come to terms with it?

**Johnston:** Oh, of course. It's our job. You can't tell anybody how to do their job. . . . It's not considered proper to criticize other people's work. And of course, everything was fine, but my characters grew and changed. So I had no choice. You either do the thing right, or you don't do it at all. I could have had the oldest dog on the planet, and that would have made readers wonder about my credibility.

**Grogan:** I think about Farley and all the dogs in the strip, but Farley was in particular a very popular character, and quite rightly. When you follow Farley around the strip, he's just this happy-go-lucky, lumbering, kind of beautiful spirit that pervades the strip.

I can see Charles Schulz seeing in Farley maybe the dog he might have wanted to have done, but never did. You know, the real dog because Farley is a real dog. He's not a Snoopy. He's not a thinking, speaking dog like the anthropomorphic dogs in so many different comics. So maybe, in a way, he felt a certain sense of—I don't know, I don't want to say ownership, but a sense of connection to Farley.

**Johnston:** I don't think so. I really don't.

**Grogan:** No?

**Johnston:** Oh no, he loved Snoopy. He loved the magic of Snoopy, and in a way, he *was* Snoopy; you know, he could be magical just by the things that he could do. He had a skating rink and he was involved with community events and things like that. And if he wanted to see something happen, he could make it happen. But Snoopy was absolutely magical. And he identified with that character to a great degree, but he loved his dog. He had a real little terrier dog that he just absolutely adored. And when that dog ran away, it just broke his heart. So he loved real animals, but I don't think he ever looked at anybody else's work and wished that he had done something similar. We all just appreciated each other. Our work is all separate. None of us really took anything from anybody else other than the joy of being in the same industry. No, I think he liked my drawing. And he often said that he liked my drawing, and he particularly liked that character.

**Grogan:** I was just thinking that he was a fan of *For Better or For Worse*, though. Even if he didn't know you. I think he was a fan of the strip.

**Johnston:** Yeah.

**Grogan:** Which is great. I think that's just a great accolade. You know, nothing's better than that, really.

**Johnston:** Well, you really want your contemporaries to feel that you are part of the team; you know that you're one of them. Yeah, it was great fun. It was fun to know him and to know so many of the other people from *MAD* magazine and people who work for Disney. The connections that you make through the National Cartoonists Society are just fabulous. I mean, friends for life. I've known these people for forty years now, and we've watched our kids grow up, and we visited each other, and it's just been a joy.

**Grogan:** Seems like a wonderful organization. And it's great. And you do read all these wonderful stories. There was a book that came out a couple of years ago by the son of John Cullen Murphy called *Cartoon Country*, which sort of was about cartoonists living in Connecticut and how they were all connected. John Murphy and Mort Walker and the Walker family and other cartoonists as well. Anyway, it's a lovely book, and you really do get a sense of community, that there is a shared connection between all cartoonists, as isolated as they are in their work.

**Johnston:** Well, I sat next to John Cullen Murphy at a dinner one time, and I looked at him and I said, "John, are you Prince Valiant?" And he looked at me with this dreamy expression, and he said, "Ohhh, yes!" [*Laughs*] You know, you have to be the character in order to breathe life into the character. So you become the character that you work with.

**Grogan:** Do you feel that way about all of your characters, that is there's a piece of you and each of those characters?

**Johnston:** Absolutely. There has to be. No question. Even the pets.

**Grogan:** Yeah, well, and even the pets! [*Both laugh*] Oh my gosh. And Elly particular. I love Elly; I think of all the characters in the strip, she's got to be my favorite character. She holds the strip together. But how did it feel to let them all go at the end?

**Johnston:** It was a huge relief. I wanted it to end because I knew I couldn't continue it. I couldn't make it better than it was. I think I was at the top of my game, and I think it's better to let something go when you know that you've told the story, rather than just sort of drag it on and drag it on. If you're not happy with it, and if you feel like you're dragging it on, then it's going to be evident in the work you do. So I stopped at the right time, and it was a relief.

**Grogan:** Garry Trudeau took vacations, took time away from the strip for a couple years, and then came back to it. Berkeley Breathed did the same thing. Do you think that that would have worked for you? Because you never did that.

**Johnston:** No.

**Grogan:** It wasn't the right thing for you, that kind of thing?

**Johnston:** No, it wasn't the right thing. I thought about it. Physically, I can't do it. I think I told you I have a growth in my right eye, and I have what's called a central tremor in my hand. So there are times when my right hand shakes so much that I can't even write a letter. Physically, it would be daunting. Even with the help from a writer, it would be daunting. But the one thing that has been presented to me recently is the possibility of doing a live-action show. So I've met with writers, we've talked about it. You need the right people who actually have a comic outlook. Somebody who does stand-up comedy could write a comic strip because they have that kind of twisted look on life right? So I'm working with people to find the right team. And if it happens, it happens. And if it doesn't, that's great, too. If it doesn't happen, it'll be a relief. [*Laughs*] If it does happen, it'll be a huge amount of work, but it has to start out fun, or you shouldn't do it.

**Grogan:** And this is retirement for you?

**Johnston:** Oh yeah. Yeah.

**Grogan:** So you're busy more. You're just as busy now as you were then almost. So will this just be Canadian National Broadcasting Company, the people who do *Murdoch Mysteries* and things like that?

**Johnston:** Yeah, I think they would be the first ones that we would approach, and it's a work in process just to get a pitch ready. So we've created one and dissolved that one, and we're in the process of creating a second one, and that may well be ready to go within the next six, eight months.

**Grogan:** Wow, that's fantastic. I feel like I just got a scoop. I'm so excited.

**Johnston:** You know, be careful what you're digging into when you think you've got a scoop.

**Grogan:** It reminds me now of the animated shows. How many of those did you do, five or six of those shows?

**Johnston:** There's about twenty, I guess, altogether.

**Grogan:** Really? Are there that many?

**Johnston:** Well, they're all Canadian animation studios, and animation studios die very easily. It's a hugely expensive project. And if you get too fancy a studio and take your family to the Cannes Film Festival, and buy yourself a couple of fancy cars and don't put the money into the shows, eventually, you say, "What happened?" as the creditors come in, right? Every animation studio I've worked with in Canada has gone belly up for one reason or another. I did one show with one company; eight shows with another company; sixteen shows with another company.

**Grogan:** Oh my gosh.

**Johnston:** . . . And all three companies went belly up. But it was not an easy process because of the financial crunch. You can run out of money pretty quickly, but you still have so many shows to deliver. And the quality gets worse and worse as money dries up. So eventually, you're turning out horrible stuff. And there's that old joke, "fix it in the postproduction." You can add sound effects, perhaps, or maybe edit things differently. But you can only fix so much in post. So "fix it in post" became my Kleenex, and I'd cry when I heard about that, you know. [*Laughs*]

**Grogan:** So from what I understand from the book, when you prepared for the animated work—at first, anyway—you went through this whole process of working out the architecture of the house and nailing down all of the details and whatnot, so it had an impact on the strip.

**Johnston:** It did. Oh yeah. You're actually creating imagery for artists to work with—they have to know, when you go in the front door, do you turn right to go to the kitchen or do you turn left? And how long is the hallway and what's out the back door? And stuff that was almost all fantasy. I mean, it was real to a certain extent because it was based on real houses, but I added rooms and subtracted rooms, and if you look at things like *Family Circus*, if Bil [Keane] wanted a kitchen on the right, it was on the right. If he wanted you on the left, it was on the left, and I think there wasn't a consistent illustration because it was done to suit the joke as a single-panel gag. But my characters would walk from room to room, so I did know where the stairwells were and what the wallpaper was like, but really, when you do animation, you need an aerial view. You need to be able to see the community, you need to float up above everything and see where the road goes, and do you turn right at the end of the road to go to town or left? I mean, it's that exact. So there was a huge amount of research done just to get the neighborhood right and where the fences were, where the neighbors were, and what shape the houses were in, and it's a huge process. And I loved the artists I worked with. They were just genius. I just loved them. I loved the writers. I loved the artists. I loved the photographers and musicians and the people who did the voices. It was a joy to work with all of them. It was actually the companies themselves that fell out of the sky. It's just too expensive. It's too expensive.

**Grogan:** Yeah, at least, certainly in those days it was. I don't know about now. But so much of it is farmed out of the Western Hemisphere and sent over to Korea to be worked on.

**Johnston:** Exactly. That's what happened to us.

**Grogan:** Oh really?

**Johnston:** Oh sure. They would send things to Korea or the Philippines or to India. And if the storyboard was wrong, the animators in India would animate incorrectly. And I would be fixing the storyboard, not knowing they had sent it already. And it was already being animated and it was already wrong. Well, how do you fix that in post? And so there were endless problems because you're farming things out. And in fact, the only way to stay alive as a small animation studio is to accept stuff that's farmed out. So you'll get ten scenes from, I don't know, Hanna-Barbera or something. You take piecework so that you can keep your artists and staff working and you keep money coming into the company. It's awfully hard for animators to get a full-time job anywhere. I mean, if you want to work in serious animation, sometimes you've just got to travel all the time.

**Grogan:** Wow. So it sounds to me like the creative process was great, but the frustrations were obviously there in the business and it would be not something you want to get back involved with again.

**Johnston:** No, I don't. And that's why any live action, any discussion of it, I'm looking at very carefully and very skeptically. Every time I got an offer to do live action or series or something in California, [the message] was, "Well, you gotta move everybody to the States." It's a Canadian show so we never did handle it that way. But it was evident to me that it was always going to be a really big project with diverse people. And it was never going to be easy.

**Grogan:** So you worked on the storyboards for the animated shows? Did you do a number of those? Did you do all of those?

**Johnston:** Storyboards are done by other artists. There is so much work to do, and I was working on the strip as well. So there is an enormous amount of work to do. And some people are just storyboard artists. I have a friend who teaches storyboard. It's a skill unto itself. It's setting up all the scenes, all the camera positions, everything. And it's done by people who do this for a living. And sometimes they misinterpret the script or they have a view of something that isn't quite right.

Here's an example. I have a bunch of kids in a school bus. The kids in the very back of the bus are shouting forward at the kids at the front of the bus. The storyboard artist makes a mistake and shows the kids answering facing forward.

The people in the front of the bus would be answering facing backward, right? Well, in the storyboard, if the artists makes a mistake and it has the kids shouting forward, that has to be changed. In fact, the whole perspective has to be changed from the backs of the heads of the kids in the back of the bus and the kids at the front of the bus turning around and shouting back to them. If that's already being animated in India, what the heck do you do? It's totally wrong. Do you cut the scene out? It's an important scene because they're saying an important thing. So do you suddenly show a picture of the bus and just the voiceover as the bus is rattling down the road? Well, maybe, except that they didn't want to show the background going by because it was expensive to do a long background to show the bus rattling down the road. Waaahhh!

**Grogan:** One problem leads to fifteen other problems.

**Johnston:** Or a really crappy show. And we ended up doing some pretty crappy shows. You don't want to apologize for your work. And people see the work and know that it's crappy. They say, "Well, Lynn Johnston produced a crappy show." But it's not just one person, right? It's just a whole bunch of circumstances. So anything that gets done, which is great and beautiful, you have to say that's an exception. That's Pixar and some of these wonderful big studios that can afford to do the best with the best people and keep them fully employed on an annual basis, which is hard for small studios to do.

Wow! We're way off on a tangent here!

**Grogan:** We are, we are! But it's interesting because I don't think people, in particular comics fans, are that cognizant of your work in animation and the story behind it. So I think it's interesting information and very worth talking about, so I'm glad we went that way. But okay, let's get back to comics and to the comic strip itself.

There's a couple of things I still want to touch on. In particular, through the course of thirty years, you had a number of storylines that had a huge impact on your audience and were very well—I don't wanna say to they were publicized; they weren't, but they were well known and had an impact in the media and in the culture. And in particular, I'm thinking first of Farley passing, which had a huge impact, and as you've noted and others have noted, I think it's probably the one thing that really stands out to people most when they think about *For Better or For Worse*. Farley's passing is probably the major thing that hits them for because we love our pets.

**Johnston:** Here's what happened at the time. When you send work out to the syndicate, it's six to eight weeks in advance right of the publication date. And you don't know what the headlines in the newspaper are going to be on that date, on any given day, right? The headline can be set, but if a bridge collapses in the middle of the night, they're changing the headlines immediately. So when Farley died, it was the exact time of the Oklahoma bombing, so nobody wanted to see anything negative anywhere. People turn to the comics page for a smile or a laugh or just to relax. And the story, which I had sent into the syndicate six weeks in advance or maybe more, it was set to run. And it ran. Because that's what packages of comics do when they are sent to the newspapers, and the editors don't change the comics page because it's the one page they don't have to worry about. Every other page changes with the headlines. If you put a brand-new headline on the front page, every other big article has to be juggled all the way through the paper, so it's a huge job. Even with electronic help now. But at one time, of course, when I first started, they'd have to reset metal type and things like that. So the page was set, they couldn't change it, the story ran. and it was a devastating story because people were crying on the subways as they read the comics, and it was awful. And at the same time, a child had died in a flood in Edmonton because they had gone down to behind their house to where a river had overflowed. And this little kid died in this flood, and the story was used in Edmonton to keep kids out of their rivers and canals as the spring runoff happened or whenever it was. I can't remember when the Oklahoma bombing happened, which maybe is a good thing. Anyways, this horrible event happened at the same time, and that's one of the reasons why the death of Farley was such a troublesome story.

**Grogan:** Hmm. Hmm. Yeah, because of the coinciding with a terrible tragedy. Yeah.

**Johnston:** I mean, the death of the dog wasn't a tragedy. He died a hero, and all that kind of thing and pets pass away. They have a lifespan of only so many years. But for it to happen at the time of a real horrible, horrific tragedy, it really was a difficult time for everybody.

**Grogan:** Farley was such a beloved animal, beloved dog, and it's funny, as we're talking about him, I feel like he's real. And that's an odd thing to say, but it's true. And when Farley passed away, it broke my heart, and whenever I go back to that story and read it now, it still breaks my heart. Such a beautiful spirit and what he did you.

**Johnston:** Well, I could bring him back to life again pretty easily, Geoff. [*Laughs*]

**Grogan:** I guess you could! If anybody could, you could.

**Johnston:** I need a pen or pencil, and he's barking again.

**Grogan:** So among the other storylines that stands out, of course, is Lawrence coming out, Michael's friend Lawrence. Looking back on it, it's amazing, really, how resonant that story is today because I think we're in a different time, a different world, a more accepting period of time—at least, we hope it is. And that particular story came out in a time when it was still controversial, still something that people didn't talk a lot about, coming-out stories, and there's a whole population who had blinders on in regard to these issues. And so that was a brave thing to do. And I think it had a huge impact as well.

**Johnston:** I didn't think it was a brave thing to do at the time. I thought it was an essential thing to do at the time. If I was writing about real people and a real community, it was part of the real community and certainly it was part of my life. My brother-in-law was gay. And of course, as an artist, you grow up, go to art school, and you're involved in the theater and music and dance and all those things, and so many people are. We're all a mix, aren't we? We're all a mix. And so when a friend of mine was murdered for his bicycle and his stereo, I decided that I was going to write this story. And it was written for my friend Michael, who the character is named for, and he was a Toronto stand-up comedian and he was a comedy writer for the CBC, which is the Canadian Broadcast [Corporation]. And he was a single fellow and busy in the theater, and busy writing and had all kinds of friends, and he was out and about, and he met this young man who was homeless at the time, and Michael gave him forty bucks, and he said, "There's a shelter down the street. You can get yourself a meal and get yourself a night there for this. So get yourself something to eat and get yourself there. You can have a shower."

Well, the kid followed Michael home, and he went and bought himself a knife with the forty bucks and knocked on Michael's door. And when Michael opened the door, he slit his throat.

**Grogan:** Oh my gosh.

**Johnston:** He took his bicycle and his stereo, and he was gone. And when he was finally found, the authorities seemed to be on the side of the young man who committed the murder because he was a homeless youth and all of this kind of thing and "poor young man."

They had an attitude that was "Well, there's another predator off the street." But Michael, he wasn't a predator. He was tiny, slender, young guy. He played the part of Peter Pan because they could lift him up on a wire and swing them around the theater. He wasn't the type of person you consider a predator. And he was a stand-up comic, for heaven's sakes. I mean, he was goofy and loving and personable. And for him to be murdered like this was just unbelievably unfair and shocking for me. And I thought, *Michael, this is a story for you. I've known you since we were thirteen years old, listening to* The Goon Show *on records at your house.* We'd grown up together. And so I did the story for him.

**Grogan:** Yeah, and it's a beautiful story. And it's a beautiful tribute to your friend in the end. One of the things I note is that you didn't think it was brave, but I think that's the hallmark of courage, really. It's that the person who shows the most courage is a person who doesn't think anything about it. And I think other cartoonists in situations. . . .

**Johnston:** If you do a movie [that makes people angry], they'll be angry with you for that day because the movie is over and they're mad. Or they might be angry with you for a few days afterwards. But if you're doing a comic strip, they're angry with you everyday that comic strip runs.

And so we got about three thousand letters from people. And in that three thousand letters, seventy percent were positive, but the negative ones were terrifying! And they were from people who didn't know who I was. Didn't know what I did. They were told to write because they were part of a religious group or part of a very negative group. And it was quite terrifying. And I heard from editors from newspapers all over North America from seven in the morning till eleven at night, every single day. I answered all the calls, and I answered all the letters; anything that was reasonable I answered, even the negative ones. If somebody had a really good point, you wanted to let them know you read them, heard them, and were responding, right? And so I was responsible all the way through this.

And the people who were most interesting to listen to were editors from really small towns in the United States who, as open-minded editors, believed they should run the story, but these people were personally attacked in their hometown. In a small hometown, where the editor is going to be at the local coffee shop or at the theater or taking his kids to school. These editors were attacked. And they would call me and say, "You have no idea what my life is like, and I'm going to have to stop running the strip because my dog was spray painted, my house was egged, my children were attacked at school." This was really something that was unprecedented, in my opinion. I had no idea that these editors would be attacked.

**Grogan:** Oh my gosh, nor would I! . . . Making your comic strip in your studio and doing what you think is absolutely right, you have no idea how— my gosh, to think that it would have those kinds of consequences with small-town editors. And then it just horrifies me to think that people would go to those kinds of lengths, whether you're upset or not. There are other ways to express your dissatisfaction with something, and those are the most terrible kinds of actions.

**Johnston:** People who don't know don't understand, right? Fear makes you do a lot of things that you normally wouldn't do, I would think. But it was fear and anger and upset. But for every negative thing that happened, the positive was overwhelmingly good. And I would lie awake at night thinking, *Why did I do this? Why did I do this?* But then you get a letter from somebody who said, "I haven't spoken to my mother for three years and today we hugged for the first time and talked." And, you know, it was wonderful. I heard from parents and kids and teachers and religious leaders, and it was a real event.

**Grogan:** It really was, and I think it moved a lot of people despite some of the negative responses. In general, it was a remarkable event, actually, because it was all over the news. And I think it's part of the civil rights movement that has led us to the place where we are today where we can speak openly about same-sex marriage and all of that. We've come a long way and still have a long way to go in many respects. But I think what you did is certainly part of that movement and contributed to its forward progress and I think that's, it's something to be proud of and it's not something that every cartoonist gets a chance to do nor would have the guts to do.

**Johnston:** You can only do it with a realistic strip, right? . . . [In some strips] you've got dogs that are talking to other dogs. Well, the cool thing about a dog strip is that you can have a small dog and a big fat dog and a long skinny dog, all different colors, and they all get along just great, you know? People are a lot more complicated. If you're doing a realistic strip, you can do realistic stories.

**Grogan:** Yeah, absolutely. And it impacts people in a real way. I was thinking about your character Elizabeth's ordeal with sexual assault and the trial that ensued afterward that ran in the strip. It's interesting to think back on that now because in the moment we are in now, Harvey Weinstein was just convicted of sexual assault and rape, and I don't know all of the charges that are against him, but he deserves whatever he gets. And I just think it's interesting to think about that how timely that story is and how resonant that story remains here today, where we're in the aftermath. We're living through the moment of the #MeToo movement.

**Johnston:** Well, for me, it seemed like a good story to do because it was realistic. And she was in a situation where she was vulnerable [and] there was somebody in that building who was going to threaten her. It was a situation that sort of developed as I wrote the story of Elizabeth working at this garden center. I don't think there's a woman on the planet who has not been threatened at one point in time. I mean, certainly, we're vulnerable. And I've felt threatened. And although nothing happened [to Elizabeth]—because of course, good old Anthony with his white hat and his charging stallion comes leaping to the rescue—she's okay, but again, it's a realistic part of life that I wanted to explore as well.

But again, I was getting to the stage where it was at the end of my comic art career in the comics, and I was getting so that I was wondering, *How many of these realistic stories am I going to tell, and is this still a comic strip or is this a saga? Am I turning it into a drama now?* And I didn't want to do that. I still wanted the comedy. And I sort of written myself out of it because I no longer had puppies and little babies, and the babies that were there now had lips. [*Laughs*] Your drawing is your signature. And so if you draw a baby a certain way, all the babies are gonna look alike. So I changed them—not just hair, but I had to make some facial changes. So, again, you get the kid's eyebrows and eyelids and lips, you're doomed. It becomes realistic.

**Grogan:** And the stories became more realistic too. Again, I know I sound like a fan, but I am a fan, and so I still think, looking back at the strip, that you did find a way all the way through the strip to interject that humor. And even while the drama was becoming more pervasive and the realistic aspects of the strip became more prevalent, at the same time you found the humor in it all. And I think that's a saving grace because it's hard to go through life. People can go through life and through all of the drama and whatnot and come out having lost that really essential spark of life. But I think you've found a way throughout the whole run off the strip to keep that humor alive.

**Johnston:** Well, you can't survive without humor. I mean, I don't know how many funerals I've been to where people have been laughing. And it's a relief, and it's a joy to be able to see something funny in the middle of something awful. And I think that's why there's so much wonderful humor that has come out of really unpleasant situations. I mean, the First Nations people here in Canada are some of the funniest, funniest, most outrageously funny people! And I'm sure it's because they felt the life around them hasn't been so great from time to time, or for a lot of time. There are a lot of people who see humor in life to the point where it becomes food and water. It really does.

**Grogan:** Absolutely. If you succumb to every awful thing or pressure that you encounter in life, and without good humor, you've got no real response. It helps you survive those things. . . . It's just one of those essential attributes of being human, to be able to find the humor in those kinds of situations, those difficulties.

So one of the things I wanted to ask you about is that your strip is one of those strips, again, where the cast just grows and grows and the characters age, and it reminds me of a contemporary of yours, really. And that's the work of Garry Trudeau and *Doonesbury*. And that's the only other strip right off the top of my head, and there may be others, but it's the only one that I think of at the moment that came out after 1970. Obviously, *Gasoline Alley* beforehand had characters who age, but *Doonesbury* shares something with you in that the characters do age, although not in real time. But they do age. And there is this growing cast of characters. What did you think of *Doonesbury*? Did you read *Doonesbury*?

**Johnston:** Absolutely. Oh no, I read *Doonesbury*. And what captivated me was his political savvy. Not only his courage—in order to do a political cartoon, you really have to know your stuff, and you also have to be prepared to defend what you and your points of views. No, I've always been impressed by Garry's work, and he works again with an artist the way I did. And together, they produce some incredibly worthy material that sees the world from a totally point different point of view that draws you in. It's not just a single panel. It draws you into dialogue, and it draws you into situations. And I think it's wonderfully, wonderfully well done. Very, very clever, but smart. And I could never do editorial cartoons because I'm not that politically savvy. I don't know the politicians inside and out, and I don't have the thick skin that is required. I have a friend who is a political cartoonist, and she called me one day and said, "Lynn, I've just had my first death threat!" And I thought, *Really?* That would not make me happy!

**Grogan:** No, it's interesting to the politics of *Doonesbury*; I mean, obviously, Canada is our very close neighbor, and you're aware of what goes on in the United States simply out of proximity. And we share a lot in terms of culture, but there's a lot about the politics of this country, about the United States, that plays out in *Doonesbury*. Did those resonate, reading it in Canada?

**Johnston:** Sure, especially at the time when he was talking about the Vietnam War and the people who had come back and were exonerated and all of that type of thing because this was my area. I know a lot of people, including my editor, in fact, who moved to Canada because they were conscientious objectors, or they had been sent to Vietnam more than once and were not prepared to go back again. That was all that was all wonderfully interesting because it was from the American point of view. We lived at the other point of view, saying, "Come on up here if you want to get away from it." And he did. So I've always enjoyed his work. I liked the characters and I like the straightforwardness. But I also love the irony. He does do a strip that grows and changes, but *Luann* has grown and changed, and *Zits* has grown and changed, and I remember Jim Borgman talking about [whether] the kids [should] actually be able to drive that old van that they're fixing up. But that means they'd have to get driver's licenses, which means they'd have to grow up. So making a change like that does add an awful lot of material to your work if you can have the characters grow and change.

I mean, a lot of characters can't grow and change. *Garfield*, for example, has to stay the same. And *Mutts*, I would think, stays the same. But these are charming and wonderful characters, and you create things around them. This is where the comic mind has to be pretty exceptionally sharp. And occasionally you work with writers, and occasionally you sit there and scratch your head and wonder why you ever got into it. But those of us who've made it have a lot of respect for each other.

**Grogan:** Sure, because it's, first of all, it's a rare group.

**Johnston:** It is.

**Grogan:** And then secondly, in order to get there, you have to obviously have a skill set that is at a certain level, and so that is a rarefied group. You mentioned a couple of different strips; are those among the favorites you have of contemporary cartoonists or your own contemporaries?

**Johnston:** Well, we've known each other. We get together once a year, or sometimes we'll go visit each other. I've gone down and visited Greg Evans and stayed at his house and I've known his kids since they were little and that type of thing. And Jim Borgman is one of my favorite editorial cartoonists, and the work that he does on *Zits* is just fabulous. Mike Peters is a great friend. I love Cathy Guisewite. There's just people all over the States and Canada who have become part of my extended family just because we do this kind of work.

**Grogan:** So you mentioned Cathy Guisewite. Let's talk about her a little bit. She sort of broke the ground for women cartoonists, syndicated cartoonists, in the early 1970s. Did you interact with her in any way?

**Johnston:** Oh sure. I mean, Cathy broke the ground for me. Universal Press was looking for another woman cartoonist to do stories about family life from a woman's point of view. All the other strips were done by men, and even though some of them worked at home and probably did some vacuuming, they still kind of enjoyed the fact that dinner's on at six and the kids are washed and in bed to kiss goodnight, right? [*Laughs*] A lot of the guys are not really in the trenches. And so when they're writing about family life, it doesn't come from the same source.

They were actively looking for somebody who would do the type of work I did. And they saw that in the books that they received, and when they offered me the contract, I was actually given Cathy Guisewite's home phone number, with her approval. We talked quite a bit on the phone, and she was wonderful! Because I had no idea how to do this. I had done single-panel gags, and I had drawn all kinds of different characters, but to do something 365 days and something that was consistent, with consistent characters and storylines or gags—I was lost. I had no idea. So Cathy was great. And she told me write the way you would write a short play: write up the dialogue first and time it out in your head, but always do the writing first. And that worked for me because Cathy was a writer primarily, her dad was in advertising, and she had written for greeting cards and commercials. She was a writer, number one, and she found it really difficult to do the drawing. I was the other way around. I could do the drawing, but the writing was a challenge for me. So talking to Cathy was absolutely essential. And I'm so grateful to her for all the help she provided.

**Grogan:** Her strip is quite different from yours. I mean, you know the story about Cathy and her foibles and the issues that women faced in the 1970s and '80s and '90s. It was very different in its approach, I think, than your strip. Did you bounce off of that, or did you get inspiration from what she was doing?

**Johnston:** What I got from Cathy was friendship. Again, when you are in this business, everybody's work is their signature. Everybody's work is their voice. And you get to know a lot about them just by the work that they do. And sometimes it's surprising; sometimes they are not the character that they draw. Maybe they get all of that out on the paper, and then they are free to be themselves at home. But Sparky Schulz used to say, "If you want to know who I am, read my work." And he literally was all of those characters. He was as magical as Snoopy and as cranky as Lucy and as introspective as Linus. And he was a loser who always wanted to be liked like Charlie Brown. All of us are characters. And Cathy is a beautiful slender woman who always thought she was fat and worried about it. I have friends who won't go shopping with her because it takes her so long to decide what she's gonna wear! [*Laughs*] There's a real affection amongst us. . . . And of course, I've known many of these people for over forty years now, which is a lifetime, right? Two lifetimes.

**Grogan:** And developed some deep friendships. One of the things that struck me in reading *The Comic Art of Lynn Johnston*, that book I keep mentioning that's come out in concert with the retrospective exhibition, is you mentioned in the book that when Charles Schulz passed away, in some ways, that had a big impact on you and on your strip, in a way. That somehow without him there, maybe the motivation wasn't as great or something along those lines. It seemed like you were deeply affected.

**Johnston:** I was. [*Pause*] We all were, really, because he died. I mean, he was seventy-seven when he died, and I'm seventy-two now. Yeah, both my mum and dad died at the age of seventy-two. So when I turn seventy-three this year, it's going to be kind of a good thing because then I've escaped that dark cloud. But the next dark cloud is when I hit seventy-seven, should I get there. Because he died at seventy-seven, and he was angry about it! "What? How can this be happening to me? I'm still working, I've got a good life. What's going on?"

**Grogan:** Yeah, yeah. Obviously, growing up with him there in the newspapers and in the culture, he's one of those folks like my grandmother I thought would always be there.

**Johnston:** I really, I really miss him. I really, really do. I really miss him. But you know, he was twenty-some-odd years older than I am. And like Farley the dog, we have our lifespan. The fact that we're not here forever makes us all pretty incredibly special, so hug your pals!

**Grogan:** Indeed.

**Johnston:** Write a letter to your mom!

**Grogan:** Yeah. Absolutely. So just a couple of other things I just want to touch on before we wrap up, and one was you won the Reuben Award 1986 for the strip. That seemed to take you by surprise.

**Johnston:** It did take me by surprise. Jim Davis was up for the award that year, and I can't remember—there was a third nominee. And I was a brand-new artist, really. I had not been doing this for very long. The strip started in '79. Jim was the all-out favorite to win, and he fully expected to, and rightfully so. And when I won, I stood up because people pushed me to stand up. And when I accepted, it took me a while to shut my mouth. I was really dumbstruck that I would win this award. And it meant so much to me. It really did. And I have it right here. I can look at it as we're speaking, and it still kind of shines even though it's lost its luster; it's all tarnished and gray.

**Grogan:** But it was well deserved, and certainly, there should be a Lifetime Achievement Award for it as well.

**Johnston:** I've received a lot of wonderful awards. I really have. The National Cartoonists Society has awarded me some wonderful, wonderful gifts, I will say, and I've had my share. I've more than my share of wonderful, wonderful awards. I have quite a few.

**Grogan:** You're very modest. So going on to another thought, now you're in a different phase of your life, and the strip is over. But do you follow the comics page at all? Are there cartoonists younger cartoonists who have come up who you admire?

**Johnston:** There are a couple people that I really do admire, and they're doing graphic novels right now. There's a young man by the name of Sean Karemaker here in Vancouver, who is doing amazing work. His work is long rolls of paper that are about three feet wide and maybe twenty, thirty, forty feet long. And he does an illustration for the full length of the paper, and it's a graphic novel. And he's on his third or fourth now. And the way it works is that when this thing is photographed, you can put on special glasses and you can actually move your way around his world because it's all on one long piece of paper. So he's created a virtual reality in black and white that you can only really see with these special glasses, but it's amazing! He's a wonderful artist, a fine young man, and his work is just exceptional.

**Grogan:** And what's his name?

**Johnston:** His name is Sean Karemaker. I think you'd have to look it up. You'll find him; he's out there. And the other is Raina Telgemeier; she's doing graphic novels, and they're wonderful stories for young people, young adults, young kids, too. She's thoughtful and caring, and you can identify so closely with her childhood and the types of things she's writing about. She's a wonderful storyteller, but she's also a very good artist. And I just wish her all the best. I see her work out there on the graphic novel shelf; she's a heavyweight for sure.

**Grogan:** Wow. And is she Canadian also?

**Johnston:** No, she's American, I think.

**Grogan:** American. Yeah, Canada has turned out some fabulous cartoonists. There's a wealth of great cartooning talent that comes from Canada.

**Johnston:** And comedy and—

**Grogan:** Sure. Joni Mitchell and Neil Young, and on and on. And William Shatner, and all other folks who come from Canada, many of whom we don't realize here in the States actually do come from Canada.

**Johnston:** The whole *Schitt's Creek* cast is pretty much all Canadian.

**Grogan:** Oh yeah, and on *SCTV*. I used to love that show. And *Murdoch Mysteries* is one of my favorite shows now. It's terrific. There's a lot. Are you familiar with Terri Libenson's work?

**Johnston:** Yes.

**Grogan:** *The Pajama Diaries*. I always thought she was kind of a successor or might be a successor to you in a certain way. She just ended *The Pajama Diaries*, to my regret. I'm sorry to see it go. She's got a very successful career in tween books, books for young people, but she's somebody I thought sort of picked up a little bit in the wake of *For Better or For Worse*.

**Johnston:** I would hate to think that anybody would be connected. It's such an individual thing. It's such an individual thing. You really can't compare one to the other, and I confess that I have not followed a lot of [strips.] . . . I used to read everything. I used to be on the comics page all the time and reading as much as I could possibly read. But once I stopped doing the strip,

I kind of pushed my interests into other directions. I like to paint and I certainly like to do these fabric designs, and we have hundreds of fabric designs now that we're putting out there.

There's a time and a place for everything. I used to play the guitar, and I thought maybe I would be a professional musician, but then there's a time and a place for everything, and I can't play the guitar anymore because I never practiced and I've lost it. I don't beat myself up over it, and I don't cry because I've lost a skill; it's just time to move on to something else.

**Grogan:** Well, I admire that attitude, which is just move forward all the time. And I think that's how you stay young, right?

**Johnston:** That is how you stay young. That's how you stay alive.

**Grogan:** Yeah, exactly. Wow. I think we've covered a lot of territory here, and I've taken up a lot of your time. But I am very appreciative, and I think it's been terrific. This has been a great interview.

**Johnston:** Geoff, I hope we meet sometime and can go have a cup of coffee somewhere because this has been such a one-sided conversation. I've talked to you for a couple of hours now, and I don't even know what you look like! [*Laughs*]

**Grogan:** I'm a little guy with a big nose and glasses. My wife would say I'm selling myself short, but I'm also short.

**Johnston:** Sounds like you'd be fun to draw.

**Grogan:** That is a compliment only a cartoonist could give. But I'll take it. I'll take it right. Heck, yes. If I had that drawing, I'd proudly frame it on the wall, that's for sure.

# A Conversation with Lynn Johnston

**ADAM CHAPMAN / 2021**

From the *Comic Shenanigans* podcast (December 5, 2021). Reprinted by permission.

**Adam Chapman:** Today we have a conversation with Lynn Johnston. She's the creator of the *For Better or For Worse* cartoon strip, which ran for just under thirty years, at least in the original printing. And it is continued to be seen in hundreds of newspapers worldwide. I was very lucky to be able to sit down with Lynn. Partially I have to give thanks to Kurtis Findlay, who is her editor on the current collection, re-collections of the *For Better or For Worse* strip, which is going chronologically from the beginning in these beautiful hardcover volumes. Volume six is coming out early next year. There's already five volumes that are already gracing my shelves, and hopefully they are gracing yours as well. Tremendous work that she did throughout all those years. Her characters aged, which definitely set her strip apart from many others; her characters grew and evolved. They didn't stay the same age forever. Unlike *Peanuts*, for example, where the characters kind of stayed relatively finite in terms of their age and never really changed too much. Whereas in *For Better or For Worse* people did change, people grew up, people had families, people had children. So things were definitely very different in that type of strip.

I got to speak with Lynn this past week. We sat down and had quite a lengthy conversation. It was really enjoyable. I really got to get into her process, what it was like working on these strips. It's interesting, I obviously talk to people who work in comic books, and I have a very good knowledge of kind of how comic books work, how the industry works, how the different companies work. One thing I don't know as much about is comic strips and how that whole faction worked, especially when she was getting started working with syndicates, et cetera. And she talks about her first contract that she got; it just kind of blew my mind because it just seems so crazy that you get such a long-term contract by selling a strip, so it's kind of interesting.

I had a great time talking with Lynn. I think you're gonna get a lot out of this interview, just a lot of insight into her process and what she was thinking and what she what she thinks about the current new collections. So strap in. This is a really fun one. I had a great time talking with Lynn. And again, a special thanks to Kurtis Findlay for helping us get together and coordinating us, or at least communicating with each other so that we could have an interview. I'm definitely, definitely very appreciative to Kurtis for his assistance in that regard. . . . So, without further ado, let's jump right into the conversation with Lynn Johnston. Enjoy.

Lynn, welcome to the comic shenanigans podcast. How are you today?

**Lynn Johnston:** I'm well, thank you.

**Chapman:** Thank you so much for joining us today. I've got to, I guess, give a shout out to Kurtis Findlay, who helped set this up. Obviously he's the editor in the current collection, the collected editions of your strip, which are currently rolling out like clockwork. We have a new volume coming out, what is it, February? That's the newest volume coming out?

**Johnston:** Yeah, coming out soon. Did you find me through Kurtis, then? That was good.

**Chapman:** Yeah, Kurtis Findlay was the one who helped put us together. I've actually been friends with Kurtis for a few years. He has another podcast, another venture that I have collaborated with him before. He was, and I remember, he was telling me about working on the editions of *For Better or For Worse*. And that's part of why I was like, "You know, I remember enjoying it as a kid. I should pick this up!" And actually, I don't know why it took me so long to get started and picking these up. I have to confess that to you. I started with volume four, and I brought it home and I was flipping through it. My son, who's now eight—so this would have been a year or so ago—he kind of came in and said, "What ya reading?" And I started reading through the strips with him, and he loved it and I was really enjoying it. And so I was like, "Well, we got to buy them all." So we picked up all the volumes except for there's one unfortunate missing volume that we just could not get our hands on, and thankfully, Kurtis was able to step in and be the hero was able to find it.

**Johnston:** It's number three, I bet. Was it number three?

**Chapman:** Number three, that's the one. Yeah.

**Johnston:** IDW is strange about not printing more. It just makes no sense at all. We've had a number of people contact us, and we have maybe four or five copies of it ourselves. But when those are gone, we won't have number three either, except for ourselves.

**Chapman:** It does seem like a very strange thing. I can understand, obviously, tapering off. Generally speaking, you stock a lot of volume ones and then maybe have less as they go on, although I think your strip is a little bit unique for that because of how the story progresses. But yeah, it's very weird. I remember talking about that with Kurtis, like "What is this about that third volume that is just so hard to get?"

**Johnston:** Yeah. Oh well. That's the way it goes.

**Chapman:** Well, again, thanks to Kurtis I have now all five volumes so far, and I'm looking forward to the future ones. And as I've said, I've really enjoyed it—not just enjoying it on my own, but also seeing how my son responds to the work as well. Because he's just falling in love with the strip. I was asking him today who his favorite characters were, and he was he was trying to think about it. And he's like, "I think it's April." I'm like "Okay, you know, a later addition, but okay."

**Johnston:** Well, she was a great character to work with because she didn't exist in real life. I was able to take real liberties with that one character because I only had two children, so the third in the comic strip was wonderfully fictional. Anything that would otherwise have been connected to my own kids were now on April's lap, and she didn't mind one bit.

**Chapman:** So obviously I do want to go back to the beginning, but I have to talk about the collected editions first. How was it for you to see your work collected so comprehensively? Because, obviously, there had been previous collections of your work before, but nothing this comprehensive and kind of encompassing the entire body of work. How do you do feel at the beginning of the project, seeing it all being recollected like this?

**Johnston:** Well, we were surprised. I'm talking about my daughter and I. She and I work together and like, I have a company called Lynn Johnston Productions Incorporated, which is aside from *For Better or For Worse* because we're doing other designs. And so she and I work together. I mean, it's wonderful to have the strip rerunning in the newspaper and we were thrilled with that. And we've sort of imagined that perhaps *For Better or For Worse* had kind of disappeared into the past. But when Kurtis approached us with the possibility of doing this series through IDW Books, we were absolutely thrilled, and the product itself is absolutely beautiful. We're so happy with the book. It's a lovely product. It's such a good quality thing. And Kurtis wanted to do something that would show everything exactly [as] it was when it first appeared so that no changes or corrections or color differences would be seen. It would all be seen exactly the way it was when it came out. And that kind of made me stand back a bit because, I wanted to change a lot of things when it reran—you know, colors I didn't like or sometimes punch lines I wanted to change. And I was able to do that in the strip as it reran, but in the books, he wanted to really be a puritan and keep it exactly the way it was. And I'm quite happy that he did that now because it's quite an interesting progression from when I first began to when I got towards the end, because you can't help but get better at something over time.

**Chapman:** Oh, for sure. One thing I've always enjoyed throughout the volumes is your remembrances that are kind of in the margin notes or the quick stories that you kind of pepper through the volumes. What was it like coming up with those and those shorter anecdotes that kind of would pepper the volume to give it a little bit more life—not life, that's the wrong word—but more context or to just point out things that you really enjoyed?

**Johnston:** We weren't going to use those little quotes. At the beginning I had started writing those for our website. We have, of course, the strip, which appears every day on our website as well as in the papers where it runs. And I just wanted to add something, because there are some really dedicated readers who come to the site every day, and I wanted them to see something more if there was something about that particular strip that I can tell them how I came up with the idea, or did it relate to something that happened to me as a child or did it really happen to our family. And some of the stories are long and some of them are really quite funny and some of them are very personal and some of them are sad. And I thought, *Well, you know, if the readers are interested, maybe I'll run it.* And when these little comments started to happen on the website under the comic strip. Some people were very upset about it. They didn't like it at all. They wanted the strip to just run and they didn't want to read anything extra. And other people were really quite pleased with the idea that they'd see something more about the actual production of the art. I only write about a strip when I actually have something to say about it. And months go by sometimes where there's no comments. And then other folks were saying, "Where are the comments?! We want to know more!" So you can't please them all, you can't please them all! But it has been fun for me to be able to remember myself where these situations came from and to write them down.

**Chapman:** How do you feel about it? It's such an interesting way of experiencing your work because obviously initially, there would have been in the dailies and then you have the Sunday strip and so that's how it was built. But now people are experiencing it all at once, so they're experiencing what used to be over a lot more time, experiencing all these events all at once. How do you think that both enriches and also maybe changes how people interact with your work compared to when they initially would have experienced it in newspapers?

**Johnston:** Well, I'm watching *Seinfeld* all over again, right from the beginning. I just love *Seinfeld*. And it's a different experience when you can just watch one episode after another. Lots of things I missed. Lots of things I find annoying. I mean, it's a different experience. It's like reading a novel when before you could just read a chapter at a time. One of the problems with reading the strip all at once, day after day, in a book, is that the stories that spun out for weeks in the newspaper are suddenly seconds long as you're reading them in a book. And there are a number of stories that were full of intrigue and you'd have to wait and find out tomorrow to find out what happened.

For example, John and Elly's brothers go out on a canoe trip, and the canoe capsizes and they're stranded in the woods on a little island and they have to be airlifted out. And that was kind of a fun little story to tell. . . . It's a few days long in the comic strip as it comes out in the newspaper, but it's just a few panels in a book and so therefore, it has no real excitement to it at all. It's resolved within a page.

**Chapman:** That is an interesting perspective. Yeah, for sure. It changes everything about the pacing. Kurtis is big into comic books, as am I, and we read a lot of collected editions of older material. We see this all the time, and it really changes how you interface with it because now, as you said, it's one after the other. You don't have that required kind of release of "Oh well. Now I gotta wait for the next one." Because there's something about that, as you said, that kind of sense of anticipation, building it up in your mind. And then you have the next chapter. It is different when you can go right on to it right away.

**Johnston:** Exactly. No, I think it's just like being able to see a sitcom all at once. It really is a different experience.

**Chapman:** When you started this strip, one thing I find so fascinating is obviously how you pace differently with the dailies and then you also have the weekend strip, and the weekend strip is obviously run in color and it feels a little bit more broad. Was that a very conscious decision from the beginning? To know that this is the one that's going to have the more eyeballs. It's going to be the more—not necessarily evergreen per se, but it's going to play maybe to more [readers] and it's going to be a little bit more vibrant and usually more about the kids, et cetera. Was that a very conscious decision right from the beginning?

**Johnston:** Yes, it was. When I started to write actual storylines where Monday started the statement and Tuesday depended on your having read Monday kind of thing, you'd have to be very careful that somebody who missed Monday is still going to pick up the storyline on Tuesday and it has to be very carefully crafted. But because some newspapers did not take the Sunday page and some papers just took the Sunday page and not the daily, you knew that there were readers who were going to miss a huge amount if they, if you, continue to story on the Sunday page, because the Sunday page gives you all those panels and there's loads of room for information. So if I was telling a series of stories, boy, that Sunday page would be great. And I remember as a kid reading, you know, *Rex Morgan* and *Gasoline Alley* and some of these other continuity strips that if that Sunday page was missing, boy, you'd miss most of the story because of all the space that you have to tell a story. So I never did continue the stories into the Sunday page. And I found that that was really helpful because if a story is serious, that Sunday page gives you a wonderful opportunity for goofiness that breaks the tension and you can get back to the story on Monday.

**Chapman:** For sure. In fact, that's how I kind of got my son into it, because I was like, "Well, maybe he won't go for the black and white"—because, you know, kids these days, they don't know appreciation for black and white for some reason. So I'm like, "I'll start with the color and I'll see if he enjoys it." And he really got taken in. Again, he really liked the color strips and then he was like, "Well, can we go back and read the ones we skipped?" And I was like, "Absolutely!" But I just was trying to kind of engage him first in the characters and again, some of the whimsy of those ones, and then go into some of the more serious strips.

It was interesting. The other day we were talking, and I was telling him I was going to talk to you, so I was asking him, "What questions would you want to ask?" And he had the typical questions about, like, "What made you bring in April as a character?" I'm like, "Well, that's a very interesting question for a child to ask," because again, it's his favorite character. And he was also asking, "Why did the dog have to pass away?" I'm like, "Yup, that's a big thing that happened." Again, he's eight years old. He's like, "You know, it was too bad, but at least I understand that the dog saved April, and everything was good," and that's very heavy stuff, but he handled it really well.

**Johnston:** A comic strip in the newspaper is supposed to appeal to a nine-year-old boy. That was what they told me when I got into the business, that they want brand-new young readers to come on board and buy the newspaper and read the newspaper. And so the comic strips were designated as an opportunity for young people to become newspaper readers, right? But of course, the comic strips appeal to everybody, mostly adults. And so to have a younger person enjoy my work is a real compliment because I obviously got an eight-year-, nine-year-old boy to read my work and enjoy it. And I guess when they said "boy," it meant all kids. At the time I remember that was stuck in my mind: I have to appeal to a nine-year-old boy.

So yeah, I think kids are reading it and they're asking great questions. I have grandchildren who are reading it and asking great questions. And the answer to the question "Why did I bring April into the story?" was because I really missed babies. The babies and little puppies and things like that give you the most laughs because they're uninhibited and they're genuine and they're off the cuff. They're so much fun. And they say and do things that are, for a cartoonist, just hilarious. This gave me an opportunity to have wonderful fun with imagery and storylines that I was losing because my characters were growing up and their vocabulary was changing and their relationships were becoming mature. And it was fun to write about them, but it wasn't goofy. It wasn't hilarious like it is like babies.

**Chapman:** So that that brings up again that one of the things that has always kind of set your work apart and been so special about it is the fact that people did age in real time. Did you know right from the beginning? "I want this to grow and evolve"? Because for a strip, that wasn't the most common of practices. Most things were kind of evergreen. I believe you were friends with Mr. [Charles] Schulz. Right?

**Johnston:** Yup.

**Chapman:** So obviously, his characters never aged. And there was a magic and beauty to that. But, also obviously, you give yourself a lot of stories as well because you do have your characters aging. But how early did you know that, "No, I want this to age in real time"?

**Johnston:** It was about three years in. It takes about three years before you really feel confident, before you get your sea legs, before you get a routine. And part of that is trusting that your ideas will always be there. Because there are days when no ideas come and you panic because you've signed this contract and you have to produce and it has to be on time. And it has to be good, right? So you're not just going to fire out something just to fill the space, although that happens from time to time. And so the pressure on you to write well and to do a good job is always there. And I found that if I got bored with my material, my readers would get bored with the material too. So I was pretty hard on myself. And at first I thought I would just keep everybody the same because I thought that's what a comic strip was. But it was based on my family and my family was growing and my kids were no longer babies and their vocabulary was changing. And they were becoming more interesting as they connected with the kids in school and they were able to do more stuff. I couldn't keep the characters in the strip the same age because I would have lost all that great material.

So I gave the characters a three-year break. I kept the characters in the comic strip the same age for three years. And my own kids grew up three years, and that gave them a nice buffer. . . . When you're in grade one, a kid in grade two seems like an adult right? Or a kid in grade four could babysit. So that three-year buffer really was wonderful for my own two real kids to feel a break from the strip. And then I allowed annual growth with the characters. And that was a super challenge because after a while you have to change their height, change their hair, change their body shape, you know. It was a challenge. And it was a challenge I didn't exactly enjoy, but I loved a challenge. Period. So when I was happy with the way the character was growing, I was feeling that I was doing what I intended to do: tell a real story from a real family's point of view and from a woman's point of view,

And I was often criticized for not changing Elly Patterson like the other characters changed. John didn't change much, but the children of course did. And people complained that she was frumpy and her hair was ugly and I should change her hair. But you know, there's a certain look to the adult characters that is a signature look that it's very difficult to change. It's fine in a sitcom with live action. You know, a major character could come in with a haircut or a pair of glasses or something that changes them and it's still them. But in a cartoon, your style of drawing is like your signature. And so it's very difficult to change hairstyles. I remember Sparky, Charles Schulz, once saying to me that if it wasn't for hair and clothing, all of his characters would look the same. And if you look at all of his characters, he's pretty well right. And that's that was his signature. That was the way he drew.

**Chapman:** A question about evolving the characters over time. Did you have like—this is gonna sound like a silly question, I guess—but did you almost have to have updated model sheets to kind of reference back to?

**Johnston:** Yes, I did. Yes, I did. In fact, one of the most helpful things was an old, old medical text that a friend of mine who's a doctor had given me, just for the heck of it. He was cleaning out his library. And I took a bunch of books that he had because they were all on babies, the development of babies, and all that type of thing. And one of them showed the relative height of a child next to an adult as the child grew. And kids are much taller than you think that they are. A four-year-old is much taller than you would imagine in your mind. And my ten-year-old granddaughter is up to my shoulder now, and if I didn't actually have a ten-year-old to measure next to me, I would probably draw her much shorter than she really is.

**Chapman:** That's very cool. So you would have to update those sheets to keep the models on [track]. . . . You're doing it every day, but I guess, as you said, you kind of have to have a reference point, especially if you are evolving them.

**Johnston:** Yeah. Well, I kept my characters three years younger at the strip. I had that three-year difference, so the comic strip characters were smaller than my real kids because they were three years younger.

**Chapman:** When you were evolving them, was it an annual thing? Was there always a specific time of year that you would usually kind of age them up? . . . Or was a not set thing? Or did you kind of move it around? How would you approach that?

**Johnston:** It was kind of a gut feeling. I would say to myself, "Gee, April has just turned five. She's got to look like this now and she's got to look like this and this should be her vocabulary and this should be her body shape and the type of clothes she likes." I'd have to think an awful lot about her as a real human being. I mean, all of my characters I thought about as being people with their own personality and their own likes and dislikes and their own quirks and stuff you didn't like about them at all. They were kind of real people for me, but real people in my imagination. They were sort of based on my family but . . . I mean, it's a story. So it has to be all you. It has to be your imagination, all of it.

**Chapman:** For sure. Now, I want to go back a second when you talk about, again, getting the strips sold to begin with. Obviously, there was a very different time of syndicates, et cetera, very different than obviously now. What was that process like at the time to get the strip picked up and to start actually seeing it in newspapers, et cetera?

**Johnston:** Well, it's one of those things that is difficult to get into. You can send submissions into the syndicates and if you have an agent, they still send your submissions into the syndicates.

I had done a series of little books on having babies and raising children. I was working as a medical artist for McMaster University in Hamilton, Ontario. And I was doing a lot of comic art for the university because students learn more from cartoons apparently than they do from graphics showing graphs and charts and numbers. It was more fun if it was colorful and full of funny images. So eventually I went from drawing serious surgical illustrations to doing a lot of comic art. One of the doctors was an obstetrician. I did a whole bunch of drawings about cartoons about childbirth for him and that became a little book. I did two other books. One was called *Hi Mom! Hi Dad!* and [the other was] *Do They Ever Grow Up?* And I was going to do these little single-panel cartoon books as an aside to my full-time job, which was working as a medical artist. And the three little books were picked up by a publisher in Minneapolis. They were first published in Canada. They were picked up by this publisher in Minneapolis who sent the books to the syndicate Universal

Press with a letter saying "If you don't syndicate her, I will." And they sent me a twenty-year contract. And I was ready to have another baby. I was walking around with a big round tummy. And they asked me for twenty comic strips—like, right away; they wanted to know if I could work under pressure. Well, there I was doing comic strips on the packing boxes since we were planning to move from Ontario to Northern Manitoba. My husband was a flying dentist. We'd bought a little airplane and were heading off to the almost the Arctic. And so I sent twenty cartoons right away, thinking I'd never hear from them again. And they sent me a twenty-year contract.

**Chapman:** Wow. Now to put that into context, twenty years obviously sounds like a lot. Was this a relatively normal practice at the time in terms of the length or . . . ? I mean, I guess they want to build up. . . .

**Johnston:** Yes, this was the normal contract at the time; pretty well all the cartoonists who signed a contract in the early 1970s or even up until about the '90s, I guess, it was a twenty-year contract and that was it. And they owned all the rights to your work and if you died, they could hire somebody else to do it. Or if they didn't like you, they could get somebody else to do it. And it was really very much in favor of the syndicate. And in their defense, they have to work hard to sell you to the newspapers because there's a finite amount of space on a comics page. You know, if the editor of a newspaper has twenty-five comics, in order to take in twenty-six, he has to get rid of one. And how do you get rid of one? And one of the problems too is that editors are very upset when people write in and complain and they say, "I really liked that strip. You put *For Better or For Worse* in there, and I've never heard of it and I don't like it. I'm angry." So it's hard at first for editors and salespeople to sell your work to the papers because it's a shuffle. Somebody has to bump you and you bump somebody else and there you go. Because there's not much space in the paper.

But after a while, if your work is really good, the newspapers hear about you and they want you. They want to get rid of a strip that might be tired, and they want to replace it, and eventually they will ask and eventually you don't need the salesman. You've got your work, which sells itself. And at that point, a bunch of us thought, *Gee, it might be a good idea if we were able to renegotiate our contract*. And so, through some crazy new rigmarole, we were able to do that. We were now able to change the contract to seven years automatic. And it was twenty years automatically renewed, if the strip was doing well. That was another thing you say: "Yeah, the twenty years, they still can't make any changes?" And changes should have been made. Because when you sign a contract, especially into something new, there's lots of stuff in that contract that you later on realize that you might well have changed if you had the opportunity and the foresight to do so.

**Chapman:** So how does the ownership of your work out, then? Obviously, you still control the work now, right?

**Johnston:** Yes, in fact, all of us own the rights to our work. We own the copyright, the imagery, everything. Today, it's ours. . . . You and Kurtis are comics buffs and your education in the comic world way surpasses mine, so you're probably well aware of some of the old original strips. I think *Nancy*, for example, *Nancy and Sluggo*, is owned by the syndicate, and they've been able to hire different artists over the years to draw the characters. And I think Ernie Bushmiller did not own the rights to his own characters at the time. I believe that's the case. You can check it out for me to find out if that's true. But after we were able to get together, and Cathy Guisewite, Jim Unger and I, and some other folks who got together, we pitched an idea and it actually worked. And we were able to get this new contract system together and all of the cartoonists now are fortunate that it's only a seven-year contract automatically renewed.

**Chapman:** When it came to, again, the idea of getting your rights back—and given that this was such a personal work and there was so much based on things that happen to you and the kind of things that happen in your life that were then funneled into the stories in different ways—did it make it that much more important to make sure that you could end up controlling your own work?

**Johnston:** Absolutely. Yeah. I really wanted to know that if I ended the strip, it ended. And it wasn't going to be picked up and done by another artist. Yeah.

**Chapman:** . . . I can't even imagine that, right? Because, as you said, it's such a personal work. It's so you. And then, again, the characters will have aged and these are characters that lived in your mind. The idea that someone else will take that over, especially because it's got so much continuity and so much built into it. It's a lifetime, right? The idea that someone else would have control of that or doing stories—that does feel very wrong.

**Johnston:** Well, I think, in some instances, the people who are publishing your work, they don't care about you as much as they care about the money that comes in. And that's the way it goes. It's a business. We're really fortunate to be working with a, I think, a very progressive syndicate that realized that if the artists aren't happy, the art is not going to be good, and we better all of us just look at this again. I think I was very fortunate. I got into the business at a time when comic strips were still a big deal. They were still selling. They were the flagship that sold the paper and there were a lot of wonderful, wonderful artists involved. I got to meet all my heroes in the industry. Now, of course, everything has changed. So much is online and a lot of newspapers have amalgamated with other newspapers or have gone out of business. The whole thing has changed. And I was very lucky to become a syndicated artist when syndication was still a really wonderful job.

**Chapman:** How did you find that you balance the craft of putting together your strip with, again, the business side . . . the deadlines especially? Obviously you're trying to tell stories and that are going to touch people in different ways and say different things and tell the stories, but at the same time it's a relentless deadline.

**Johnston:** It is, and I'm glad you said that because so many people think, *Well, you just do a drawing a day and you're done. Right? You could spend the rest of the day out picking lilies in the field.* I mean, they don't like you to turn in anything that's not finished; they want a week at a time. I think Garry Trudeau was the only one that was permitted to send in a couple at a time because his was so political and so close to what was going on in politics at the time, so sometimes he was able to send just a few in at a time. But the rest of us, and rightfully so, were required to send in no less than one week at a time, and it had to be six weeks ahead of the publication date for the dailies and eight weeks ahead for the Sundays. And that was because the Sundays were pretty well all colored in Buffalo. And a lot of it was we had to send a hard copy. We didn't send GIFs and TIFFs and whatever on the internet now, these high-resolution files, and then you keep all your original art now. At the time, we had to send a hard copy, and one time I lost a week and that was devastating. I had to scramble like crazy to catch up. But after I retired, I found out that I was one of the very few artists who actually was six weeks ahead of the dailies and eight weeks ahead of the Sundays always. And that deadline was relentless. It really was. Because, you know, if you want to go on a holiday for two weeks, you have to be eight weeks ahead on your Sundays plus two weeks. Six weeks ahead on your dailies plus two weeks so you can take those two weeks off. And so I was working on trains and planes and hotel rooms and on beaches. If we were on a holiday sometimes I might be in the room writing or drawing. And one time I went to visit a friend in Florida, and I was there for about three, four weeks, and I had to take my drafting table with me. It was a portable drafting table. And I worked. It just never goes away, and that's part of the stress of it.

And again, I think I said after three years you trust the Muse. You know that you're going to be able to write again. But there will be a full day when you're supposed to be writing when nothing will come. And if you don't sit there and think, if you go off and buy groceries and visit a friend instead of taking that day to think, it doesn't come the next day. You got to spend a full day just focusing, being a fly on the wall or being the characters. And you run over all the dialogue in your head, and you try to figure out which character have I not focused on and what subject matter can I explore and all of this stuff. It's like wakeful dreaming. That was my process, anyways. And I wrote as if I was writing a script for a play, but it's very small and very short.

And a lot of my process actually was suggested to me by Cathy Guisewite, who did a strip called *Cathy*. Cathy is a wonderful writer, and her dad was in advertising and she did a lot of writing for her dad before she got the job. And meeting other people in the industry is so helpful because they're wonderful when it comes to support and advice. So before I even signed my contract, I called Cathy and said, "Help! How do you do this?" And she said, "Well, to begin with, do not call it *The Johnstons*. Do not call the main character Lynn." Because she called her character Cathy, and she said, "I've always wondered if that was a good idea."

**Chapman:** That's funny. So the question about, again, that sense of process, especially raising a family and then having the stress of a relentless deadlines schedule. How did you find the creative process? Did you find that you did try to keep kind of traditional daytime hours in terms of when you would be creative? Did you find that you would do it more at nights? When did that Muse hit you?

**Johnston:** Well, I couldn't work nine to five. . . . My little girl would go to a babysitter from nine to noon, so I could work from nine to noon, and then she would come home for the afternoon and my son would come home from school. So I would be a regular mom during those hours, and then after dinner, after the kids were in bed, I would work. And I would often get up at four in the morning. That was a great time to work. No phones. Nobody bothers you. It's quiet. I would work at four in the morning. And, of course, I was a lot younger and had a lot more stamina then. I could work longer hours.

But anytime you get a chance to work, boy, you grab that chance, and it does interfere with your life because part of the time you're living in a fantasy world. So if I was drawing, for example, and one of my kids was in my studio, they'd come over and talk to me and I would say, "Uh-huh, uh-huh," but I wasn't listening to anything they were saying because I was so focused on what I was doing. And I remember one time, it was just before dinner and my son said, "Can I have a piece of cake?" and I said, "No." And he's standing right there eating the cake right beside me. Like going *chew, chew, chew, munch, munch, munch*, holding the cake under my nose. "Can I have a piece of cake?" "No, it's too close to dinner." And he's eating the cake and I didn't even notice it right there.

There were times when that was awful for the kids because I was there, but mentally I wasn't. And there were times when I did a lot of traveling for book tours and speaking engagements and going down to Kansas City to the syndicate, things like that. I had an airplane ticket on my desk all the time. And I remember one time dressing up to go out with my suitcase and my airplane ticket and my son standing between me in the doorway with his hands on his hips, saying, "So are you turning into Lynn Johnston again?" There were times when it got in the way. And I was pretty arrogant for a little while. My strip was doing well. People wanted my opinion. I was getting interviewed. And I thought I was pretty hot spit. And so my family nicely pulled me down to earth. "You turning into Lynn Johnston again?"

**Chapman:** When you were being creative like that, were you more excited about the actual drawing and penciling and inking and doing all that work, or were you more excited about the story generation and just thinking about what the next plot was going to be? Which part, if you could delineate between the two, was the part that made you most excited to get started every day?

**Johnston:** This is a great question. And it can only come from somebody who writes and draws, right?

You must write and draw. You must do this process, aside from the fact that you do podcasts and that you're interested in media. These are the kinds of questions we asked each other. You know, "When do you work? What is your routine? How do you get your ideas?" and that type of thing. And it's not a simple question. And it's a good question. And the thing that I guess I enjoyed most about the writing part was the fantasy that led me through all of the body language and facial expressions that I was going to need for the actual drawing. If my writing was good, I couldn't wait to get to the drawing. And the pencil work was a joy. . . . I called it "ghosting" because the characters and everything about the artwork was done in pastel gray with your pencil so it was easy to change, and it was almost like a ghost—you could see through the images. But then when you ink it, you touch the characters and they come alive. You put that in the ink and you touch the paper and you push the pen onto the paper and you're touching the character's cheek and you're running the ink over their shoulder and you're combing their hair with the tip of your pen and you're bringing them to life. And to me that was just wonderful fun. That was a great opportunity to just be grateful for the skill that you have.

**Chapman:** When you're doing this strip—obviously, as you said, you'd done the books before you started the strip—even the process of doing the pencils and inks and bringing it to life, that's obviously not just an amateur. You're applying your craft because those are two very different skills and to be able to do both of them competently is extremely good. And then when you're doing the weekend strips, you're doing colors as well. Did you find [adding] colors was a harder challenge to adapt to or change? Because obviously it's different than the starkness of the black and white with the whites and the inks.

**Johnston:** In the beginning we had very few colors to work with. And what you would do, and this is years ago before we had a lot of this electronic stuff, my process was to copy each Sunday page on a on a photocopier, and that copy would be colored with pencil crayons, and each color had a number. Like the skin was six and hair was forty and sweater was sixty-two and all of that. We had about sixty-two colors. And then you would send that chart with the original art to the syndicate. And I think they put it on microfilm at the time, and they somehow got the black line to Buffalo along with the color chart, and they would use that color chart. And when I first started they were still using Amberlith and Rubylith, which your listeners are going to have to look up online. Amberlith and Rubylith are two of the really original ways of putting color into print. And you had to use Exacto knives to cut away this stuff. It was a real difficult process and there'd be rows of people, mostly women, cutting this transparent paper in order to put the color into the comics.

When I had been there for about two years, they developed this computerized coloring system. And I went down to Buffalo to find out what it was like. And it was a room that was very small, but it was actually a huge room, but it was all computers. You stepped up onto the floor and the room buzzed and hummed with the smell of electricity and lights. It was like walking into a computer. And there'd be a couple of people sitting there with these screens and putting the color into the artwork, and it was like magic because the color would sort of bleed into the line, and they could shade a little bit here and there, and the whole room hummed. Literally, you walk into a computer.

So that was the first of the coloring system, and now of course you can do it on your iPhone, for goodness sakes! That was groundbreaking. That first little palette of colors that we had, they were able to put colors in between those colors. So it went from sixty to, you know, it doubled it. And then it went again and again, until finally the colors were endless. It was just endless. And it didn't take long for me to discover that I could hire a colorist myself and I could stand beside him and I could say, "Could you change this to green, and could you shade a little there?" And so the coloring became something that you had a lot of control over. Whereas in the beginning you were lucky if you got anything like what you wanted because you were doing pencil crayons or felt pen or whatever you did to send it to Buffalo to get them to do it. And they were great. They tried to figure out what the heck we were indicating and they did the best they could.

**Chapman:** So about colors, I was thinking about when you were developing and choosing which colors to use, and then obviously you're seeing it in newsprint and that's going to look different than on your drafting table, what your original conception for that color was. Now seeing it in these collected editions—where, again, you're seeing it on crisp, white pages as opposed to original newsprint—how different an experience [is that] for you? Not just the color strips, but also the black and whites, to see what they actually look like in a nice, white, really bright, crisp paper as opposed to the newsprint that they were on all this time?

**Johnston:** Well, to begin with, they were a pretty good size, but . . . the editors shrink the strips or they stretch them to get to fit more work in there. Your artwork looks different in almost every paper. So to see it pristine the way it is in these books by IDW, it's beautiful. Everything is clear and crisp. And, as you said, it's the way the artists would like it to appear.

**Chapman:** One skill that I'm curious about in terms of your ability to kind of adapt over time was just lettering. How did you find lettering work?

**Johnston:** The lettering I really enjoyed. I was always happy with lettering. And after I practiced it for a while I could do it quite, quite easily. And I found that the Rapidograph pens were the best. And I don't think people use Rapidograph pens so much; they're using a lot of these felt tips now. But I eventually was able to hire another artist to help me with the artwork and this was, maybe, I don't know, maybe twelve years in. And because I was hiring somebody else to work with me, I was able to put more detail into the art and they did all of the lettering. But I also have a font. Nowadays you can have a font of your own lettering, which is great fun.

**Chapman:** Absolutely. So I'm curious about the iconic title of *For Better or For Worse*, the font that you use—how long did it take to develop that distinctive look? Because, obviously, that's going to be everywhere, that's going to be on every strip, that's going to be identified with the strip forever. So was that stressful for you to come up with not just the name of the strip, which is in and of itself enough of a stressor, but also the look of the title?

**Johnston:** I think anybody who eventually finds themselves doing comics for a living has drawn and written in a comic style since they were five years old. I was doing lettering since I was very, very young. And my dad was a wonderful letterer, and my mother was a calligrapher actually, and she did a lot of hand lettering for different companies and things like graduation gift

Johnston's real-life friendship with Charles "Sparky" Schulz slips into the *For Better or For Worse* strip on what would have been his one hundredth birthday. FOR BETTER OR FOR WORSE © 2022 Lynn Johnston Productions. Dist. By ANDREWS MCMEEL SYNDICATION. Reprinted with permission. All rights reserved.

certificates and things like that. And she also did beautiful hand lettering for stamp collectors' albums, things like that. And my dad was a good cartoonist and a good visual artist and loved to do lettering. They were both very proud of their handwriting and their lettering. So I came by it quite by the DNA. But again, by the time you're actually working as a graphic artist, your lettering should be pretty good.

**Chapman:** For sure. . . . Was that always how you wrote your name? Or is that specifically something that you adapted for the strip?

**Johnston:** I adapted it later. I signed my full name for a while and I wrote it like in script like a signature for a while, but it just was too much space. And I decided that I would just use my first name because I've been married a couple of times and my last [name] changed. It had gone from Ridgway to Franks to Johnston and I felt, well, one thing that hasn't changed is Lynn. So I just put Lynn on the bottom because it didn't take much space and it was easy to poke in there.

**Chapman:** You spoke before about the idea there's this kind of community of cartoonists, and you mentioned Sparky specifically. So I'm curious. What was your relationship with Sparky like and how did it begin?

**Johnston:** Well, Cathy Guisewite introduced me to him in Washington the year that I won the Reuben Award, which was 1985, I think. And he was sixty-three and he was about to turn sixty-four. And we were walking behind him and his wife, Jeannie, and we were singing "Will you still need me? Will you still feed me?" Right? And he turned around and said, "I don't want to be sixty-four! I don't want to be any older than I am!"

Right away we had a really good connection, and he invited me to visit him at his home. And once you go visit somebody in their home, that makes a huge difference to your relationship, you know. Once you feel that you can put your feet up on the sofa and make yourself a cup of tea, then you know you're really comfortable with each other. And I got to know Sparky really well. There were a couple of times when I wrote speeches for him, when he'd be invited to do a speaking engagement somewhere. And I wrote a couple of speeches for him and I got to know a lot of his friends and his family, and it was a great relationship. I missed him terribly when he died.

**Chapman:** Obviously he was this huge icon by then, he'd been doing *Peanuts* for so long. So when you met him, how quickly did it go from "Oh, my goodness, it's Charles Schulz" to "Now he's Sparky"?

**Johnston:** He was very welcoming, and most cartoonists he'd asked them to call him Sparky. He was very friendly and very kind. He was less friendly and less kind to people who were his serious rivals, if your work was seriously rivaling him. I know that Snoopy and Garfield did not get along that great because *Garfield* was pretty darn powerful. And at one point, I was in two thousand papers. And I said to him, "Well, Sparky, I'm catching up to you." And he looked at me, and he was mean! He said, "I'll see you in the Louvre!" He was very competitive and although he had this kind of apologetic exterior and [seemed like] kind of a meek and mild and humble guy. Oh no, he was very proud of what he'd done and he was very competitive.

**Chapman:** Now similar to Schulz, you also had your work adapted to various different media formats. What was that like for you, to see that happen? Because obviously, that's a reflection of how much people are engaging with your own work and really enjoy it, that they're willing to adapt it into other mediums. Was that a fun experience? Obviously, it's happened multiple times. What has that been like on the whole?

**Johnston:** I was really lucky that the first show we did was a nice show. And I met a Canadian author in a coffee shop one day and he'd written a number of plays, and Gordon Pinsent was his name. And I walked right up to him, and I said, "Mr. Pinsent, how do you write a play?" I wanted to write a television show for animation because I'd always wanted to be an animator; that was where I was headed at the beginning. Anyways, he was reading a paper, having his breakfast, he looked up at me and said, "Just do it." [*Laughs*] What else is he going to say?

So I went home and I wrote a play. I wrote a story. And I submitted it to a fellow that had a small animation studio in Ottawa. And that evening, I got a phone call and it was Bill Stevens, and he said, "I just read your story, and I'm going to do it." And he signed me up and we did the first little television show and it was called *The Bestest Present*. It was a Christmas story. And they didn't change any of my script. And I worked with them through the whole process, and it was an absolute joy. And that doesn't happen very often.

I have since done a number of other animated shows and the process was gut-wrenchingly awful. I mean, you can get angry with your kids, but I have never been as angry as I was when we were doing these. . . . I literally bit a telephone book in half one day. You know, you can split the back of the telephone book, just rip it in half? Yeah, I bit one in half, I was so angry. But the first show was an absolute joy. And I remember being in the animation building, walking down a hot hallway, seeing all of the artwork stuck to the wall as the storyboard is often all stuck up on a wall. They were running the soundtrack back and forth in one of the rooms. They were checking the music, a whole group of young, wonderful animators who were all drawing my characters. And I stood in the hallway and I shut my eyes and I said, "If you don't say to yourself, 'This is the best day of your life,' you're going to miss it. It will go by." Anytime somebody says to me anything about what it was like with the animation, I remember that day because it was an absolute joy. So many people were working on *my* stuff. And I loved the process. I loved the artists, the musicians, the voice people, the foley people—everybody was great to work with.

The management often sucks in these things, you know, and the money disappears. And that was a problem with the shows that followed. It was always a struggle, because they'll promise you one thing and then your budget disappears. They go to the Cannes Film Festival with their family and friends, I guess. I don't know where the money goes, but it certainly didn't go into the shows. And the shows suffered terribly. You know that old gag "fix it in post"? "When the show is finished, we'll just get the sound people and the music people to fill in what is missing." Well, there's a lot of stuff you cannot fix in post, and I look at those other shows that we did and I can see all the flaws. The first show had some flaws too, but it was a joy in the end. And it won a Gemini Award for children's programming. And I think that if we had just done one show a year like Sparky did, it would have been good. But these production companies want to do twenty-six. They want to do a series. And once you do a series, it's terribly hard to keep your quality up because it's too much and too fast. You're still writing the script when they're trying to animate it. And they'll send it to Taiwan or they'll send it to Peru. I don't know where they send it, but it's out of your hands. And if somebody animates the scene, and that's totally wrong, it's cut into the show and it's wrong and you don't have time to change it and it's awful.

**Chapman:** I have a question. You mentioned hearing the music loop back on the special, so I want to actually get into the concept of music for a second as an abstract. When you were first working on the strips, and you're drawing and you're coming up with the stories, what was on in your background when you were at your drafting table? Is there a TV on? Is there a radio on? Are you listening to music? What was giving you the vibe to keep you locked in? What was the soundtrack of your work life?

**Johnston:** No, no sound at all when I was when I was writing. It had to be absolutely quiet. Birds maybe outside. But [when I was drawing] I used to listen to the CBC, which is you know, the Canadian Broadcasting Corporation, and many, many artists do. I know that Bob Bateman, Robert Bateman, who is the wildlife painter, he listened to it. So many artists listen to the CBC because it makes you feel as though you're part of a group, you know. These talk shows and discussions and news and stuff. And if the CBC was running something I didn't want to listen to, then I had a stack of CDs. I had all my favorite CDs and I would listen to them.

**Chapman:** Now when you eventually decided to end the strip, what was that relationship with your strip like at that point? Was it something that you knew [about when] you might end it? Because that's a big decision to end something like that that's obviously taken up a huge aspect of your life. Was that a difficult decision to be like "This is going to be the moment," or did you feel that coming for a little while?

**Johnston:** With my last seven-year contract, I knew at the end of that contract I would end the strip. It was a story that was going to have to wind up because it wasn't something that I could keep on going forever. Mostly because everybody grew up. All of my funny characters were gone. You know, the dog died; and the second dog wasn't as funny. And all the kids grew up. And Michael and Elizabeth, when there were children born to them, I had to change their look so that they didn't look like April and Elizabeth when they were young. I had to change the looks, and once you changed the look to the point where it's a totally different character, it's not as goofy and it's not as much fun. Once you add lips to a character, you can't open that mouth like a drawer. It has a finite space, right? And so it became too realistic. The backgrounds became too realistic. The characters became too realistic. You know, I was drawing every leaf on the tree. And I was looking at clothing magazines to make sure that the clothing was on trend and all that kind of silly stuff. And that became too exacting and there was too much research done. I was having Elizabeth dating a helicopter pilot, so I went to the helicopter school and I took photographs of the inside and outside of the helicopters and asked all kinds of questions about the program, and I was doing research that was crazy. And I thought, *This is not fun anymore; it's turning into a really serious sitcom. And I just can't sustain it.* There has to be a time when you end something. It's not going to be good forever. And it was good, but it wasn't going to be good forever. And I think I did the right thing.

And during those last seven years, I was able to wrap up the story quite well. I was able to tie up all kinds of loose ends and end it.

**Chapman:** . . . Obviously, Sparky was a big influence in part of your life. So one question is, when he was going to end *Peanuts*, did you ever talk to him about what had led to his decision to do that? And then the next question that will dovetail into is, when you were preparing to end yours, did you ever think about what Sparky would have thought or what advice he would have given you to end it?

**Johnston:** Nope. No, we didn't. We didn't take each other's advice. We're awful people about taking advice, you know. "This is mine. I'm going to do it my way." [*Laughs*] And I remember talking to him once he started to get ill. We talked about ending the strip and writing a story that would end it, and he felt he felt that would jinx everything. He thought, *If I write a story that ends the strip, then I'm going to die right now.* And he didn't want to do that. He didn't want to have Charlie Brown kick the football or have anything happen that would sort of wrap it up. He thought he might do it someday, but he put it off and put it off. And I don't think he thought he would ever die. He was certainly very upset about it when he was in the hospital. He kept saying, "This isn't fair. I'm not ready. I want to keep going. I've been doing the greatest work I've ever done and I love what I do and I am not ready for this. It's not fair."

**Chapman:** Actually, to jump on the Sparky kind of remembrances for a second, I had an interview last year with cartoonist Judd Winick, who spoke very highly of you. I guess you helped introduce him to Sparky, and he said that he couldn't believe he was at the table with him. And he couldn't even believe that he was supposed to call him Sparky.

**Johnston:** Oh yeah, Sparky was very generous that way. He was very approachable. And again, you know, unless you were sort of threatening his position on the head table [*laughs*], he was quite happy to be part of the crew.

**Chapman:** In terms of where you were, did you find yourself competing with anyone or feeling that anyone was like a direct competitor of some kind when you're all kind of competing for, as you said, space on the newspaper page? Did you ever feel that sense of competitiveness, and how did that drive you, if it did?

**Johnston:** I think you always have a sense of competitiveness, especially with yourself. You want to be better today than you were yesterday. But I think the one person that made me catch my eyeballs and sharpen my pencils was Bill Watterson. I mean, *Calvin and Hobbes* was wonderful. Beautifully drawn, beautifully written. It was an exceptionally good strip. And I just thought, *Boy, there's a new bar right there.* And so if I competed with anybody . . . it was more of an intellectual competition than anything. You admire somebody's work and you say, "Boy, if I'm going to stay in this job, I better keep on pushing myself hard," right?

But the competition really is between syndicates and their sales staff because their sales staff again has to go into a paper and say, "Listen, *For Better or For Worse* is better than *Blondie*. Get rid of *Blondie*," or *Blondie* would say, "*For Better or For Worse* is garbage." You know. "*Blondie* has been around for ages; take *For Better or For Worse*." *For Better or For Worse* would bump *Blondie*, *Blondie* would bump *For Better or For Worse*. And yet I can be friends with Dean and Charlotte Young, go have dinner with them, and have a lot of laughs as our syndicates beat each other up over who got that little space in the paper.

**Chapman:** Do you remember kind reading [newspaper strips] when you were younger? Would you point to any as being a specific inspiration point or a thing where you learned something from that specific strip that you actively wanted to emulate on your own? And obviously you're telling your own stories, but which strip would you say was the most impactful on the type of strip that you ended up wanting to do?

**Johnston:** I think that's just probably super politically incorrect, but the strip that most affected me was called *Henry* and I absolutely hated it. I thought it was terribly drawn, terribly written, and I thought, *Man, if you can get a comic strip into the newspaper, so can I.* and I was about eight years old. [*Both laugh*]

My brother is a professional trumpet player. And I remember saying to him, "So Al, where are you on the on the scale of good?" And he said, "Lynn, if you want to be good, go where people are bad." Right? I mean, it's competition everywhere when you're an artist. . . . But yeah, seeing something really bad [*laughs*] made me feel that maybe I could get there.

**Chapman:** Over the years obviously there's been *For Better or For Worse* merchandise. Was there a specific piece of merchandise that you that was your favorite, that you were like, "Now I've made it. That happened"?

**Johnston:** You know, we have almost no merchandise, to be honest, very, very little. Mostly what we have are the books because my characters grew and changed all the time. It was very hard to license them. You know, you can license Snoopy and Charlie Brown and all these characters that don't change, but something that changes really is difficult to license. The one character that we actually had produced ourselves was Farley the dog. And we had him made in China by a great company and we had a wonderful guy who was working with us on this, but we did it because there's a group of veterinarians in Ontario and they have a foundation called the Farley Foundation. They asked if they could have the dog's name and the dog's image as a mascot for their foundation. And we heard about what they were doing, and what they did was they raised money so that people who could not afford to have their pets taken care of could have veterinary care that was covered. There's always senior citizens or there are all kinds of situations where your pet is the most important thing in your life. And if you're sick and you can't look after your pet, you might have to leave the pet in pain or the pet has to be put down, and that's devastating. And these veterinarians don't want to euthanize your pet. They want to keep your pet going. But some of these operations are six hundred or thousands of dollars sometimes. And so the Farley Foundation is only in Ontario, which I think is too bad because it's such a good group and they've been doing for many years. And Farley has been their mascot, and we had the Farley plush made so that they could sell him and the money would go to the Farley Foundation, and that's the nicest product we've ever had. And we only have about twenty Farleys left.

**Chapman:** Oh wow. One of my last questions before I let you get back to your evening after spending so much time with us—and I'm very appreciative of that—is when you were developing the strip and, as you said, your characters were kind of three years behind your own kids, what did your family think of being somewhat represented in these strips that were inspired by your own life? Were they happy about it? Did they like seeing things that had happened to them represented in the strips? Were they mortified by it? Did they eventually become more okay with it? How did they feel about being having their lives in some way interpreted as part of your work?

**Johnston:** Well, to be honest, when they were little, they didn't read it at all. For example, my son Aaron was Michael. Now and then, there would be somebody saying, "Do you really have a girlfriend called Martha?" And he would come home and get angry and say, "Why do you have to do this? Why do you have to have us in the strip?" But for the most part, they really didn't pay much attention to it at all. Mostly they were affected by my traveling. But they were also affected by the fact that I knew all these really cool people. I mean, we went to visit the Schulzes a number of times and saw the [*Peanuts*] ice show. We would go down to Disney World or Disneyland, and we would be able to go through the back alleys and behind those shows and see how things were done and put together and ride that train. We had all kinds of privileges that other people don't have—you know, flying in Garfield's airplane. They had all kinds of wonderful adventures. I got to know Phyllis Diller quite well. For my daughter to say, "Yes, well, you know, I met Phyllis Diller," that was a privilege. The kids really had a wonderful time with that. And I tried so hard not to hurt them or expose them or say anything that was true and that they would be embarrassed by. I worked really hard, and that's where April came in. April was a wonderful foil because she didn't exist.

**Chapman:** Yeah.

**Johnston:** What's happening now is that my daughter, who's in her forties, has two kids. And she's saying, "*Now* I understand." She's reading it with a whole new point of view. It's completely from a mother's point of view now. And your son is reading it at the age of eight, right? And he's seeing it differently now from how he will when he's a parent himself.

**Chapman:** For sure, even just watching, reading it with him now . . . I can see the humor in things I may not have seen before. And I'm like, "Oh my God, that's totally true." I'll sometimes point to him and say, "That's exactly what you're like." And he's like laughing at the characters and saying, "I guess so, Dad." [*Laughs*]

**Johnston:** Well, it was realistic, which was what I really wanted to do, in all directions. Everything from the sad stuff to goofy stuff to relationships. I wanted to be believable. And it was all from the woman's point of view. And I guess I was hired because the dad would come home from work in these other strips, and he saw a very idealized family; the kids were cleaned and dressed and dinner was on the table. Whereas from the mom's point of view, she had to clean and dress those kids and peel those spuds, right? [*Laughs*] So, you know, it fit in quite nicely. And it was the career of a lifetime. I will never stop feeling lucky that I was able to do that.

**Chapman:** What is it like now, having your daughter kind of working with you? Because obviously there's still intellectual property, you're still creating products, et cetera. What is it like to have her working with you?

**Johnston:** Oh, it's wonderful because she's grown up with the strip. A lot of comic artists, their children somehow or other are drawn into the business just because they grew up with it. She's wonderful. She's also a business mind. I mean, a lot of artists just are completely lost when it comes to marketing and business and contracts and the serious stuff around the production of a feature like this. So she's great.

And what she's doing now too is, she's working with my colorist and they're making all kinds of changes to the strip as it runs again. And so they're putting helmets on the skiers and seatbelts on the people in cars and erasing cigarettes. Things like that. [*Laughs*] You don't see that anymore. So it's great to have that. And we get along great. I'm very lucky. A lot of folks don't get along with their kids, but I get along with mine.

**Chapman:** That's fantastic. Well, again, Lynn, thank you so much for spending so much time with us today. I really appreciate it. It was great understanding more about your process and what kind of went into those books. So thank you so much.

**Johnston:** You're welcome. And thanks so much for the interview. This was a real pleasure and an honor. Thank you.

**Chapman:** Thank you so much.

# Are We Good? Conversations with Lynn Johnston

**JEFF McLAUGHLIN / 2023**

Interview conducted on April 8, 2023 via Zoom. Previously unpublished.
Printed by permission.

**Jeff McLaughlin:** It is April 8, 2023. . . .

**Lynn Johnston:** Are we good?

**McLaughlin:** I can hear you, but I cannot see you.

**Johnston:** Okay. I don't know why.

**McLaughlin:** Okay.

**Johnston:** Katie, would you mind coming up and helping me with this? Please.

**McLaughlin:** I don't use this [video] system that often, so. . . .

**Johnston:** Yeah. Well, my daughter does all the time, and she is on her way up to give me a hand with it.

**McLaughlin:** Okay.

**Johnston:** He can't see me. I can see him. We can hear each other, we can hear each other.

**Katie Hadway:** Oh, sorry! Right, right here in the corner. What? Start here? Okay, you can unmute. And you can start the video. Okay, so good morning.

**McLaughlin:** Oh! Here we go!

**Johnston:** This is my daughter, Kate.

**McLaughlin:** Hi!

**Kate:** Hi, Jeff! Nice to see you.

**McLaughlin:** Okay, so pressing right now, it says, "record on this computer." So hopefully, this will work. Okay. And I also have another computer running where I'm trying to do the same thing, so I have a backup. Okay. Again. I just want to thank you for taking the time to talk to me. I hope you enjoy our conversation today. I know I will. It's been a great pleasure to dig into your past—

**Johnston:** Not too deeply, I hope.

**McLaughlin:** —and I found out so many interesting things about you, and one of the things we'll get to are some of those things that you've done that are quite astounding, not just in terms of doing the strip, but simply the matter of how much time and energy you spent with other things that you've done. So I've talked to lots of people. I've read lots of things, so I know your time is precious. So my plan is for today, I have a lot of things to hopefully cover. And it's been quite fun when reading many of your interviews or watching you answer questions when you have an audience, as you're often refreshingly and intriguingly open and forthright. Is that just who you are, or is it because you got used to being inspired by the personal issues that you dealt with in the strip?

**Johnston:** It's just me. I mean, I know a lot of people who do public speaking and comedy. Most of us talk about ourselves because it's easier to rip yourself apart than it is to attack others.

**McLaughlin:** Well, it's been very interesting to find out you, and this Conversations book series put out by the University Press of Mississippi is really enjoyable to learn more about other people.

**Johnston:** Most of the comic strip artists that I know are very open, very easy to talk to, very revealing about their family and their work. And it connects us.

**McLaughlin:** But it's also very useful to learn about what you folks do. For example, in your presentations, my favorite thing that I've seen you do is when you work with a circle and dots and the letter C and a little line for a mouth, and you demonstrate how moving these basic pieces around can suggest so much, such as age and different emotions. I'm wondering where that came up or where you learned that.

**Johnston:** Through teaching, I guess. Through teaching young students, very young kids who use all of these very simple elements, and by taking those elements and showing them how they can move. Take the eyes, move them apart, move the position of the nose, move the mouth, tip the mouth a little bit. And because I worked as an animator years ago—I was an apprentice here in Vancouver; we worked on acetate all the time with the lines. And you could see one layer over the other. And so it worked very well, especially on an overhead projector. And it's really quite fun to watch. So now that you can no longer get an overhead projector—try to find one of those things [and] you're covered with dust in school basements now. But that was the horse that I rode onto the stage. I could hide behind my overhead projector, and I could draw and talk at the same time, and it was fun.

**McLaughlin:** You seem to have a lot of fun when you're doing your presentations.

**Johnston:** I love learning, I love comedy, and if I can make people laugh, that's great. And I got into trouble all through my life because I was the class clown, and if you can put that silliness to work for you, it's good for everyone. As long as you're not hurting anyone. I mean, there's a lot of comedy that's hurtful, and I guess when I was younger, I was caustic and mean because I didn't know how to . . . I didn't know how to use words, and I didn't know how to make commentary that was direct without nailing someone else. Right? And so it takes a while before you lose that cruelty and learn how to use comedy in a really healthy way.

**McLaughlin:** Speaking of using words and so on, with the strip, you're restricted to how many words you can use to convey the ideas. You have three panels and a few moments to capture the reader's attention. How do you go about narrowing down your verbiage? How do you say what you want to say without being too wordy or too false?

**Johnston:** That's a real art. And it took me a long time to learn how to do that. In fact, I was lucky that I was given a six-month creative contract before the strip began, and during that time I would learn how to write, and it's almost like writing poetry. You have to. It has to have a cadence. You have to have an economy with the words. You have to get to that punch line easily, quickly. I call it "a log on the highway."

It has to flow, and you have to get that punch line in there, plus you have to write so that it's easy to illustrate, because each little panel is like a glimpse into a movie set, right? So you're taking your audience from the face of the person to the background, looking at the dog on the floor, and then the punch line at the end. And so it was a real skill set that challenged everything. I had to write, to draw, and to actually try and be funny. If you were lucky. I mean, a lot of the punch lines weren't funny. They were just colloquial expressions, or they were wordplay puns. Things like that. But when you're on a deadline, you take whatever comes through the Muse.

**McLaughlin:** Can you think of an example off the top of your head of a sentence that you might want to shorten?

**Johnston:** I wish I had thought about that earlier, but often you're describing things when you're writing. If you're writing a letter, for example, and you wanted to explain a beautiful sunny morning, you can fill that sentence with far too many adjectives—startlingly, brilliantly, reflectively, *blah blah blah*—and you want to take one of those words and use the best one rather than fill that sentence with all these different descriptive words. And of course, if you're drawing at the same time, you can fill a lot of that description in with your artwork. But it's a skill.

And right now, I'm working on a series of children's books. And I find that I'm a much better writer for a story with a beginning, middle, and an end. If I write in prose, I go on and on and on, but poetry forces you to have an economy of words, and to also use words that you normally wouldn't use. You have to you know search a vocabulary and find something that works right with the cadence. And again, it's a punch line. So yeah, the strip taught me how to write within an economy of words. And poetry forces me to do that again.

**McLaughlin:** And you worked with editor Lee Salem.

**Johnston:** Yes.

**McLaughlin:** Could you tell me what an editor does for a newspaper comic strip?

**Johnston:** Well, to begin with, he supervised all of my efforts to learn how to write sequentially. I had been used to doing a single-panel gag and a comic strip is four panels usually or three. And you need to write dialogue, statement, statement, gag.

And so it was an economy of words that I needed. I needed to write in a certain poetic style so that the words flowed. And you made sure that you used words that were easy to read and led you from one panel to the next comfortably.

You know, there's certain things that you can and cannot do in a newspaper comic because it's read by families. So there's criteria about what you can and cannot do. If I wavered from that, he would catch me. He was very concerned about cigarettes. If I showed a bunch of people standing at a bus stop, he did not want to see anybody with a cigarette in their hand. I would argue with him and say, "Yeah, but—. Yeah, but—." You know, things like that. But really we were on the same wavelength and he was very supportive of what I did.

I was not edited much. There was another editor that I worked with, and she was much more interested in punctuation and that type of thing, the nitty gritty of actual construction of a sentence. Mary was more [interested in] did I use a semicolon or a period or something.

**McLaughlin:** In one early newspaper article they noted that you were "a soft-spoken Canadian, nervously stumbling through your first public presentation to an audience which just so happen to be disinterested psychiatrists."

**Johnston:** Yes, oh boy, I remember that.

**McLaughlin:** I know how hard can be to speak in front of a crowd. How did you get over that? That fear, for lack of better word, of speaking to the public.

**Johnston:** I really wanted to do it. I wanted to learn how to be a public speaker, and I knew that it would be hard. It would be. It would be tough, because the number of times you get out of a theater, and you just say, "Why did I do that? Why, why, why, why?" You lie in your hotel room bed, and go, "You idiot! You stupid idiot!" And it's like a mantra over and over again. But, damn, a phone call comes and you accept another speaking engagement, right? And eventually I got so that I had a routine. I had a thing that I could do, and I used the overhead projector, which, again, was my Dumbo's feather. I could hide behind that and I could draw while I talked. But then I realized, even though I was pretty good at it, I realized that I couldn't do this as a career, because your audience would get bored to death if you didn't change your presentation. I had a good presentation, I could do it over and over again. But if I had to change it—which you would have to do if you're a comedian—you have to change what the audience is hearing, and that's a lot of hard work. And so I was never willing to put that kind of work into it and just do public speaking. But I enjoyed it. It was fun. I traveled. I met some wonderful people. I learned about audiences. It's like a classroom.

You're a professor, right? So you know that some classrooms are receptive and warm. And you just get in there and it's like you're with a bunch of friends. And others are cold and brittle and reject what you're saying, and you just don't feel as though there's a connection. And audiences are like a classroom. And so one of the things that I found that I could do to warm up an audience was that I wanted to talk to the teachers in the room because the teachers saved my bacon. If I had not had such good teachers all through school elementary school, high school, art school—wonderful, wonderful people—I don't know where I would be now because that kind of comforting strength and guidance was so important to me. So I would look at the crowd, and I'd say, "How many of you are teachers?"

And the people would put their hands up, and I'd say, "Oh, I just want to thank you all!" and that would start to warm everybody up. It would also warm me up. And I also I had a chance to work with sign language interpreters. On each end of the stage there would be these sign language people who were fabulous to watch and at points I would speak faster and faster, and it would force them to sign faster and faster, and as they were signing, I'd walk over behind them and just keep talking and they'd be so oblivious that they keep on signing, and then I would just say, "Aren't these people incredible?" And everybody would cheer. So after a while you get a routine together and you become a performer. But I knew that it wasn't something that I could recreate over and over again and do it as a career.

**McLaughlin:** One of the things I discovered about you is that you did a lot of research when you were doing the comic strip and a lot of design work, consulting various experts [on topics] from how buildings burn to medical issues to how the court system works. Why was that important to you?

**Johnston:** Authenticity. Because your work goes out there to millions of people, and in that crowd of people there's going to be a helicopter pilot who says, "Well, that's not what the inside of a helicopter looks like." And that immediately destroys the strip. It destroys your work. And I know that really talented authors do huge research. In fact, I think James Michener sent out a crew of people to do research on the amazing books that he wrote. You cannot put something out there if you haven't researched it. And I think it began a long time ago when I saw a single-panel comic strip that was done by somebody, and I can't even remember the joke, but it involved a chainsaw and the chainsaw was so badly drawn. I thought, *You stupid idiot! Get a catalog and figure out what a chainsaw looks like. Don't draw something out of your head that absolutely doesn't work!* And so that realization that I couldn't remember the joke but I remembered the bad drawing made me realize how important it was to draw things with authenticity.

Not only did I research things that were imagery, but I would go to the police department and ask questions. I would go to a courthouse and take pictures. I would go to the helicopter school and find out what really happened there. And it was fun. It's great fun! You meet some great people. You go into an office and you ask somebody about what they do, and they're very happy to show you. You go into a veterinary clinic and you really ask questions and you look at all the equipment that they have, and as long as they're not too busy, they're more than happy to explain what's going on. But yeah, the research was part of the fun of it.

**McLaughlin:** [That] leads me to ask: Did you have this all sort of mapped out beforehand? You know where the story arc was going to go? Or did the characters take you to places that you didn't know or expect that you would wind up at?

**Johnston:** Well, that's a good question, and you have to be an author yourself to ask that question, because your characters do take you away, and sometimes to places you don't want to go. You say, "No, I do not want to go in that direction. I want to go here." But the characters take you there, and you go with that flow, because again you're on a deadline. You're expected to get material out, and if the characters take you in a different direction, that's where you go. And I found that that was part of the exciting, almost spiritual part of this. It's like spirit writing.

**McLaughlin:** An article quotes you as saying the creative process is "like writing a letter to a lover and an emotional outpouring. And suddenly, it's just there. And the worst thing that can happen is if you're working on a story and right in the middle of it, it just stops." Then you have to scrap it, and that's hard to do, because it could almost be a whole week's worth. Do you ever recall changing a story where it went off the rails, as it were, and you just put it aside?

**Johnston:** I had so many characters that I had too many characters for the panels that I had for the one statement a day. So, for example, Elly's neighbor, Anne, was married to a guy who was a salesman. He traveled, and he was a salesman, and he was unfaithful to her, but he was also a hoarder. Their yard was full of stuff—only drew that once. But the stories of Anne and her husband, they were all here, and I just couldn't . . . there was too much. And it was the same with Lawrence, who as a mature man now owns a landscaping company. But there's all kinds of interesting stories about that. And as the characters grew and connected to other people—like Mike and Weed, for example—you're adding all of these new characters in there. There were too many characters and too many stories. And many stories I wanted to write, but I just didn't have the space or the time.

**McLaughlin:** A lot of the characters names that you use were based upon real people over the years, and as you mentioned about your admiration of teachers . . .

**Johnston:** I was kind in my work. If I named somebody or if I used a story that they had given me, they were very happy about it and would share it with their friends, and I often gave them the original strip that it was in. But I think one of the nicest situations was when I wanted to find my grade one teacher because she meant so much to me, and I was able to reconnect with her family. The last name was Hindmarch, and I had put Hindmarch Hardware [in the strip]. Whenever Elly went to the hardware store, it was Hindmarch Hardware. And that's an unusual spelling of the name. I think it's usually *s-h* the end. And I got a letter from the people in Michigan, and they said, "Where did you get this name?" And I said, "I'm looking for my grade one teacher." And they said, "That's our aunt!" So they connected me with my grade one teacher, and she phoned me, and she said, "Huh! How could you remember me?" And I said, "Not only do I remember everything about you—I mean, your hair, your clothes, the shoes, and your voice, and everything—but you drove a pale blue two-door Studebaker with the license plate number CBJ 386." And that was the license plate on Elly Patterson's car. I said, "You meant so much to me that I just wanted to tell you how much I love you and I appreciate you while I still can." It was wonderful. What I mean is, that was such a gift, and I have been able to connect with lots [of people]. This was before Facebook, right? So I was able to find some friends and family through the strip.

**McLaughlin:** You spent a lot of the time living in small communities. Did that have any impact on your perception or how things were at the time? And we're talking the 1980s and '90s.

**Johnston:** Living in a small town means you have to be a kinder person because you can be found very easily. You're putting your trash out with everybody else. So if you start to be cruel, or you say unforgivable things—and we all do these things in the privacy of our home—in a big city, you might be able to get away with it, but in a small town you have to be careful about what you say, and who you say it to. And you also know a lot of people in a lot of different areas. I mean, you get to know the mayor and the police chief, the doctors, the dentists, and the lawyers. You know all the infrastructure. If you need help or you need advice, there's always people you can easily find. It's not the same in a big city. You might have to go through a number of people before you get the right one. In North Bay, for example, I could just drive down to the newspaper office and talk to the folks there, right? In a small town you get to know a lot of people intimately. You get to know their private stories. You get to know a lot about their families that you can use actually as a storyteller without ever revealing your sources.

And so yes, living in a small town had big pluses. One was that I was connected to a lot of people in a small area where I had the confidence that I could talk to them openly, but I was also kept away from publicity in the big city. And you can tell I'm a bit of a ham; I don't mind being interviewed, and I don't mind being on the stage. And in the early years, when I had an opportunity to get out of the small town and fly to New York or Los Angeles, whatever, [I'd say,] "Yeah! Call me up! I'll be there!" But you know it doesn't do you any good. Publicity does not do you any good, and eventually you turn into something ugly and awful, and you're pretty self-centered and develop an "aren't they lucky?" mentality, and I didn't like that. So, again, living in a small town keeps you honest and keeps you okay; humble.

**McLaughlin:** And what was it like returning to some of these places after you became successful?

**Johnston:** Well, I lived in North Bay, Ontario, for years, so coming back here to North Vancouver, I was anonymous. It was lovely. I liked that a lot. What was strange was to go to a place like Milwaukee[, Wisconsin], or Bellingham[, Washington], and for people to know who I was and to connect to me and to have a relationship with me, and these were complete strangers. . . . I'd be signing books in a bookstore and a complete stranger would come up and say, "You are living my life," and they'll tell me intimate things about their relationship with their kids and their family; and this is in a lineup at a bookstore, right? So that kind of intimacy was surprising, rewarding, and it made me realized just how connected we all are.

The best letters came from people who were living in Guam and people from other countries who were with the American military because they got the *Stars and Stripes* newspaper, and I was in the *Stars and Stripes*. They would write and say, "It's a little slice of home, and I feel connected to home. I feel like I'm able to see something that's really happening in real time at my home." So I felt welcome everywhere, which is great.

**McLaughlin:** And speaking of feeling welcome and feeling connected, you were given an honorary membership award from the Ontario Veterinary Medical Association for your involvement in the Farley Foundation, which provided funding for necessary veterinary care for pets of people who couldn't afford it.

Another project you worked on was the Connections group for young people who were in danger of dropping out of school, and you captured your own identification with these kids by saying, "The Connections program is saving little me's over and over again." Can you explain a little bit more about why you wanted to get involved in these sorts of organizations?

**Johnston:** Well, again, this was in North Bay, Ontario, which was a fairly small town. I think it's about fifty thousand people, if you count the folks in the surrounding area. And so you get to know a lot of the people that are working to improve the downtown and with different associations that are working with kids at risk. And I did recognize myself in some of the kids at risk because I certainly was.

I was a kid that had all kinds of emotional ups and downs, and there was a situation in North Bay where they were trying to get kids to graduate from high school and to get that diploma. And a lot of kids didn't have a lot of resources; they didn't have a lot of support at home, and they didn't have food. They didn't eat, and so they might steal to get food. They might therefore make some bad choices, just because they were hungry and isolated. And there were some great people in town who had ideas that just needed funding. And if I could provide a small amount of funding every month . . . these resources would continue; you'd have a space to meet, you'd have a classroom available. You'd have a teacher and psychologist available. You'd have help. And these programs worked very, very well. And I had a little bit left over that I could share. So we were making T-shirts for these young people, and we were getting the kids out and into the public and helping people carry their groceries. And they would put dimes in the parking meters at Christmas time. And they would go in and out of the shops and help the shopkeepers unpack their materials at the back of the store, and they were given positions where they had to be honest. Okay, you had to trust these young people. You give a kid a handful of dimes. Is he really going to put those dimes in the parking meter? Is he going to buy himself some cigarettes?

But because we trusted them, they became trustworthy, and they finished school, and they thrived. And it was a wonderful program. I was so proud of that. And it wasn't me; it was a little bit of funding and a little bit of my time, but mostly it was all these other people that saw potential in these kids. And it worked really well. I've been involved in all kinds of stuff, and anytime that little bit of funding in town would help, I could help out. It's not much, and more than anything, it's just your interest, your support.

**McLaughlin:** Any of these programs still running, do you know?

**Johnston:** I don't think so, because a lot of the people that initiated them are gone. There's always a core group of people that start something and then they get older and move on, and if there's nobody there to take on that project. . . . But there were some wonderful initiatives in town, really good things to help young people, especially getting through school to get that diploma. . . .

**McLaughlin:** What's interesting is you're pointing out the importance of teachers, but also the importance of helping the kids get through that process.

**Johnston:** Yeah, you just have to say, "I believe in you" to some people. I mean, I needed that. I was a mess when I was a little kid. I needed that. And my teachers filled that space.

**McLaughlin:** Speaking of having resources, and this is a big stretch, your website is remarkable. Why have you and your team put up so much? You didn't have to. Yet it's a site you can get lost in with so many different treasures that your fans can discover. One can find out about real people, the real places you've used in storylines. There's frequently asked questions, your own commentary on strips, and so on. What was the drive to do that?

**Johnston:** I have to say the drive and the thanks go to Stephanie van Doleweerd, who is my website designer. She's an absolute gem. She's a fan of the strip. We are very good friends. We've worked together for at least twenty years. And Stephanie has created that website and it's through her diligence and her pressure, actually, because she'll call me and say, "Please give me some more stuff. I need more stuff." So we're constantly creating more and more things. Because if people are interested and they ask the questions, then I'm happy to answer it. And it makes you approachable as a person.

I would like what I did or anything I do now to carry on to the next generation, so if somebody looking at the site says, "Gee, they're just a person that drinks coffee, and slips up from time to time. Maybe I can do it, too." . . . The trouble with being in an entertainment industry of any kind, whether you're a dancer or a singer, musician, performer of any kind, is that the audience tends to think that you're exceptional; that you're not like them, you're something that's magical; that you can do it all the time; that you're always capable of being funny or singing on key. You see someone on a stage on Broadway and you say, "Well, that person is great! I could never do that." But you can because we're just people.

And I guess one of the best things that ever happened to me was visiting Len Norris, who was the editorial cartoonist of the *Vancouver Sun*. The people I had made arrangements to meet Len had not told him that I was meeting with him. It was on a Thursday afternoon, and I was seventeen years old. Mr. Norris was coming down the stairs at the Sun Building and as I was going up, I was too nervous to say, "Wait! I'm here to see you!" Instead, he said, "Good day," and I said, "Good day," and I went upstairs to his office, and I thought, *Well, I'll just wait here, and maybe he'll come back.* But he'd gone for lunch. So I walked around his office and I didn't touch a thing. Oh, but what I saw was his pens and his pencils and his brushes and his paper and his mirror and his glasses and whatever was there on the desk! And I said, "I can do that. I got all that stuff." So maybe it was the right thing that I hadn't met him. And years later, when I finally did meet him, I was well into the strip, and he said, "Why didn't you stop me on the stairs?" But you don't have that kind of courage, right?

**McLaughlin:** Definitely.

Like other successful cartoonists, you have many, many collections of your work. And you have been able to go back and look at your work more closely with the project you're doing now with the American Library, who's publishing the complete run of *For Better or For Worse*.

**Johnston:** Oh, I can't believe you've gone to all this trouble to look this stuff up. You're amazing, scary!

**McLaughlin:** And I just wonder what it was like to look back. Did you see things that you didn't see before or character developments or themes or points of view that you didn't realize before?

**Johnston:** Well, the strip ran for years and years. And yeah, you forget stuff. You forget story arcs. You forget certain character traits. And especially in the later years, when the strip became very complicated, it was no longer kind of a funny, cute family thing. It was more of a saga of a community, and it became very complicated. . . . I mean, we've just now gone through the very last of the strips, right to the day that I ended the strip—and for first couple of years there I was learning my own work. And it was surprising.

Naked Ned figure appears in the background. FOR BETTER OR FOR WORSE © 1997 Lynn Johnston Productions. Dist. By ANDREWS MCMEEL SYNDICATION. Reprinted with permission. All rights reserved.

**McLaughlin:** Did you have to give up anything in order to appeal to everyone? Because you commented once that you were told that you needed to appeal to the nine-year-old boy, who is not probably the person who would be most likely to read it.

**Johnston:** I'm a nine-year-old boy. I love burps and farts. And I get along great with my grandson, who's into video games. And [for his ninth birthday] I took him to a joke shop and I bought him all the stuff. The rubber chicken, the plastic poop, and he doesn't use it properly. I told him, "You know, your teacher is ripe for a plastic puke. You gotta put it just so. . . ." But you can't. You can't point to it. You have to walk away and wait for it to be discovered. So there's a nine-year-old boy in here that wants to do silly things in a comic strip format but because it has to go out to millions of viewers, you have to be very careful what you actually put in the strip. You can't put in a butt crack. For example, certain words you can't put in there. Well, I did manage an X-rated word, and I managed to do the butt crack, and the editors never caught me. . . .

It's that kind of challenge and stupidity that's what got me in trouble all through school. That's why my teachers, who tolerated me and put me to work, were the ones who actually steered me towards a career as a cartoonist. Because they could see that that's where I couldn't help myself. That's where I was going. But there were all kinds of stuff I could not do because it was a family strip, and nor did I want to, really.

But now, if I was to write a play, for example, I could do all kinds of things because it's not going into all of these households. Newspaper comics, I think initially, were set up to bring in the next generation of readers. The newspaper manufacturers wanted more eyeballs, and they wanted the young people to be coming. And so they started out with some of these illustrations, and the illustrations were more popular than the text—which is where the old quote about you can say more with a picture than with words seems appropriate—so they put more and more illustrated pictures, because photographs couldn't go into the newspaper yet. And so comics became a force to reckon with, and they found that it wasn't the nine-year-old boys that were tuning in and being the next generation; the adults love the comics as much as anybody! So the comics page became the seller for the newspaper. I mean, people would maybe not subscribe to a paper if they didn't have *Blondie* or *Peanuts* or *Wizard of Id*. They really thought that comic strip artists were heroes for the longest time. They're really well-known people. Their names were in your mind when you thought about comic art, and I was lucky to get into the industry just as it was sort of cresting and just before it was over. It's sort of over now.

**McLaughlin:** Yeah, that actually is my next question. Some newspapers don't run many comic strips at all, which is very disappointing to me. At least it's a nice break from the horrible news that you've been reading about. What's your thought about their continued existence within papers that are themselves struggling?

**Johnston:** Well, a comic strip space, that little chunk is called "real estate." And when you think about real estate in the city, it's very, very expensive. And so every time they give up that piece of real estate to a comic strip, that comic strip had better be good enough to bring in more readers. It has to be good. And so they're expensive. And a lot of small papers can't afford it. And I know that when I first started, *The Dundas Valley Journal*, I think they spent ten dollars a week on comics, but the *Chicago Tribune* might spend a hundred dollars for the same comic strip. It depended on the size of the newspaper and on the circulation that you had. But even so, they're very expensive. And so unless that real estate is making is doing good things for your paper, they would probably rather put advertising in there or a column or maybe not even have that page at all because it is expensive.

**McLaughlin:** One of the things I noted, and you alluded to it a moment ago about how people knew the artists as household names almost, is that there are literally hundreds if not thousands of newspaper articles about you or your strip and events that are going on within it or in your own life, whereas with comic book artists or comic book writers, we typically don't see that. For example, when you switched syndicates and then you went back to Universal Press, that counted as news. People wrote about it, and I'm wondering why. Is it just that you are a celebrity?

**Johnston:** Well, a comic book is a huge effort. The amount of work that goes into an actual comic book is enormous. You have more than one writer, you have more than one artist, you have more than one editor. It's a big group of people that are putting together a comic book. You might see the name of the originators of *Superman*. . . . [Jerry] Siegel and [Joe] Shuster's names might be recognized, but I've known people who worked on *Archie*, for example, and they were just one of many, many people. And usually the property is owned by the syndicate or is owned by a publishing company; it's not owned by an individual. Whereas the comic strips are very small. They are created and produced by one individual who owns the copyright usually.

Now, at least, some cartoonists work with writers because you can't maintain a really good quality strip if you're not getting good quality writing. . . . And it's very difficult if you're doing characters that don't change. I mean, how often can you come up with something really clever about a cat and a mouse or something like that after a while? And I would say three years is about the limit for somebody with characters that don't change. So we'll probably need some help, and one of the very few people that never got any writing help was Charles Schulz. He refused to take anybody else's ideas ever. And so he was one of the ones whose characters never changed. But he created everything himself. A lot of the others, well, family members might be writers, friends might be writers, professional writers are involved, and it's necessary. It's not a downfall. It's necessary in order to keep the feature current, and it's necessary in order to keep the feature good.

**McLaughlin:** And so you think, then, that people who are reading the paper would have more of a connection—that they would know that it was you who was writing this as opposed whoever is handling a certain comic book.

**Johnston:** At the end of the comic strip, you'll see the name "Mike Peters," and so you remember Mike Peters from *Mother Goose and Grimm*. While in a comic book there's a whole crew of people that are doing the illustrations, and maybe there's a list of their names. I don't know. I haven't read a comic book in a while, but certainly graphic novels.

**McLaughlin:** Many of those are written and drawn by the same person. So graphic novels are like the newspaper comic strips?

**Johnston:** But they're huge, right? It's a huge effort. People will know Raina Telgemeier for example, who's doing some of the most wonderful graphic novels now. But comic books? And manga is a huge consortium of people. That's an assembly line. If you look at a manga book, you'll see. Maybe the cars are beautifully drawn, but the people are crap and it's because the guy that drew cars can really draw cars, but the guy that did the people couldn't draw a stick figure if they tried. But they got to get it out. It's a machine. You gotta get it out, get it out. . . . That goes from one guy to the next, and one guy's doing backgrounds, one guy's good at mountains, and one guy's good at trees, one guy's good at cars, one guy does color. . . . You got people producing a book because it's gotta be out there, and people are eating this stuff like hamburgers.

You go to a train station in Tokyo, and there's kiosks filled with manga, and people are eating this like hamburgers. You go there and people are taking them off the shelves and reading them on the trains and handing them over to someone else and taking another one. It's hamburgers, right? I don't know how good the stories are. Some of them are really graphically horrible, but it's a concern of a group people. It's a team; it's teamwork. And a comic strip is one person.

**McLaughlin:** So do you think it's okay, then, for the newspapers to write "Lynn Johnston was seen over here," and "Lynn Johnston did this"? Is it because it's important for the reader?

**Johnston:** Yeah. I think so. If they're interested in your work, they're interested in you. I mean, I saw Carol Burnett on a show the other day, and I was thrilled to bits because she meant so much to me as a performer, and there she was again! And I wanna know more about her. I want to know what her house is like and what she does on the weekend. And is she writing? And what's going on going on with their family? I want to know more, because I like her so much I and I loved her work so much, and I think if you love a particular musician or if you're a fan of a particular actor, you want to know more about them. Because you care.

**McLaughlin:** Speaking of caring, lots of people cared about many of your characters and your storylines. I want to talk about Farley for just a moment. You may know where I'm going with this. In reference to when Farley died, you had a lot to say about the reaction that you got. I think one of the best things that you said was quoted in the *Toronto Star* that starts by noting that "Johnston doesn't blame herself for Farley's demise." You said, "You don't know what joy and happiness are unless you experience some sadness. And the strip is called *For Better or For Worse*." So here we have a situation where you brought up many "for worse" type scenarios. Here it's about the dog, but you tackled many tough events and situations, including various health-related issues. Why did you want to include those sorts of things later on in the strip's development that early on really didn't appear?

**Johnston:** Well, once the characters started to grow older, once the children grew up, it became a family story, and I wanted to show reality as I saw it from my eyes as a mom and as a member of a community. Whatever was possible in my life, I wanted to put into the strip. And of course, when you're dealing with characters growing and changing in real time, you have to deal with lifespan. And that meant the dog could only be a certain age before you had to seriously deal with his death, and the dog was thirteen years old, approximately. My sister-in-law at the time was a veterinarian, and she said,

"I hate to say this, but old English sheepdogs don't live that long; only about twelve years, maybe. You really have to deal with this. If you're going to be true to this aging thing, you have to deal with the death of the dog."

And she said, "Please, I'm a veterinarian. It's the saddest thing when I have to euthanize a pet, so have him go a hero." Let him go a hero. And I heard that. And I thought, *Yeah, that's it's going to be interesting to craft a story that allows him to go a hero*, which I did. And it took about two weeks to tell the story, because it's one panel, one image at a time, and the dog is in the river with the little girl, and he's holding her head above water, and all of that drawing is very challenging and really exciting because I was so into it as an illustrator. I had done my grieving well before I had written the story, and so, as I wrote and drew the story, it was perfecting my craft. And when it went out there I was surprised by the shock that happened. And of course, Charles Schulz said, "If you killed that dog I'm gonna have Snoopy hit by a truck and go to the hospital. And nobody will care about your stupid story." He literally said it that way, right? So I didn't tell him [that I had done it], and he was blindsided when it when it happened.

It had quite a big impact, mostly because I don't know how many characters have died in comic strips. Probably *Rex Morgan* and *Mary Worth* and some of the ones that were a storyline strips. They probably dealt with that. But this was different.

**McLaughlin:** Was there another storyline that you liked and that you're especially proud of that didn't make the news?

**Johnston:** Hmm! I don't know. I think aging the characters was difficult; aging the mom and dad was difficult. The children, the hairstyles, the shapes of the faces. . . . Things like that were a challenge, and people talked about that. But it was only other cartoonists that would come to me and say, "If I do this, how do I do it?" or "What's the best way to change and grow a character?" It was mostly amongst ourselves that these conversations happened about the craft and altering the appearance of a character in terms of that sort of impact.

**McLaughlin:** The Lawrence coming-out story was significant. Because of it, some newspapers would later warn readers of upcoming strips or stories that you are going to be introducing. One headline I came across was "Gay Theme Will Appear in Comic Strip." And then it goes on to say, "Today through Saturday the strip *For Better or For Worse* will involve a gay character. Lawrence is the best friend of Michael Patterson, and the college student in the Patterson family, around which the strip revolves. . . . Lawrence announced his homosexuality in the strip years ago. In this sequence his partner, Ben, is pondering a move to Paris. About thirty papers have decided not to run it and will rerun a strip from 1995. *The Augusta Chronicle* will use the sequence."

I'm wondering what you make of this announcement. Is it advisable? A good compromise? Or is it offensive in itself or perhaps a bit over the top?

**Johnston:** Perhaps. You know, living in a small town was really helpful for me because I got to know the newspaper editors and the features, writers, and people like that. You learn something about the workings of a newspaper because you're part of it. And so what happens in a big paper like the *Chicago Tribune* or *The New York Times*, or whatever, is that they have such a massive readership that they're going to be able to put something like that out there, and they enjoy a little controversy. It's fine with them. But you have a small-town newspaper like *The North Bay Nugget*. And if you have a very conservative audience such that the editor or the newspaper owner is going to be assaulted at a coffee shop if people don't like what's in the paper, then they're very, very vulnerable.

When the Lawrence story ran, I got phone calls from, say, seven in the morning till eleven o'clock at night every day. And it was overwhelming. But I decided I was going to answer all these questions. I was going to speak to all of these editors, and I found that for the most part, every editor I spoke to was accepting and they liked the story. But they many of them couldn't run it because they were living in such conservative communities. And one guy said, "My children have been assaulted at school. My dog was spray painted, my house was egged." You have to think about these small-town community newspapers and what the editors have to deal with. So I understand about warning people at the time. Today, it's almost a nonissue. We've had too much of this information now, and we're ready to sort of put it aside and just carry on with life. But at the time it was a bit of a news story, and so I could see why, through conversations with all of these different editors, some papers had to warn their audience or not run the story at all.

**McLaughlin:** I read a quote from Tom Batiuk of *Funky Winkerbean*, and he was talking about the social issues that were coming up in comics or the lack thereof. And he said that with the Lawrence coming-out storyline, comics strips were now dealing with social issues or being more topical in the way that other forms of pop culture, like books, movies, and television, had already been doing for decades.

Given that you're also known for taking special interest to make sure you had diverse characters in your stories, be it, ethnicity, age, and so on, what do you think about newspaper comic strips tackling these sorts of social issues?

**Johnston:** Well, again, when you have that job and you have that real estate, you're still dealing with you as a creator. A jazz musician probably is not going to write folk music, right? And so if you're in comics, if you're a writer and you're creating comic art, what comes out of your hands and your head is very personal to you, and if these social issues are something that nag at you and make you want to cover them, you will. Or if you're doing a story about a donkey and an ant, you won't. It's all what is in your heart and soul, which comes out on the paper. Sparky Shulz used to say, "If you want to know me, read my work." And he absolutely was all of those characters. He could be as magical as Snoopy and as cranky as Lucy. It's what comes out of you. It's what the editors approve of. It's what works. It's what your audience is accepting. And it doesn't take long before you realize what doesn't work. And you put that aside, and you go for what does. It's very personal. A comic strip is a very personal expression.

**McLaughlin:** Did you find that your colleagues in the profession when these sorts of storylines were coming out were being given a bit of a push forward? Or did they hold back because of some of the negative responses, even though you had overwhelmingly positive responses to all of these storylines?

**Johnston:** The comics creators, it's a small community. It's like any other niche group of people who are connected emotionally and personally, and we would often get together a couple of times a year. We had opportunities to get together; there would be book events every year. It would also be the Reuben Awards, which is the comic art Oscars. So we would all get together, and what we talk about in the bar, after the events, is process and responses from readers and what's going on with your syndicate and that type of thing. I don't even know how to say it, but you don't want to copy anybody else or get into a routine that anybody else is in. You want to do something that's unique to you, and there were a couple of strips that were very realistic, and one was *Zits* and it's still running, and one is *Luann*, which is still running. And we would talk about how real to make these characters and how to grow the characters and make them get older and things like that. And so because I had already done that, we talked about having the characters in *Zits* grow up and actually go to university. They were in high school; now they're in university. Luann grew up a bit, and she was more than the schoolgirl. She was now in university, things like that. In that respect, I talked to colleagues who were interested in carrying on in a sort of tradition that I had, but their strips weren't so annually updated. My characters grew up year by year by year, and they would go for six years before they would do an increment of change. Another six years, another eight years before they would change the characters.

But my relationship with my colleagues in the industry has been absolutely stellar. The people in the industry are wonderful, wonderful people. They're smart. They're caring. They're supportive. They're honest. I just love the friendships. They are lifelong. When I first got into the industry, I thought maybe it would be a bit unwelcoming: "We hope you fail." [That] sort of thing. But that's not the case. It's very supportive because each comic strip is an individual signature and an individual voice, and it's not an easy job. It is all-encompassing, all the time. Twenty-four hours a day, seven days a week. In order to take a holiday, you have to be eight weeks ahead of your deadline before you can even pack your suitcase. It's one of those jobs that not many people have, and those of us who do, we have a lot in common.

**McLaughlin:** Putting this altogether with talking with your colleagues, how do you balance your creative desires to explore with having to appeal to the general readership?

**Johnston:** I had a lot of characters, so I would try and balance the young kids and the puppies and the household chaos with the more serious adult relationships and people trying to decide whether they're going to rent an apartment or not, or which courses to take at university. Some of these things were pretty serious and dry, and so you'd have to balance everything, and I did the best I could. I would sometimes be the character. I would sometimes be a fly on the wall, listening to the character. I would sometimes have nothing at all, nothing, nothing. I'd be absolutely empty, and I would sit. But if you take that day of emptiness and you go out into groceries and clean your car, you lose. You'll have another day of emptiness. You have to sit and think about the characters; you have to be the characters; you have to hear their voices. You have to walk through the front door, sit down on the couch. You have to open the fridge, even though no gags are coming and no writing happens and you have no direction to go. You have to be there for that day. The next day you'll write three weeks. It's shocking the way that works. But until you trust that to happen, it's terrifying . . . because you don't want to turn out garbage; you don't want to send out something that is not good enough.

Again, I knew Charles Schulz really well, and he would say, "All you can do is do the best you can possibly do each day." And sometimes the best you can possibly do is not great, but you've got a deadline, and you have no choice. You have to get it out there. In order to do the best I could possibly do every day, if I had a day of nothing, I would dedicate that day to thinking about everything in the strip. All of the characters whose voices needed to be heard from next, et cetera. And I love the Sunday page because the Sunday page was a respite. It was never part of a story because some of the papers just carry the Sundays, some of the papers just carry the dailies, some carry both. To run a story through Sunday would mean that many readers would miss a whole chunk of the story. So every Sunday page for me was a break. I could have fun with the babies or the dogs, the silliness of something falling out of a shopping cart at a grocery store. I could have fun with imagery. It was fun. The Sunday comics page was always my day of rest. You can call people type A or whatever. But if I sign a contract, I'm going to do the best I can every day, even if my best is not great.

**McLaughlin:** You got started at the Vancouver Art School, and then you worked on animated versions of *Abbott and Costello*, which I think it was in the same studio that did *Rocket Robin Hood*.

**Johnston:** Yeah.

**McLaughlin:** I don't know if you remember that one, but I remember even seeing *Rocket Robin Hood* as a child and going, "Wow, this is bad, and really cheaply made too!" Was that frustrating for you to be there and see how animation was being treated at the time? Or were you able to learn that this was sort of just this fast food-slash-hamburger type of thing that you mentioned earlier?

**Johnston:** Well, Disney and Warner Bros. had the luxury of having teams of people to work on these beautifully complicated, animated shows. Whether it was what you saw at the matinee, at the theater, or whether it was what you saw on the Disney Channel, they had the luxury of time, and they had money.

But when television was in everybody's living room, they had to feed that beast. You have to feed that insatiable beast and to feed it constantly. And everybody wanted Saturday morning cartoons. You had to simplify the cartoon. For example, generally a walk cycle is twelve drawings, and you double click each drawing, which gives you twenty-four frames a second. So that's a luxury to have that. When you have *The Flintstones*, it might be three frames. But they had no choice because they had to get it out. What they did have was great writing. I mean, *The Flintstones* is gonna run again and again and again, as will *The Simpsons* and some of the other less complicated animated shows for Saturday morning. Some of the ones that I worked on were really awful because the writing was awful. We did *Abbott and Costello*, and throughout the building we worked in, you could hear the soundtrack. We got *so* tired of that, and if you ever saw the Abbott and Costello films, that was not a big part of it. Once in a while? Fine, but it became sort of a crutch.

But because it was simple and because I was working, getting income painting and learning, it was a great way to learn. I learned from the ground up. And I learned from great people. And you couldn't get into the business by going to school at the time; you had to apprentice. You had to get into the studio empty garbage cans and clean brushes, and then slowly, you would be trained if you had any skill at all.

**McLaughlin:** You point out some of the significant differences between animation and doing a comic strip. With animation, you have sound, you have visual effects, you have voices, you have environment, you have music. What makes a comic strip stand out from this?

**Johnston:** Time. You have time to look at it as a reader. You have time to look at each panel. You have time to read it again and again. You have time to think about it. Whereas in animation, it's there and gone in a blink of an eye, literally. If the story appeals to you, or if the sound effects appeal to you, you might remember that show. But a comic strip often will have a punch line that's memorable. You're a philosophy professor, and I'm sure this is what's brought you into comics, because there are many, many punch lines that are full of real reason and they are good words to live by. Often they're memorable. And I think the time it takes you to read through it and to get to that punch line and you say, "Well, I like that thought" or "That made me laugh"; it's different in animation. It might be funny relationship gags with eyes and big mouths, and the bigger the eyeballs and the bigger the mouth, the smaller the brain space, right? So that goofiness is thrilling.

I love it. I love Goofy. I can still do Goofy, the way he talks. I mean, love it. And so one brings it to life in a way that is visual. One brings it to life in a way that's, I think, intellectual. If that makes sense.

**McLaughlin:** Trying to put a positive spin on your animation experience [Editor's note: Lynn discusses the process involved and her disappointment with the results in other interviews in this book], I have this image of you as a grandmother watching *The Bestest Present* with your own grandkids.

**Johnston:** You know, I've never done that. I have never watched *The Bestest Present* with my grandkids, and I should, because I think it's funny, really. If you're in a certain business, all of this stuff is like shoes on a shelf, right? You'll only wear them once in a while, and sometimes not at all. And then you forget about them. So I have not done that with my grandkids, and I will. Thank you for the good idea.

**McLaughlin:** Another observation you made, and this is not that long ago, was about your art exhibit that went around, and you said that you wanted people to see your mistakes, to show them the magic behind it, as it were, and the hard work that goes on to it. For example, you noted with the Lawrence coming-out story that you had to wait until you had enough papers behind you to do it. You had to wait till you were strong enough in the industry because it was an important topic, and you also said that a lot of editors didn't like Canadian artists anyway. So with your art exhibit, were you happy with how it came out?

**Johnston:** Putting together a show for a gallery is a huge job, and we worked with the folks at the Sudbury Gallery, whose idea was to create a show that would tour. My daughter—thank goodness—was able to give me tremendous help with this, and we put this show together. It didn't do a lot of touring, but it went to a number of galleries. People were interested in the process. Mostly it's interesting to kids because they get to see it. All kids draw. And what I love about kids is that their heads go faster than their hands can go. If they want to do a comic strip, by the time they've drawn the first panel, their mind has already gone to the next story. And they can't understand why they did one panel but the story's finished. Well, they finished it in their head.

And when you see the kids walking at the exhibit, they walk right up close to the artwork, and they see the lines, and they see the white-out on the edges, and they see the pencil lines in the background. It's this opportunity for a kid to say, "I can do that." I love the opportunity to show art students that it's a very fallible career. There's a lot of mistakes in it. You just don't see it when the line art comes out in the paper.

**McLaughlin:** Speaking of students and teachers, you've been granted honorary degrees, and your addresses to graduates typically offer practical skills rather than philosophical, abstract ones. For example, at Western University [in London, Ontario] you said, "You have to show up on time. You have to be good at what you do. You have to charge a reasonable price. You have to be honest, and you must respect others." Why was it important for you to get those messages out rather than, say, talking about the more abstract value of art?

**Johnston:** When my son was setting off on his own at the age of eighteen, he had just finished school. We were living in North Bay, Ontario, and he wanted to move to Vancouver, which is on the other side of the country, and I wanted him to be safe. And I wanted him to be employed. And those were the guidelines I gave him: "Show up on time. Be good at what you do. Charge a reasonable price. Be honest. Be good to work with. Communicate." There was a list of about seven commandments, and I said, "You do these things, and you'll never be without a job."

I grew up in my dad's jewelry and gift shop, and I cleaned the jewelry, and I wiped down the counters, and I cleaned the floors on the weekend and did the windows, and I sold stuff, and I was good at it. And I know that if I could not draw, for a living, I could always work in retail. I knew that because I showed up on time. I gave a little more than is expected. I'm honest. I charge a reasonable price. I follow those guidelines. And that's another thing; I think it's on the list: "Do a little more than is expected" because that makes you outstanding. If somebody is calling you in to sell their merchandise, and you fold all the blankets and you clean the dust off the window sill, that's a little more than they expected, and they're happy because they know that you respect their place of work, and you want to be there, and you care. And so those were the guidelines I gave my son when he took off at the age of eighteen, and he's still working.

**McLaughlin:** I found more practical wisdom from another honorary degree speech that was addressed to fine art students, where you say, "Listen to good criticism and accept it. Draw for the love of it. The money comes later. Be willing to draw something again and again, because you can always do better." So more good practical advice.

One of the things I also found in reading up on you, in newspapers primarily, is that journalists would often reach out to you for a comment on something. For example, Charles Schulz helped liberate the concentration camp at Dachau, and your parents—your father was in the RCAF [Royal Canadian Air Force] and met your mother in Britain—sometimes partied because no one knew during the war if they would ever see each other again. Extremely challenging times. Given your expertise, do you think comic art, and graphic novels in particular, could do a really good job of capturing these significant moments and events?

**Johnston:** Absolutely, You can say so much in a graphic novel that you can't say in a comic strip, or probably even in a book of prose where the imagery has such impact. Art has always featured in war, hasn't it? You know those massive paintings of war. . . . We've always been fascinated by it, and if [the war] affects you personally, you're traumatized for the rest of your life. And so, like that car accident that you slow down to look at, you're always glad that you can keep on going. But if that car accident involves you, it's gonna affect you for the rest of your life. I think, as long as there are artists on the planet, there is going to be depictions of everything that we experience, from war to love to sex to childbirth to fantasy, outer space, you name it. That's the magic that's in people. There are so many people who are capable of taking those fantasies and putting them on a page for others to share.

**McLaughlin:** Did you ever have the feeling when you received negative letters about your strip that you weren't being appreciated?

**Johnston:** Quite right, or there's something missing there. Most of those letters are from stupid people with stupid ideas, and you just laugh at them. I answer every letter that makes sense. I answer every letter that has credence and strength. Anybody who's got a good idea, even if it totally opposite to mine, I will respond to those letters because I think they're valid, and I think that's insurance in the future. If people know that you've heard them and you answer them, then they know that you're out with them.

Whereas some of the other comments are bothersome. I mean, the trolls are idiots. God knows what they do with their lives. If you have nothing better to do with your life than criticize somebody who's doing something? Do something, idiot. It's easy to criticize. I just laugh at these people. I really do.

But the people whose messages affect me, I will respond to them. I will respond to all of them, and I think part of the reason why I'm still in the newspaper is because there's a loyalty with the readership; and part of that is due to the letters I wrote. I wrote literally thousands of letters. I had about 150 answers, and eventually you get a team of people to help you. But I did a drawing and a signature on the bottom of each letter, and each letter answered that person's questions because I would answer it.

Their letters would come in the old days before email. I would write letter number 12, which would have "Dear so-and-so, Thanks very much for your kind letter. I was particularly interested in *blank*." "I was particularly interested in your story about your dad that would go into the *blank*." The people who helped me knew that I had read the letter. I was responding and responding to particular concerns. In that letter, the reader who wrote would receive my reply, and it was a personal reply with a cartoon handwritten on the bottom of each one. I did thousands of those over the years, and for every person who would receive that, they would show it to a friend, and that friend would tell somebody else. And if that newspaper in that community decided to drop *For Better or For Worse*, those people would say, "Wait a minute, you can't! She wrote me a letter!"

One time I was sitting in a bar, which cartoonists are often doing. [*Laughs*] And there's two young new guys, just got a contract. They were just starting to do some good work, and they were joking about all the letters they got, and I've got my beer in my hand, and I turned around and I said, "I hope you're answering those letters." They said, "Well, it is too much work." And I said, "For each letter you answer, that's a dedicated reader that you've connected with, and it's worth your while. Not just because it's polite, but it's insurance. It connects you to your readers in a way that nothing else can." They blew me off. They're gone now. Those guys are gone now. Because not only do you connect with your readers by writing back to them, but you connect with them through your work anyways, right? If your work is not connecting with your readers, they're not gonna be there for you. And why would you read something that does not connect?

I think one of the funniest letters I got was from a woman who just berated me for a particular comic strip. She just hated it. It was a very angry letter. And I thought, *I'll go back and find the strip she's angry about*. When I read it again I thought, *This does not merit this response*, so I wrote back to her, and I said, "I've read your letter, Carol, and I think you probably had a really crappy day, because I don't think that comic strip is that bad. So I hope everything's cleared up and you're feeling better and good luck to you, and thanks for reading my work," and whatever I said. . . . But it was a handwritten letter. I got a handwritten letter back from her, and she said, "Oh my God! I didn't think you'd read that. I thought it would go to some editor, and it would be thrown in a garbage can!" She said, "I had a terrible day, and I took it out on you. When I dropped it in the mailbox, I couldn't get my hand in to get it back, so I'd hoped that you wouldn't read it." So then I wrote back to her. We had this wonderful exchange, and here was somebody who had a really bad day, who fired off a nasty note to someone she thought would never hear it.

**McLaughlin:** What this tells me is not only how much time you spent on the strip material, but also how much people connected to the material because they would have to actually take the time to write you a real letter with a real stamp.

Universal Press brought in vacation time for cartoonists. I hope that helped a little bit in giving you a bit of a break.

**Johnston:** Nope! I didn't take vacations. I was always weeks ahead on my strips, always, and I would work in airports and hotel rooms. When I was in the bath, I was thinking of gags. You know, my checkbook was full of punch lines. I'd pull over on the side of the road and write a punch line in my checkbook so I wouldn't forget it. So no, it was an all-in, all-time-consuming job.

It is full time. People just think, *Oh, you do a drawing a day, and then you're free*. It's a big job, and very few people manage it. Many people burn out in three years.

**McLaughlin:** When did you first know you were successful?

**Johnston:** Right off the bat.

**McLaughlin:** Why was it that?

**Johnston:** Oh, they were hoping to start with 150 papers, and we started with 150 papers right away. Yep, it did well right off the bat and it just kept gaining papers until I was in over two thousand papers, and it happened fairly quickly.

**McLaughlin:** And how did that feel for you?

**Johnston:** Comforting. . . . At the same time, it's a terrifying experience to be assigned to a twenty-year contract where you're expected to be good. All the time. You have to do your best work all the time. I mean, for anything that you do in life, that should be your criteria, right? Do the best you can do at all times. But for something like this, where thousands of people or millions of people are reading your work every day, the pressure is really profound. And whatever positive feedback I got I was balanced, I would say, by the amount of pressure that was on me to do something that was outstanding. And could I do it? I don't know. I gave it my best shot.

**McLaughlin:** Well, you did wonderfully, of course. Everyone knows you did wonderfully. Yet with that twenty-year contract, that is so intimidating. How did it work? Was it just that your salary would go up on the number of newspapers who signed on?

**Johnston:** Yes. Yes.

**McLaughlin:** And what would happen if it didn't go off like you planned? If, say, your numbers went down?

**Johnston:** They would watch as you lost papers. And as your papers dwindled, there would be an agreement at some point that you would cancel mutually. I can't imagine trying to kick a poor dying horse if it's not gonna get up. So I was prepared to have the contract canceled if I couldn't fulfill their requirements.

**McLaughlin:** And with your success, you had a team that was working and helping you. When did you start bringing other people in?

**Johnston:** Well, coloring was quite a big process, and so I first hired some-body to help me with the coloring. If you hire another artist who's got a good color sense, you give them the color chart and you give them a copy of the original art, and they fill it in with the colors and the numbers, and that was sent to Buffalo for the colorists to use. And so that was the first person I hired.

I later hired another artist to help me with the actual illustration of the strips because I was being pulled in so many different directions. I just didn't have a number of hours in the day required to do this job because I was rais-ing two kids; I was involved with the community. I needed a life. I was doing books and book tours and speaking engagements and animation. . . . There were all kinds of other things that pulled me away from the drafting table.

So I met a wonderful illustrator who took over drawing the backgrounds for me. I would put everything into pencil, and she would do the lettering of the dialogue balloons, and she would also do all the background, the trees, and the cars. It was drawn for her. Her pen line was excellent and her work mirrored mine very closely. I didn't let anybody else touch the characters but [she did] the backgrounds. It was great fun.

She hated things like drug stores and grocery stores and libraries that had so much stuff in the background, all the details, but eventually I took advantage of her skill and put every brick in the building and every branch on the tree, and the drawings became very complicated.

**McLaughlin:** I've read so many letters to newspaper editors from *For Better or For Worse* readers that were either praising you or criticizing you. It made me wonder why they would take the time to complain about something such as "How dare John step on a spider!" or something trivial along those lines. Whereas they don't take the time to complain about something horrible in the real world that's actually going on.

**Johnston:** Well, they can get their head around it. You can get your head around John stepping on the spider or I think it was Elizabeth's cat eating a spider. Elizabeth goes out of her way to protect this spider, and the cat eats it in the end or Farley does, or something. Anyways, people will get all in a knot over something like that. But if there's a headline like a child is kidnapped, and there's a terrible story, then you can't get your head around that. You just retreat into silence and in awe and shock. But honest to goodness, I don't know why people take the time themselves to write a nasty letter to a cartoonist.

I really don't. What if it makes them feel good? I guess it's like having a shower or taking a dump. Just get it out there and get it over with. Just make me feel better.

**McLaughlin:** I don't know. I don't know.

**Johnston:** I think a lot of them live in a basement somewhere. Actually, there was one person who was trolling me, and it turned out that she was a really bright person. Stephanie was able to figure out, triangulate this person's living space; and found out that it was a quite an accomplished woman who was a teacher. And you know, we couldn't understand what was going on with this lady, but . . .

**McLaughlin:** Yeah.

**Johnston:** Fine and dandy. Do what you need to do. . . .

**McLaughlin:** And it's so much easier now just to spew something online, and imagine the poor cartoonists nowadays who must deal with that.

One of the things that that struck me as very important is the backstory to Lawrence about the reality of the situation, about your friend being murdered. . . . And I thought when I was reading about that and then reading about these people complaining about this particular storyline, what if they actually knew why you had done that, if that would change their views? And I don't know.

Showing the warmth of the Indigenous community. FOR BETTER OR FOR WORSE © 2006 Lynn Johnston Productions. Dist. By ANDREWS MCMEEL SYNDICATION. Reprinted with permission. All rights reserved.

**Johnston:** Probably not. I doubt it. I doubt that there's a family on the planet who does not have a family member who requires some extra thought and care. We all have family members who are dealing with life-changing issues, whatever it may be, and that was part what of our family was dealing with—the issue of how do you tell your parents, how do you tell your friends? And so, when Michael died, I wanted to do this story for him, and I've known him since we were kids in about grade eight.

We formed a comedy troupe, a bunch of us, about four of us, and we would listen to *The Goon Show* records. We'd go down to Michael's house at lunchtime at school—he lived close to the school—and we made up plays and drew cartoons. Michael wasn't a gay guy. He was my close friend. The fact that he was gay was part of his wonderful persona. He played Peter Pan on stage because he was tiny and feminine and light and funny, and he was a wonderful, wonderful comic. He and his partner were doing blackout comedy in Toronto at Yuk Yuks, and through them I met Robin Williams and all kinds of people. He was not a gay guy, he was a guy, for goodness sakes! And so when his death was treated with sort of a cavalier, "Well, there's another one off the streets." I thought, *Nope, this is for you, Michael. This is from the heart. This is for you.*

And I had the help of my brother-in-law, who had gone through that whole [coming-out] process and was very happy to just tell me what he thought and how he felt.

**McLaughlin:** I think that sensitivity about others is one reason why you've been recognized, not only by your fans, but also by your peers, which we'll talk about in a moment. But you were awarded the Order of Manitoba, one of the orders that you received, because of your doing a story of a northern community. I was wondering how that particular storyline, where Elizabeth moves up North to become a teacher, came about?

**Johnston:** Well, I wanted to include northern communities, these tiny little remote northern communities. Each one has a heartbeat. Each is all unique to itself. And there are so many different Native communities; there was Chipewyan, Ojibwe, Cree, Oji-Cree—which was a mix of the two—and they're up in Northern Manitoba, and there were a number of different languages.

We had a float plane, and my husband was a flying dentist. We would go into these very remote communities and provide dental and medical service one week out of every month. I would go quite often on these trips. And a lot of the elders didn't speak English. They lived very traditional ways. They really do rely on hunting and fishing. And it's a different way of life all together, but the sense of community and the sense of camaraderie is incredible, and the sense of humor is incredible. First Nations people are the funniest people on earth. And I guess all kinds of folks who had to deal with the good old white guys, they have to have a sense of humor.

I really enjoyed the privilege of being able to go into the communities. And then, when we moved into North Bay, there was a big community right close to us and it was Ojibwe, and it was very accessible. Beautiful powwow grounds. Wonderfully funny people. Welcoming people. And I would go to the powwows all the time. I just love powwows. I love the action and the jokes and the outfits and the dancing. And I just wanted to be able to incorporate some of that, because to me, being able to have that in my life was such a privilege. We don't know each other well enough. That's one of the biggest problems I found with the so-called settler, white guys and the First Nations people; we don't know each other. We don't get together enough. We don't talk enough, and there's that separation happens when you are strangers. Right? You try to imagine what the other person's life is like, but you'll never know it if you're not part of it.

So I felt it was such a privilege to be able to go to the schools and to see the kids learning their own language and to know families who are putting together the outfits for the dancers. From my point of view, I have no tradition. I'm from a British background. Bangers and mash, "Hail to the Queen," whatever. But there's no real ceremony to my background. I would love it if I had a Dutch cap or a Ukrainian dance, but there's no history to my background . . . a tangible history, aside from my dad's limericks and stuff like that, and God knows what. But I loved the tradition, and I loved the ceremony, and I really got to love the people in order to bring that to life.

Realistically, you have to live in the community. I've had friends who were teachers who worked and lived in small Native communities. And this is their story. What they went through. Often the kids won't even come into class because they have to be out on the trap line, so you work around that. I thought it was great fun, and I was able to go to the powwows and ask people lots of questions.

And the town of Mtigwaki that we came up with was designed by a friend of mine who was one of the Band council members, and he and his family got together with me on a number of occasions, and we planned out the town, where it was in Ontario, how the community would thrive. . . . It was a fantasy town, but it was based on real Native communities and how they operate, what makes them work. Most of them have a nursing station and a school and an airport. Some of the airports are just gravel, but the sked airplane comes in once a week and brings in the doctor and the supplies, and the teachers sometimes too.

It's an interesting life, and it's a powerful community in that the relationships are so strong and so meaningful. You can live in a community and never talk to your neighbor. But if you live in one of these tiny little towns, everybody relies on everybody else in the community. And the stories are incredible, and there's tragedy and hardship there too. And you learn all about that. And you know there's trouble, but there's trouble everywhere. It was the good stuff that I wanted to connect to.

**McLaughlin:** Have you been back to the North at all?

**Johnston:** Not to the Manitoba or Ontario North, but I've been up to Atlin [, British Columbia] and Skagway and White Horse and the North in BC. It's all very similar. It's like a small town anywhere, but the isolation makes you unique. And there's a certain arrogance to living in the North because the southerners really don't know what life is like up there. You can have some bozo politician come up and be there for a day and pompously say, "I know what's going on in that little town, and I'm gonna figure it out." They don't know anything about life in the North, and part of it is difficult, part of it is joyful. You make your own fun. The difficulty is like living on an island, getting in and out in the bad weather, and all of that. And lack of services and lack of infrastructure. And all the stuff that goes on. But it makes you stronger. But the people that move to the North are unique people, they are adventurous, they are outgoing. They're outspoken. They are hardworking, and I love small towns in the North.

I grew up in Vancouver and never thought I'd leave. Who'd leave Vancouver? Huh? So my first point of call was Hamilton, Ontario, and I was obnoxious. I was a West Coast snob. "You called that a mountain? [*Laughter*] It's an escarpment."

"You call that a fish? Okay, it's a minnow, right?" And people would say, "Lynn, go home. Just pack up your stuff, go back to Vancouver. Eat your sushi and go walk around the sea wall and go home."

Okay, so then, from Hamilton—and I got to love Hamilton—it was a steel town, and it was a place where they said you could open your windows so you could hear the birds cough because there's so much pollution. But, oh my God, my best job was as a medical artist from McMaster University. And I wouldn't have done the comic strip if it wasn't for wonderful people in Hamilton who encouraged me.

I divorced, remarried, moved to Northern Manitoba. What an adventure that was! I learned how to fly! I went into all these tiny little communities. All of these experiences have helped me be a better comic strip artist because I'm not a Vancouver West Coast snob anymore. I've lived in a little town. And one of the interesting things about Lynn Lake, for example, was that there was a man who used to fall asleep in the doorway of the of the pharmacy, and his name was Hyacinthe. And you would step over Hyacinthe, go in and buy what you needed to do, step over Hyacinthe again. Say, "How are you doing?" And maybe buy him a coffee. But we knew who he was. We knew who he was, we knew about his family. We knew that his family loved him. We knew that he had problems, but he was a good guy. And we knew his name. And we knew that he didn't mean to be sleeping in the doorway of the pharmacy, but he just was. And here Vancouver, I can step over a guy on a doorway, never know who he is, and not care. *I care now*. I care, because I lived in a town where you got to know everybody.

**McLaughlin:** You mentioned some of your beginnings a moment ago. At McMaster you started out doing anatomy drawings and adding pictures and cartoons to the slides that the medical professors were showing in class, and apparently students would remember the information better. Any idea why that was the case?

**Johnston:** It was visual. You have a blue diazo slide with graphs and lines on it and numbers. Or you have a cartoon character. Let's see. Hmm, I've got to do an analogy here. I did a whole series of cartoons on water and wind-born particles that would cause health problems. And this was everything, from bacteria to fungus to pollen. Whatever. And it's carried by the water. It's carried by the wind. Will you show a guy underwater, holding his nose and fish coming up to him? And each one is a different kind of pathogen. That's far more memorable than a blue chart with lines on it. In fact, the most work I did was for epidemiology, which is very dry and it's all text.

Sociologists did a project in which they had a bunch of students try to learn the same material from blue diazo slides, and the others learned from the comics. One of the doctors, who was very anti-comics, was suddenly asking me to do cartoons for them. So I did a lot of comic art for the doctors at McMaster, and one doctor that I did a lot of work for was Dr. Murray Enkin, who was head of pediatrics.

**McLaughlin:** So we've been talking a lot about connections and communities. And I know one of the personal highlights for you was to meet some of the cartoonists who were your heroes and have them accept you as one of their own. Can you think of something that they might have taught you?

**Johnston:** Well, it's kind of funny, because I learned from all of the people that I wanted to meet. I don't know if they ever learned anything from me, but these were my heroes! I was dedicated to *MAD* magazine. As a syndicated cartoonist, to walk into the *MAD* magazine offices in New York and have people say, "Come on in Lynn, I'd like you to meet Sergio Aragonés. I'd like you to meet Mort Drucker." Holy suffering . . . ! These were people I learned from! These people I admired, and for them to say, "Oh, we like your work. Come on in!" Whoa! You can't ask for more positive feedback. That's even a crappy way to put it. But you can't ask for a more wonderful reception! I've really done what I never thought I could do, and here I am. Sergio, he's the guy! Very funny. It's magic. He draws better than anybody I know.

**McLaughlin:** Speaking of people who are important to you, I know you've spoken a lot about Charles Schulz in other interviews. What was special about the relationship you had? Why was it so important to you?

**Johnston:** I guess for me he was a bit like my dad. He was twenty-five years older or so, and he was somebody that I enjoyed being with. He was very, very supportive. And I guess being accepted by somebody like that was reassuring. But we just had a great friendship, and a friendship is up and down. You fight, you complain, you don't speak to each other for a while, you get back together again, and whatever happens strengthens the relationship. I got to know his family, mostly his wife, quite well. I didn't get to know his children too much because they were adults and had families and were very busy. One of his children, Jill, is an athlete who's just incredible to watch. His life was rich. And I loved his friends. He had some wonderful friends.

It was a family that I became part of in a way, and I'm still in touch with Jeannie and love her to bits. But Jeannie herself is an amazing person. All these people aren't just amazing themselves. All the people around them are amazing. Like Jeannie's a pilot. She flies an airplane. She's in her eighties now, but at the time that I knew her, she was exercising with Cirque du Soleil. They would strap her into a trapeze, and she would literally fly! This is Jeannie

Schulz! You don't know about that, but all of the people around the cartoonists that I knew were really interesting people with incredible stories themselves.

Jeannie is quite amazing. She's a real athlete, and he needed to marry an athlete because he was as well. Tennis and golf all of the things that he liked to do. But Jeannie's pretty impressive. All these people were a privilege to know. They really were.

**McLaughlin:** When you won the Reuben Award and being the first female *and* first Canadian, did you find that it was perhaps a burden to win it relatively early on? Or was it just reaffirming your own confidence that you were doing well?

**Johnston:** I won it too soon. I didn't think I was ready. I didn't think I had produced enough material. I didn't think I had earned it. And the year that I won, Jim Davis, who does *Garfield*, was also up for the award. Now he *did* deserve it. He had done the work. He had really earned it. And I felt that he should have won that year. And I didn't know whether it was political. . . . I wondered because he does a character that doesn't change. He has a set number of characters, and after a while you really do need help. If you're going to keep your work current and worthy, you need help. He had a couple of writers. He had a couple of artists, and he worked with them. But he never stopped working on it himself. You know, he was one hundred percent part of it. But maybe there was, I don't know for sure, but at the time I thought, *Are these people voting against Jim and for me? Or did I really earn it?* And I had not earned it yet, I felt.

**McLaughlin:** How does that award process work?

**Johnston:** At the time they would put out the word that it's time for the Reuben Awards. Nominate whoever you think should get it for the year, and it's the Cartoonist of the Year. Well, in order to honestly vote for Cartoonist of the Year, you, as the voting public, have to know what's out there, and how much can you read? As one person. And there's thousands of comics out there. There're comic books, there's animation, there's greeting cards, there's magazines, there's editorial, there's strips, there's books. I mean, the categories are endless. Really. How can you honestly vote for Cartoonists of the Year? So it ended up being a popularity contest: "Oh, so-and-so hasn't won. Let's vote for so-and-so" or "I really like so-and-so's work. I haven't seen any anybody else's, but their work is good for the year. They should get it this year." It was a very difficult thing to vote for. We tried. We all tried to honestly vote for Cartoonist of the Year, but it wasn't until quite a few younger people came in and were willing to put the time in. Again, it's one of those jobs, it is all-encompassing. You have no spare time. To be the President of the Board takes time and takes commitment, and it's hard to do. Finally, there were some young new people who came in and said, "We've got to change the way we vote." And now there are categories.

So there are chapters, and, say, a chapter in Los Angeles might get together, and they might do the comic book, and there might be a few people in Minneapolis, and they get to do the editorial. And you get an award. And it's much more fairly judged now. But it's still difficult to choose cartoonists of the year, because again, it would have to be one of the category winners. . . . If you win top of editorial, you should be in line for the Reuben Awards. But I can't see editorial in comic books, as a voter, so it's still flawed. But in the end, I think everybody who deserves it wins it, and everybody is supportive of the winner.

There are very few real bozos in this industry. Everybody I have known and loved and cared about is caring back. It's a small group of people and it's a difficult industry, and we're all very supportive of each other because we all know how much hard work goes into it. Even if you didn't do better than anybody else on the planet that year, you probably did deserve it.

You know, before we end, I wanna know why you're doing this.

**McLaughlin:** Oh well, we're not done!

**Johnston:** I know, but I wanna know why you're doing this, Look at the amount of reading you've done in the research. And I'm very flattered, and it's wonderful for me, but you're a professor. My head is spinning. . . .

**McLaughlin:** There's a number of reasons, so when we get together in person I'll share many of them with you. But you've mentioned some of them. You know the importance of comic strips and what they can do. As an educator, I love hearing stories because we learn from other people. One of the things you mentioned early on in your career was "Am I doing something that is just about my life?" But then you hear back from someone who writes and says, "Oh, I dropped a frozen turkey on my foot too, just like in your strip!" So it's recognizing the impact that your profession has and what value you're adding to society.

**Johnston:** Well, thank you. Because cartoonists don't think about what their impact is often. And it's people like yourself who actually care and read and write about it that keeps us alive and well and comfortable in our own skin because, if you don't have an appreciative [readership] . . . most of the audience doesn't get back to you at all.

**McLaughlin:** There are the trolls and the letter writers, but millions of people that read your work don't or can't get back to you all, but they love and connect to your work.

**Johnston:** Thank you. But you're still a person working in your basement at a drafting table, so it's wonderful to have somebody who's certainly got your educational background to really take this work seriously, because so many gallery owners don't. They'll say, "This is not art. You call this art? This is not art." And you want to say, "Well, my friend, you're a curator in a little gallery somewhere, and I'm doing just fine."

**McLaughlin:** Another reason why I want to do this is when you were doing the strip and living in Northern Manitoba, I was growing up in Winnipeg. And I thought, *How cool is it that there's this woman up in Lynn Lake, Manitoba, who has captivated the world and has millions of readers, and she's up there?* [*Pointing northward*] I don't want to sound too odd, but I was like, "I'm pretty proud of there being someone around here doing this."

**Johnston:** Well, I have to say, I love Winnipeg. One of the great things about living in Lynn Lake and being in Manitoba was the support that Manitobans give you. People joke about the flat prairies and the long winters and the mosquitoes in the summer. But you can't have a better city or a better province for theater and art and comedy and music. The Winnipeg Folk Festival in the summertime, and all the all the absolutely wonderful, spontaneous, comedy that comes out of Winnipeg. I was very fortunate to live in Manitoba, and again, I was a Vancouver snob who was just gonna say, "You call that a mountain?" [Editor's note: There are no mountains in Manitoba.]

Yeah, I love Winnipeg, and I love being able to stand on the corner there in front of the Hudson's Bay store and be blown apart by that winter wind. "That's it. I'm here. This is it! This is what they talk about. I'm in Winnipeg!"

**McLaughlin:** I just finished rereading the canoe story arc, and John's canoe tips over and everyone is worried about whether John and his buddy made it. But before that, they're out paddling, and there's a can of Old Vienna beer floating by, and I was thinking, I wonder if, when you're revisiting that particular strip for the collection, whether you'll change it to a brand of beer that people would know now.

**Johnston:** Did you ever drink Gimli Goose wine?

**McLaughlin:** Yes! And Baby Duck!

**Johnston:** Oh, Baby Duck! Yeah! I love the label on the Gimli Goose wine, because the goose has gigantic gumboots on. Yeah, good old Manitoba. . . .

**McLaughlin:** Did you get any pushback for the Canadianisms?

**Johnston:** In the beginning one editor at the syndicate, who eventually was fired for various very good reasons, said that he would refuse to allow me to use Canadianisms. And I said, "Well, then, tear up the contract, my friend, because that's gonna happen. If your editors don't like racket with a *q* [racquet] or check with a *q* [cheque], then they can change it in their editorial efforts. But I'm going to do what I know." The other editors and the owner of the company were on my side and they said, "Yeah, you're a Canadian citizen. Do what you need to do."

**McLaughlin:** How did you come to be the president of the National Cartoonists Society?

**Johnston:** Because the guys didn't want to work hard enough to do it. It was the old boys' club. A bunch of old guys would get together and they'd smoke cigars and they drink their beer and they would eat and chew the fat. And one woman who was the secretary did all the work to organize the Reuben Awards, chaired the meetings, did everything. She did all the work. And when she became ill and retired, nobody wanted to do the work, and I had been brought in as the Canadian delegate—somebody other than an American. They wanted to go international. So I was pulled in by Bill Hoest, who was the president at the time, to be the international member, and Bill got sick. Bill had cancer and he was dying, and he was becoming more and more ill.

It was evident that nobody was taking over the range of the of the society, and there was no president, and so I started taking on more and more. "This has to be done." Okay, I'll do it. "Well, this has to be done." Okay, I'll do it. Eventually, I was doing everything. And so they voted me as president.

One day it was like a kangaroo court in one of the guys' living rooms. Somebody else was saying, "We can't have her as president. She's a woman. She's Canadian. We can't have her. I'll be president!" They say, "Shut up! Sit down! She's President!" It was that kind of silly, silly thing. I became the president, and I was president for a year, and I did a really good job because I had some great help. You pull in people that you know you can trust who are going to work on something for it. I worked hard. And it was a very crazy year, and as much as it was an old boys' club, and they treated me. . . . They used to draw naked pictures of me. . . . They wouldn't give me the gavel for a while. So my husband made me one. They would draw nude pictures of me while I'm trying to conduct a meeting, so I would draw nude pictures of them. And some of those guys are pretty ugly, and they didn't want to see themselves in the buff by my hand. So it was even-steven. And I worked hard, and eventually I gained their respect for that.

Fortunately, there's a pretty equal status there amongst the cartoonists now. But these were *New Yorker* guys. They're all in their seventies and stuff. Pretty staid in their ways.

**McLaughlin:** What was the society responsible for, or your role as president? What sorts of things were you looking after?

**Johnston:** Well, at the time when the National Cartoonists Society began, it was a group of people in New York who loved to get together. They were friends, and they would get together at a bar. Then it got bigger and bigger. There's cartoonists in Los Angeles and cartoonists all over the country, and they started coming from LA or Florida or other communities to New York, and they started to say, "Well, we want to get together with you guys, but we don't want to come all the way across the country. Can't you have a meeting in Los Angeles or elsewhere?"

And Bill Hoest, who I took over for, was beginning to organize different events in different parts of the country so that cartoonists, most of whom don't have the money for airfare and hotels and expensive meals, could meet. And [they felt,] "It'll be nice if it came to my town for a change." So when I was president, I hosted it into Toronto. It's a huge amount of work, but people remember that as one of the best, because they got out of their own backyard, and they came to a different country and got to meet a lot of different cartoonists from up here. So, again, it's a wonderful community of people, and it's international. There's a cartoonist association in Australia. There's certainly one in England. I could go anywhere in the world and be welcomed by the comic artists.

**McLaughlin:** Was it primarily just a social thing, or were there assorted initiatives?

**Johnston:** Well, it started out as a social thing, as these things always do. I'm sure the masons started out as a social thing. But yeah, it started as a social thing. And then they realized that as a large group, certainly, if you want to take it off your income tax, there has to be some value to the meeting, right? You can't just go and drink beer and shake hands and have fun. You have to make a presentation. You have to invite a guest speaker. You have to have a cause. You have to support the children's hospital. You have to do something that legitimizes this gathering, right? And we didn't want to spend money on guest speakers, so we started to guest speak ourselves. . . . And it turned out that we loved hearing from the other cartoonists. And it's great fun having, you know, name a cartoonist—they get up on the stage, talk about their process, do some drawings, and we all learned about each other! And we got pretty good at these presentations. And that led into the Comic-Con in San Diego. So it got bigger and bigger, and now it's quite an established and really well-run organization.

**McLaughlin:** You mentioned the nude sketches, as it were. And I know that when you're signing your name, you sign it "Lynn," because your last name has changed through marriages, but you're always "Lynn," which points to the fact that women have different issues that men wouldn't think about. Being one of the very first well-known female cartoonists, were you comparing notes with Cathy Guisewite?

**Johnston:** Sure, Cathy and I know each other quite well. And Cathy was one of the first people I called when I got my contract. But what people don't realize is, there are millions of women cartoonists. You just don't see them. They're doing comic books or doing greeting cards or doing children's books and illustrations. They're doing some amazing editorial work. There are a lot of women out there, and they just are not heralded the way the men are. And often it's because they don't have the freedom because they've got families and other commitments. But come on, men! Vacuum more often! Clean the dishes, for heaven's sake! It all falls on the shoulders of the wife. Right? . . . Lots of women in the industry. And I've met quite a few wonderful, wonderful people and been on panels with them. And it's a joy to know all this talent. It's a privilege.

**McLaughlin:** One panel that you were on was with Kate Beaton, the graphic novelist. I think graphic novels are one way that women have been able to be recognized more and be out there more in the public eye.

**Johnston:** Well, you can say more. And I think, unless you have a contract with a publisher that's demanding you get a manuscript in on a certain date, you can work at your own speed a little more perhaps. I don't know. I've never done a graphic novel, so it's not right for me to talk about it because I really don't know what I'm talking about. But the people that I know who do graphic novels, they don't turn one out at every year. It's every couple of years, and they have the time to perfect their craft, and they're doing very well.

**McLaughlin:** It must be fun for a cartoonist to know that a particular strip of theirs is on someone's fridge and it's been there for years. But I want to take it up to the next level and ask about your thoughts on when scholars refer to your work when they wish to highlight some position or argument that they're making or when they want to analyze your strip specifically. So, for example, there's *Typical Girls: The Rhetoric of Womanhood in Comic Strips* by Susan E. Kirtley.[1]

In terms of actual content, Kathy Turner, a Tulane University professor, spoke about how she admired *Cathy* and *For Better or For Worse* and their literal portrayal of their main characters. She argues that the way you both draw women is different than the way men do, in that "men draw women because women are more self-conscious about their bodies."[2] What do you think about academics looking at your work or using your work?

**Johnston:** It's astounding! In fact, I don't think I've read any of those articles you just mentioned, and I'm blown away that you know about them! But you're an academic, and you do research. And this is what you do. But I have not followed any of this. I don't really know where it goes and who uses it. I'm glad that they do. And I'm glad that they find value in it. But I have to confess that I haven't paid much attention, and especially since when the strip wrapped up, it was like I moved on, and for a while, I didn't want to even draw a *For Better or For Worse* character. "Please leave me alone. I never want to see these characters again." But now I'm enjoying them again as the strip runs again. It's kind of daunting to think that people would analyze your work and find stuff like that to write about.

**McLaughlin:** These scholarly works also answer part of your question to me earlier about why I do this. It's to promote the recognition that some academics are looking at this type of work and different types of pop culture in a rigorous and intellectually fruitful manner and pulling important ideas from it. I will send you some of the articles I just mentioned, so you can have a glance at them if you'd like. But I'm glad that you like the idea, that is, because you see the value perhaps in this approach—if not necessarily knowing what these people are talking about, but that they are using your work as a way to learn. You were already doing educational work with your drawings at McMaster University. . . .

Still, what if someone reads into something that you did, but you don't think that's the right interpretation? As an artist, do you say, "No, that's not what I meant—this is what I meant"? Or do you just sort of say, "Take whatever you want from it"?

**Johnston:** I think people have to take whatever they want from it. I mean, you make a statement. It's out there. If it's in black and white, you can't take it back. If you're proud of the statement, great; if you're not, you take the lumps. But when it comes to content and the meaning of speech and thought. . . . I think about George Carlin, who, I think, was one of the most brilliant stand-up comics ever. And I wish that he could have been president of the United States, because I think he's one of the most brilliant minds and clear thinking and objective and a funny, funny, funny man. But the things that he said were things that people think and know don't say out loud. And that's what made him so hilarious. Because you'd say, "You are absolutely right! I would never say that! I wouldn't really be caught saying that. But, oh man, are you ever right!" And so if, from time to time, your work can have any impact at all, it's beyond gratifying, and you can't let it change you. You can't start to think that you're clever because then the magic will go away. Once you think, *Oh, yes, it all comes from me. I'm brilliant*, then I think the magic goes away because it comes from out there somewhere.

My partner is a jazz musician, and he writes a lot of music. And the music comes from out there, just like comedy comes from somewhere else. And there are times if you think of something great, you have to look up and say, "Thank you, whoever you are, for being with me today because I could never have thought of that ever!" So great ideas come from somewhere. And those of us who write cartoons and do comedy are a conduit from that "somewhere." Wherever it comes from.

**McLaughlin:** Will Eisner once said that comics were perceived as being in a ghetto. And that he had a hard time imagining how a newspaper comic strip artist could be creative for themselves and keep pushing and yet do the same thing over and over again when you are trying to develop your own style and becoming more proficient as an expert in your work. What sort of little tricks did you learn about yourself in terms of doing Elly's hair or other shortcuts, as it were?

**Johnston:** Oh, that's a great question, because I want other cartoonists or kids especially to know some of the tricks of the trade that I use. You can use your iPhone now, but I used a Polaroid camera. So if you have a kid cutting their own bangs, for example, their hand is up like this, and they're holding a pair of scissors, how does that look? You can't make that up. You have to have that information in a photograph in order to do it right. Or somebody's taking the handles off a kitchen drawer. You have to reach inside with the screwdriver. How do you hold the screwdriver? You have to use a Polaroid camera. I have albums full of Polaroid photographs that if they were uncovered by some archaeologist in a dump somewhere, they'd say, "What in the world? Why would these be here? Why would anybody photograph [that]? This is insane!" But many, many of the comics that I have been looking through lately, I can identify one after the other that were done well because I had a Polaroid camera. The other thing that I do is that I buy toys that are three dimensional. I'm wondering if I have any of them around here right now. . . .

**McLaughlin:** I recall seeing you with all these little airplanes and little cars. . . .

**Johnston:** Yes, yes, I had a car for each one of the characters that owned a car, and bicycles too! And one of the hardest things to draw is a shopping cart. When I found a shopping cart —it was a little magnet—I was thrilled to have it because I could then turn it around. For example, if you have a school bus and you're doing a comic strip, you can imagine the comic strip as a long piece of real estate. A school bus will fill that piece of real estate if you show it side on. But if you buy a model of a school bus, and you can get those in any good hobby shop, you turn it to the side, and you can hold it in any position. You want a really good diecast car that has all the anatomy under the car to show you what a real car looks like so you can actually turn a car over in a ditch in a comic strip. And your diecast model is going to give you exactly what you want with the perspective that you want, because you're holding it.

So I have diecast models, and I have all kinds of toys. I have cowboy hats. . . . And when you think about a basketball, for example, there are lines on a basketball. Can you imagine where those lines are? Would you be able to? No. But I've got a toy basketball, and I can hold it in any position I like. And if those lines are going to change when they are holding it in the first panel, it's in a different position than it would be in the last panel because you move things around. If I'd taken a photograph out of a magazine, it would never change; I'd always have to use that image. But holding a toy basketball? I can turn it, and so it becomes more real in my drawing. So toys and Polaroid Cameras, and even having people pose for you—it is *so* important to get the art right.

**McLaughlin:** In terms of "getting the art right," there was a one-day event called "Swap Day" when you took over Michael Peters's *Mother Goose and Grimm* and he took over your script.

**Johnston:** Oh, sure. Oh, lots of fun! Yeah, we did those four times when we swapped around. And we also did things like saying happy birthday to Charles Schulz. Jan Eliot, who did *Stone Soup*, has put Elly in her comic strip a number of times, which is great fun. I have them sitting on my wall right here. It was a way to say "Hello!" and give a hug to one of our friends.

**McLaughlin:** In 2006 you signed a petition with 450 other cartoonists to have the original artwork of Dina Babbitt returned from Auschwitz-Birkenau where she was forced by Dr. Mengele to do drawings. And a letter was sent to the Auschwitz Memorial Museum. Do you recall this?

**Johnston:** I do.

**McLaughlin:** In that letter it states "the fundamental principle that art belongs to the artist, and who create it is recognized everywhere except in totalitarian countries." And in the report from *The New York Times*, it states that the letter was "Signed by Stan Lee, the creator of Spider-Man; Lynn Johnston, the cartoonist of *For Better or For Worse*; and so on." I don't know if you know that the end result was that they were not returned. She eventually received copies of the work, but not the originals. And I'm wondering what's your philosophical view about that particular area of ownership and copyright and the whole situation.

**Johnston:** Yes, well, it's a super complicated situation. It comes to ownership and copyright. Some people believe that it belongs to the artist, and some people believe that it belongs to the syndicate or the entity that hired you to do the work. And it becomes mired in a lot of heavy-duty conflict, and you get legal people involved. But ultimately I think just voicing an opinion was about all I could do, and I don't know what the outcome was, so I'm glad to hear that you've researched that as well.

**McLaughlin:** Milton Caniff said that drawing was like eating and drinking—namely, he couldn't do without it. What is it about drawing that is so important to you?

**Johnston:** Well, I express myself through drawing quite often. I can't explain something unless I am drawing. If I'm telling somebody about a situation like designing a backyard, for example, rather than try to explain it with my hands, I will take a piece of paper and I will draw the backyard or a hairstyle or any number of things.

When I went to Peru and to Honduras and to Mexico with the Medical Missionaries, I could speak enough Spanish to be a translator at the time, but the fact that I could draw was super helpful because a lot of medical procedures you can't describe very well. If I could draw the procedure for the patient, it made all the difference in the world because then they could see what was going to happen and they could get their head around it. Fear is the worst thing in the world. You've got some person who comes from a small town in the mountains, and everybody's going to have a medical procedure in the city. They're terrified. They've never been out of town, right? And so that was super helpful. Language can't do it all. Illustration is very helpful.

**McLaughlin:** Talking about when you were retiring, you have mentioned in other interviews that you wanted to work on your Spanish and that you wanted to travel with medical teams. Where does that interest come from?

**Johnston:** I've always been interested in medicine. I always thought for me to get into the medical school at McMaster was a gift. And I've always wanted to learn more, because aren't we a miracle? We're a living, breathing miracle, every one of us, every dandelion, every mosquito, every dog, cat, bird. We are miracles. And how does that work? You know?

And so I've always been fascinated by how our body works. What that pump actually does and where the air goes and how we survive. I mean, we're a miracle. So working at McMaster was wonderful. I was connected to all kinds of amazing people. I could go into surgery and see stuff that the average person just doesn't get to see. And it made me realize even more that there is a soul to each one of us. Because when you open up a body, it's just like the textbook; except for a few people who have the heart in the wrong side or an extra kidney or something, we're all pretty much the same. It's like taking the back off of refrigerator. The components are pretty much the same in each refrigerator, but when you plug it into the wall it does something. And so when you see an autopsy, for example, you become very detached because you're looking at a textbook image. It's all there. They weigh it. They cut it up, they check it out, they put it back in, they sew you up. But what makes that? What makes that biology project a person with a personality and talent and history and facial expressions and just all the funny things about them? You look at Rich Little and some people who could parody others, like Robin Williams, who could become any number of characters. Well, each one of the characters that you become is an individual. They are so unique that you can parody them. What makes that happen? And is there not a spirit? Is there not? Magic isn't a word that covers even part of it. When I came away from my first autopsy, I was so filled with a spiritual awakening. Not that I'm a religious person—but I guess I am, in that I have to say there is more to us than just this meat-and-potatoes vehicle sitting on a chair. There's more to it than that when I'm gone. I want to know where I'm going.

**McLaughlin:** I think you also commented when you saw that first autopsy, and they had removed the internal organs, that it was like an empty canoe. That was an image in my head that it's hard to get out.

**Johnston:** Yeah, and it was. Having that background made me better at what I did, ultimately, as a cartoonist. Because having anatomy and learning how to draw the body from the inside out is imperative. You can't be a sculptor unless you know how to draw a skull. And so having that, and also having this spiritual connection, made all the difference for me in what I ultimately did as a career.

**McLaughlin:** And as you moved beyond your career and have had the opportunity finally to take a vacation, it was Peru you liked.

**Johnston:** First, I went to Honduras with my husband and his medical team, and then I went on my own to Peru. And I just love the people. I love working with the people, especially the people in the mountains. Their areas don't get a lot of medical help, and I was just enriched by that whole process, and I got to use the language, which I love. I love the Spanish language. I love the music, the food, the people. I just love it. And that to me was another bucket list thing; I want to work is with the medical missions and use Spanish and draw pictures of surgeries and keep people who were vulnerable from being terrified by medical procedures.

**McLaughlin:** It's nice that you are able to bring those loves together.

**Johnston:** Yeah.

**McLaughlin:** That's very, very special. You moved back to North Vancouver some time ago, and you downsized quite a bit. First of all, what was it like returning home?

**Johnston:** Wonderful, best thing I ever did. Yeah, it's a good thing to go away. It's a good thing to live away from your place of birth, because you really do need that experience. But coming back, it's been wonderful. It's a beautiful place to live. I can manage the rain, and I like being anonymous. Nobody really recognizes me out here, which is great. I like that, and I'm comfortable. I still have family here. I have high school pals that I kept in touch with, and we get together and enjoy the fact that we've known each other since we were little kids. My partner I've known since grade five, and we would not have met if I hadn't come back here, and life is good. My daughter lives within walking distance, so does my son, and we're all very happy and productive. It was a good move.

**McLaughlin:** And part of moving involved downsizing. You donated a lot of work to the National Archives and to the Ohio State University. How did that come about? And what do you hope for those collections?

**Johnston:** Well, you can imagine drawing for year for years, plus calendars and greeting cards and advertisements and just stuff like spot art. Thousands, thousands, thousands of drawings. What are you going to do with all of that? And I gave it away. I sold some of it, but there were boxes of it, boxes! It's hard to imagine how many boxes of art. And if the archives wants that material, they're not only going to display it, they're going to look after it in hermitically sealed containers and people are going to touch it with white gloves. I throw it around like it means nothing. But it's wonderful to know that it's kept and appreciated and respected. So yes, I've given a lot away to the Canadian Archives, the American Archives, the Ohio State University. It's great to know it's there, and I know it's accessible. If we want to do a show, we can contact the archives, and they will certainly, with great effort, allow us to take a few pieces and display them if we wish. It was very nice that I was able to do that.

**McLaughlin:** What do you hope the collection will do for other people?

**Johnston:** Well, there's nothing like original art. You actually see the paper. You see the pressure of the pen nib on the paper; you see the Wite-Out where they made a mistake. You see the word that they didn't like and crossed out and put something else in. You see all the vulnerabilities. But you also see the power of the work itself, and there's nothing like seeing [that]. Winsor McCay did those massive drawings for the old *Little Nemo* pages, and I remember one of the first times that I was at Ohio State. It was a display of his material up there. I was so fascinated I didn't want to talk to anybody. There was a reverence there, just standing and looking at his work, and he didn't use a lot of Wite-Out and stuff like that, just the original art. It's like seeing a handwritten letter. If Abraham Lincoln or the Queen wrote a handwritten letter, wouldn't you want to look at that and say, "Wow!"? I mean, anything that's done by hand . . . even when you go to Mexico and you see the carvings in the temples. That was all done by hand. Isn't that thrilling to know somebody before you, an artist, actually left their signature right there in stone? It's rewarding and comforting to know that your work is kept in the archives. It's an honor.

**McLaughlin:** When you retired, you went into what you called "new-runs" and then into reruns. And now you're revisiting the strips again for this complete collection. Why is it important for you to tweak some of these original strips that you're doing?

**Johnston:** Well, you can always make your work better. And if you have an opportunity to make it better, you should take that. When it was announced that they would be running my work from the beginning, I was thrilled, but the first thing that came to mind was, *I don't want people to see that old work again, because it's not good enough.* I wanted to fix some of it. I wanted to add better stories, flesh things out. Because in the first year, for example, I may make a statement, and then that would be lost. Then I'd make another statement, and then that would be lost. But after the characters became real, living, breathing images, I wanted to go back there and take that statement and flesh it out a little bit more. And so I added a lot of new material to the early work, and that was a good thing mostly because it gave me an opportunity to improve what I had done, but it also gave papers who were going to run the strip again something new to work with. They weren't just repeating the same old material. After about two years, I think I allowed it to just go ahead and run again.

But we are editing still. And because we're living in a different age now, some things have to be changed. You have to put helmets on everybody, take cigarettes away, put seat belts on people. And recently, we had to redraw a number of strips that showed April sitting in the front seat with her mom. And she's just a little kid of about four, so she has to be in the back seat. So the conversation has to happen. All the artwork has to be changed to show [April] in the back seat, and I'm very grateful to my graphics and colors guy, Kevin—thank you, Kevin—who takes a lot of these things, and he adds the helmets, and he adds the seat belts, and he's doing all the "repairs." And now and then, some of the dialogue has to be changed, especially since it has to be reconfigured to fit into a new calendar because calendars change. A Father's

Day strip that might have been on the twelfth of one month might be on the sixteenth of another month. Or Easter. So things have to be reconfigured and juggled so that they hit the same date again, which is something my daughter and my colorists do. But yeah, we're still working on it.

**McLaughlin:** You mentioned your bucket list a moment ago, and we are now pulling up to the present time. What sorts of things have you been exploring and working on?

**Johnston:** Yeah, I'm working on a series of children's books right now. I can show you. Here's the cover. [*She holds up the cover*] I hope you can see that. Okay, so it's a story about a little robot boy and his family. It's Mom, Dad, Grandpa. It's a family with family stuff going on, but it's all written in rhyme. And I will have six done by September.

**McLaughlin:** Wow!

**Johnston:** I have four done now, and three are colored. And I'm also working on a series of video games. And this is again starring these robot characters. It's a project that we're able to do because the strip is running again. We're paying for this from the money that I get from the comic strip that is running a second time. It's allowing us to do this, and it will launch in September. It's called *Alottabotz*. You have to come up with the title, and then you have to register the title and own the copyright for the title. We have an animator in Mexico who's animated the title and is animating the characters.

We decided to do some video games, which is a new industry, even though it's been out there for a while. But the actual nuts and bolts of the industry is changing daily, moment by moment. We started to work with a very young group of mostly men who are video game developers. Their talent is in their ability to create movement and the game philosophy, but they don't draw pictures. So they send me stick figure sketches. But I can draw, so I still have a job. [*Laughs*] I've been drawing the most amazingly complicated backgrounds and infrastructure for them. You draw the background as if you're doing a giant map, and the character starts at one spot and they go through it. And there's waterfalls and territory. But then, over top of that, you have to put all the trees and the buildings and the bridges and the volcanoes and whatever else the characters are going to encounter on a second level, so that can be cut apart and moved. And some of these can be animated. It's a huge process. And the funny part is that these guys are all in their twenties. Some of them are younger. Some of them are students in Winnipeg. I keep telling them, "You're working with a 1947 Ford here." I can still get the job done, but I ain't gonna use a tablet. This is old technology. So their headlights are shaky, the exhaust fires off sometimes in inappropriate times. . . . I finally got a very respectful relationship with our team of creators. And I'm learning how to do backgrounds for video games. You can't get any more up to date than that!

Oh, and I'm also playing harmonica again. My dad taught me to play the harmonica from when I was a kid. My husband's a jazz musician, and so harmonica and jazz guitar go well together. I'm playing my old button accordion again. Physically, mentally, I'm keeping in shape and having one hell of a good time.

I just hate how I look!

**McLaughlin:** You look fabulous!

**Johnston:** Well, thank you very much. Don't we all, don't we? As long as you're alive and well and breathing, you have all your teeth and both eyeballs working. Maybe that's okay. But man, I look in the mirror and say, who the hell is that?

**McLaughlin:** Oh yeah, but it's better than the alternative, though.

**Johnston:** But the alternative might be more interesting than we think.

**McLaughlin:** My last couple of questions, then I'll let you go. After all the success, after all the accolades and the honorary doctorates and the different Orders of Canada, Manitoba, and the Hall of Fame awards, what would you like people to think about you and your strip?

**Johnston:** What do I think about me and the strip? The strip is over. It's like a novel I've written, and I've put it on the shelf. I would love to pass on any of the skills that I have to the next generation. I've enjoyed working with students, but I don't think I have ever in my life being happier than I am right now. I'm happy with my life, my family, my work, my partner.

**McLaughlin:** That's wonderful!

**Johnston:** I'm happy, and I cannot be more lucky or be more grateful for a situation than that. I'm happy.

**McLaughlin:** After so many years, what value did you learn that comic strips provide?

**Johnston:** Well, they were initially put in the paper to draw new young readers in, and I guess each comic strip was a different voice.

Each cartoonist had something different to say. Whether it was about an animal, like *Garfield* or Snoopy, or whether it was a family bickering like, I don't know, *Blondie*. Everybody had something to say, so there was a real variety of ideas and information on the comics page. But, again, you had to adhere to certain strict rules and content and all of that, so you know it couldn't get too out there. And none of us really wanted to cover any one particular topic.

I think at one point *BC*—that was done by Johnny Hart—everybody loved *BC*; it was such a popular comic strip. And John started to insert an a lot of

ELLY, IF WE COULD GO BACK IN TIME, I MEAN … IF I ASKED YOU TO …

YES, JOHN

FOR BETTER OR FOR WORSE
By Lynn Johnston

… WITH ALL MY HEART, I WOULD!

ELLY AND JOHN PATTERSON RETIRED TO TRAVEL, TO READ, TO VOLUNTEER IN THEIR COMMUNITY AND TO HELP RAISE THEIR GRANDCHILDREN!

GRANDPA JIM LIVED TO WELCOME ANTHONY AND ELIZABETH'S FIRST CHILD, JAMES ALLEN. JIM PASSED AWAY AT THE AGE OF 89, WITH HIS WIFE, IRIS, AT HIS SIDE

ELIZABETH CONTINUES TO WORK AS A TEACHER. SHE'S DEVOTED TO HER WORK AND TO HER FAMILY, LOVING ANTHONY MORE EACH DAY.

ANTHONY MANAGES THE MAYES MOTORS EMPIRE, HAS DRAWN HIS BRIDE INTO BALLROOM DANCING, AND LOOKS FORWARD SOMEDAY TO OPENING A SMALL BED-AND-BREAKFAST.

MICHAEL PATTERSON HAD 4 BOOKS IN PRINT BEFORE SIGNING A FILM CONTRACT. HE CONTINUES TO WORK WITH JOSEF WEEDER AND TO WRITE FROM HOME — WHERE HE SAYS HIS INSPIRATION AND HIS CONFIDENCE LIE.

DEANNA WORKED AS A PHARMACIST UNTIL SHE BEGAN A SMALL SEWING SCHOOL. SHE TAUGHT SON ROBIN HOW TO COOK. THEIR DAUGHTER MEREDITH WENT INTO DANCE AND THEATER. THE FAMILY GOES ANNUALLY TO THE MONTREAL 'JUST FOR LAUGHS' FESTIVAL.

APRIL PATTERSON GRADUATED FROM UNIVERSITY WITH A DEGREE IN VETERINARY MEDICINE. HER LOVE OF HORSES LED HER TO A JOB IN CALGARY AND AN OPPORTUNITY TO WORK WITH THE CALGARY STAMPEDE. COUNTRY LIVING AND A COUNTRY BOY KEEP HER "OUT WEST"!

THE EXTENDED FAMILIES, FRIENDS AND ACQUAINTANCES OF THE PATTERSONS CONTINUE TO LIVE AND GROW, LOVE AND LAUGH AND EXPERIENCE LIFE AS WE DO ….

AS IF PART OF A COMPLEX NOVEL, WHOSE PAGES ARE CAREFULLY CRAFTED AND THEN TURNED BY ANOTHER HAND.

8.31  www.fborfw.com

THANK YOU - TO MY SYNDICATE, PUBLISHER, FAMILY, STAFF, READERS AND FRIENDS FOR ENCOURAGING, GUIDING AND ACCOMPANYING ME THESE PAST 29 YEARS - AS "FOR BETTER OR FOR WORSE" GREW FROM SIMPLE SKETCHES TO AN INTRICATE "SAGA" INVOLVING MANY CHARACTERS.    IF I COULD DO IT ALL OVER AGAIN … WOULD I DO SOME THINGS DIFFERENTLY? … I'VE BEEN GIVEN THE CHANCE TO FIND OUT!!
PLEASE JOIN ME ON MONDAY AS THE STORY BEGINS AGAIN … WITH NEW INSIGHTS AND NEW SMILES. LOOKING BACK LOOKS WONDERFUL!

Lynn Johnston

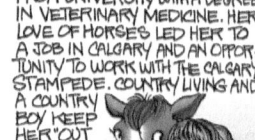

The last Sunday, August 31, 2008. Lynn Johnston says goodbye. FOR BETTER OR FOR WORSE © 2008 Lynn Johnston Productions. Dist. By ANDREWS MCMEEL SYNDICATION. Reprinted with permission. All rights reserved.

his religious beliefs in *BC*. And although this was something he really enjoyed and really wanted to do, they didn't go over that well with the readers. Some of them were just not interested in his point of view, right? So you have to be very careful about putting messages into the comics. You can put subtle messages in like "be nice to your neighbor" and "don't bully the kid in the next class." I had a gay character, and I showed people in an old folks home and what they were dealing with. . . . I did have my little crusades, but more than a crusade, it was just part of life and just whatever I experienced in my own family; that was it. I rarely deviated from that.

**McLaughlin:** Hmm. And you brought a lot of humor to the strip. Speaking with you, I know you're very funny. What value do you think humor has for society?

**Johnston:** I go crazy when people analyze humor. It's like analyzing music. It's whatever makes you laugh. I very rarely laugh at stand-up comedy. I very rarely laugh out loud at a movie or anything that is filled with comedy because I'm so busy saying to myself, "That was good, that worked. That could have been better. I really like the way they delivered that, but maybe they used a few too many words." I'm so busy analyzing it that I very rarely laugh out loud, but now and then I do. I laugh out loud, and it's often it's something I never expected to laugh at. But there you are.

George Carlin made me laugh out loud a lot. And there are other comics that just made me laugh out loud, but other people might not have found what I found funny. It's so subjective, and this is so subtle and so diverse. Who doesn't want to laugh in this world? And it doesn't matter whether you live two thousand years ago or whether you're being born tomorrow. Comedy lightens the load. You know, it's that piece of helium that pulls you up when you need a lift, right? That's what it is.

**McLaughlin:** There! You just gave an excellent analysis about why we want laughter and why we need laughter. And you clearly brought it to us for decades.

Last question. Do you ever read the strips over with your grandchildren?

**Johnston:** No, but they're reading them on their own. And that's the way it should be. And if they're entertained or impressed or interested, that's great. That's the next generation. It is great to see young kids reading my work and that there's another generation of people reading my work. A lot of folks were children then, parents now, and their children are reading my work. So that's pretty nice. That's rewarding.

**McLaughlin:** Well, it's rewarding just to spend so much time with you today, Lynn.

**Johnston:** Thank you.

**McLaughlin:** So thank you so very, very much. I appreciate all this time you've given me.

**Johnston:** Well, Jeff, thank you. I know how accomplished you are, and I know how hard and how long it's taken you to achieve the career that you have. For you to be interested in my work is an honor, and thank you so much for all of your research and your great questions. Thanks.

**McLaughlin:** Well, it's been great. It's fun!

**Johnston:** This *is* fun!

Notes

1. Susan E. Kirtley, *Typical Girls: The Rhetoric of Womanhood in Comic Strips* (Ohio State University Press, 2021). Other works discussing or referring to Johnston's strip include Margaret Morganroth Gullette, "Menopause as Magic Marker: Discursive Consolidation/Strategies for Cultural Combat," *Discourse* 17, no. 1 (1994): 93–122; Christine Schreyer, "Messages from Mtigwaki: Lynn Johnston's Cartoons and Their Impact on Canadian Culture," *Canadian Journal of Native Studies* 34, no. 2 (2014): 181–96; Sue A. Lafky and Bonnie Brennen's "For Better or For Worse: Coming Out in the Funny Pages," *Studies in Popular Culture* 18, no. 1 (1995): 23–47; Roger M. Downs, Lynn S. Lieben, and Debra G. Daggs, "On Education and Geographers: The Role of Cognitive Developmental Theory in Geographic Education," *Annals of the Association of American Geographers* 78, no. 4 (1988): 680–700.
2. "Women's Roles in Comics Stronger: U.S. Professor Gives Credit to Female Artists," *Toronto Star*, November 29, 1986, G4.

# INDEX

Page numbers in **bold** refer to figures.

# ABOUT THE EDITOR

Photo courtesy of the editor

**Jeff McLaughlin** is professor of philosophy at Thompson Rivers University, Kamloops, British Columbia. He is editor of the groundbreaking *Comics as Philosophy* as well as *Graphic Novels as Philosophy* and *Stan Lee: Conversations*, all published by University Press of Mississippi. His teaching and research interests include applied ethics, critical thinking, popular culture, and the Holocaust.

www.ingramcontent.com/pod-product-compliance
Lightning Source LLC
Chambersburg PA
CBHW030409030726
47497CB00002B/537